W9-CIQ-482

99

The
Life
of
Jesus

THE
LIFE
OF
JESUS

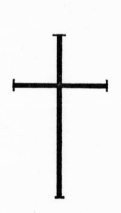

JEAN STEINMANN

Translated from the French by PETER GREEN

An Atlantic Monthly Press Book

LITTLE, BROWN AND COMPANY · BOSTON · TORONTO

UNITY SCHOOL LIBRARY
Unity Village
Lee's Summit, Missouri 64063

DISCARD

ENGLISH TRANSLATION © BY LITTLE, BROWN AND COMPANY, INC.,
1963. COPYRIGHT © CLUB DES LIBRAIRES DE FRANCE, LES LI-
BRAIRES ASSOCIÉS, PARIS, 1959.

ALL RIGHTS RESERVED. NO PART OF THIS BOOK MAY BE REPRO-
DUCED IN ANY FORM WITHOUT PERMISSION IN WRITING FROM THE
PUBLISHER, EXCEPT BY A REVIEWER WHO MAY QUOTE BRIEF PAS-
SAGES IN A REVIEW TO BE PRINTED IN A MAGAZINE OR NEWSPAPER.

LIBRARY OF CONGRESS CATALOG CARD NO. 63-17426

FIRST EDITION

First published in French by Editions Denoël in 1959
under the title *La Vie de Jésus*.

ATLANTIC-LITTLE, BROWN BOOKS
ARE PUBLISHED BY
LITTLE, BROWN AND COMPANY
IN ASSOCIATION WITH
THE ATLANTIC MONTHLY PRESS

Published simultaneously in Canada
by Little, Brown & Company (Canada) Limited

PRINTED IN THE UNITED STATES OF AMERICA

BT
301
St36l

To
my
brother
André

Author's Note

As is made clear in the Afterword, this *Life of Jesus* is based on the evidence afforded by the synoptic Gospels, St. Mark's in particular. My own presentation of the narrative derives very largely from this latter source. I hope in subsequent works to study the evidence of the Pauline Epistles and the Gospel according to St. John.

Bibliographical references are in the Notes section following the Afterword; references for Bible quotations are listed in the section Biblical References in the Text, which follows the Notes.

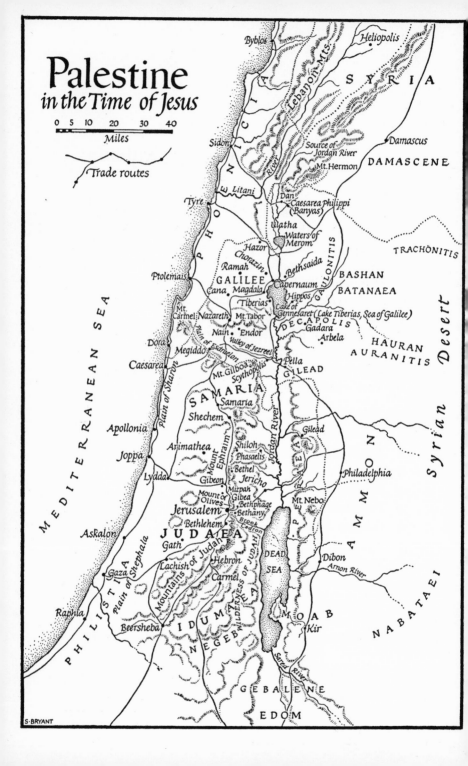

Palestine
in the Time of Jesus

0 5 10 20 30 40
Miles

Trade routes

Byblos   *Heliopolis*

P H O E N I C I A

Sidon

S Y R I A

Lebanon Mts.

*Source of
Jordan River*   *Damascus*

Mt. Hermon   DAMASCENE

Tyre   *Litani*

Dan
*Caesarea Philippi
(Banyas)*

Uatha
*Waters of
Merom*   TRACHŌNITIS

Hazor
Chorazin
Ramah   *Bethsaida*

Ptolemais   GALILEE   *Capernaum*   BASHAN

GAULONITIS

Cana *Magdala*   *Hippos*   BATANAEA

Tiberias

M E D I T E R R A N E A N   S E A

*Mt.
Carmel* *Nazareth*   *Mt. Tabor*
*Lake of
Gennesaret (Lake Tiberias, Sea of Galilee)*

DECAPOLIS

Nain *Endor*   *Gadara*

Dora   Valley of Jezreel   *Arbela*   HAURAN
AURANITIS

Megiddo   Plain of Esdraelon

Caesarea   *Pella*

Mt. Gilboa
Scythopolis   GILEAD

Plain of Sharon

S A M A R I A

Samaria

Shechem

P E R A E A

Apollonia   *Arimathea*   *Gilead*

Joppa   Mount
Ephraim   *Shiloh*
Phasaelis

Lydda   *Gibeon*   *Bethel*   *Philadelphia*

Jericho

Mizpah
Gibea   *Mt. Nebo*
Mount
Olives   *Bethphage*

Jerusalem   *Bethany*
Bethlehem   Brook
Cedron

A M M O N

Askalon   J U D A E A

Gath   *Dibon*

P H I L I S T I A   *Lachish of Judah*   *Hebron*   DEAD
SEA   Arnon River

Plain of Stephela   *Carmel*

S Y R I A N   D e s e r t

Gaza   I D U M A E A   WILDERNESS OF JUDAH   M O A B

Raphia   N E G E B   *Kir*   N A B A T A E I

Beersheba

Sared River

G E B A L E N E

E D O M

S·BRYANT

Contents

Author's Note   vii

Palestine in the Time of Jesus   viii

Part I John the Baptist   1
  1   The Country and the Period   3
  2   The Dilemma of the Jewish Conscience   10
  3   The Baptism of John   14
  4   Jesus of Nazareth   20
  5   The Temptations in the Wilderness   25

Part II The News of the Kingdom   33
  1   The Return to Galilee   35
  2   The Fishermen   41
  3   Teaching in the Synagogues   46
  4   Incident at Capernaum   51
  5   Two Healings   55
  6   Publicans and Sinners   58
  7   The First Parables of the Kingdom   62
  8   The Twelve Disciples   67
  9   The Charter of the Kingdom   71
 10   Inner Justice   78
 11   The Problem of the Sabbath   81
 12   The Mission of the Twelve   86

13   The Gadarene Swine and the Healing of
      Jairus' Daughter   91
14   The Prince of Evil   96
15   The Sign from Heaven   101
16   The Death of John the Baptist   105
17   The Cursing of Galilee   109

Part III *The Hunted Messiah*   115
 1   Among the Pagans   117
 2   Faith in Caesarea Philippi   119
 3   The Son of Man   125
 4   The Temptation of the Son of Man   128
 5   The Transfiguration   134
 6   Our Father   140
 7   The Great Parables of Divine Mercy   146
 8   The Wealthy   152
 9   Jericho   158

Part IV *The Tragedy of Jerusalem*   165
 1   A Triumphal Entry   167
 2   Uproar in the Temple   170
 3   The Sanhedrin   175
 4   Some Devious Questioning   179
 5   Jesus Defends the Samaritans   183
 6   Further Parables   187
 7   Jesus Attacks the Scribes Again   191
 8   The Temple and the Coming Ordeal   196
 9   The Parables of the Ordeal   199
10   Preparation for the Passover   202
11   The Last Supper   205
12   Gethsemane   207

CONTENTS

13 Before the Sanhedrin   211
14 Pontius Pilate   215
15 The Cross   218
16 The Resurrection   223

An Afterword   227

Notes   233

Biblical References in the Text   235

one

John the Baptist

The Country and the Period

WHAT WAS AFTERWARD to be known as the Christian era began during the reign of Augustus: a period of Roman history stamped with unprecedented greatness. The all-powerful sway which Julius Caesar's heir exerted over the entire known world had a decidedly sobering effect on him. Republican *libertas* — the so-called "freedom of the Forum" — was dead; but the only people to have benefited from it were the aristocrats, whose sanguinary quarrels had dishonored the very name of the Republic. Thanks to the Imperial Peace, the arts were now able to attain a high degree of refinement and sophistication. Artists modeled themselves on Greek masters: the native Roman tradition had never achieved anything of aesthetic value, unless we count the grave and melodious Latin language. Augustus extended his patronage to Horace and Virgil, and the latter was already a recognized classic by the time he died. But after the accession of Tiberius, in A.D. 14, the Imperial regime became an organized reign of terror, which stooped to such exquisite cruelty as only a civilized race can conceive, and latterly became the target for Tacitus' stinging, all too well-merited invective.

With the single exception of Mauretania (modern Morocco), the Empire encircled the Mediterranean from shore to shore. It extended northward to Belgium and westward to Lusitania (Portugal); its southern boundaries embraced upper Egypt, while in the east it held a line running from Damascus through Palmyra to the southern shore of the Euxine, which we now call the Black Sea. Like any modern colonial empire, it was a complex mosaic of provinces annexed by conquest, plus various federated or allied dependencies and a number of protectorates. Within its boundaries were to be found men of every known race: Asians and Nubians, Gauls and Numidians, Greeks, Jews, Egyptians and Pannonians. There were also Roman citizens proper; and these — leaving aside for the moment the urban populace — formed the backbone of the army and the Imperial administration.

The tongue normally spoken in the towns was Greek, which formed a commercial *lingua franca* throughout the Empire. But in the country districts and the more distant provinces the peasants adhered to their local vernaculars — Latin in Italy, Punic (Carthaginian) throughout southern Spain and the African littoral, Egyptian along the Nile Valley, Aramaic in Syria.

There was as great a variety and diversity of religions as of races. Rome's traditional pagan cults remained the prerogative of the aristocracy, who paid skeptical lip service to them. It was not long since Cicero had written his tongue-in-cheek treatise on divination; yet as a consul he had solemnly taken auspices from the sacred chickens, and the cynical Augustus had himself held the office of Pontifex Maximus. The Greek deities were revered by the common people, and also by artists and prostitutes. The animal-headed gods of Egypt, the fetishes associated with Cybele and the mystery cults, the demons conjured up by magicians and sorcerers — all had their devotees. On top of this there were the "revelations" of diviners and bogus thaumaturges, the speculative talk of the philosophers and mages, and the moral disputations of Stoics and Epicureans.

Roman law was by no means universally applied in the affairs of daily life: only a privileged minority who could claim Roman citizenship had the full benefit of it. Slaves had no legal rights;

though they formed an over-all majority of the population, they were considered on a par with cattle. Those who kept their free status remained subject to local laws, which varied from place to place. Many cities had autonomous self-government. The Empire's internal frontiers were legion — and matched by a bewildering array of rival taxes, customs tariffs, legal systems and political authorities.

But one institution was ubiquitous: the Roman army. It kept the peace — the *pax militaris* — throughout the provinces, and backed its decisions by superior force. The secret of its efficiency was an unrivaled communication system. Those broad, well-paved highways radiating from Rome throughout the length and breadth of the Empire — like arteries in some vast living body — bore witness, then as now, to the building genius of Rome. Anyone who has ever strolled along the Via Appia on an autumn morning, between the dark cypresses and the crumbling tombs, must surely have meditated on the destiny of these great trunk roads, which bore to the farthest corners of the known world not only the legions but also Christianity itself.

The Jews were the most distinctive of the many races which went to make up the Empire. They were scattered everywhere, or nearly everywhere — in Rome, Corinth, Macedonia, Asia Minor, and, above all, in Alexandria and Egypt, where, a million strong, they formed one-eighth of the entire population. Jews were also to be found beyond the Imperial frontiers; a sizable Jewish colony flourished in Babylon.

The Jews' own country was Palestine, but they had been emigrating throughout the Near East for several centuries. Their capital was the cramped, swarming fortress of Jerusalem, built on two adjacent hills in Judaea, some twenty-five hundred feet above sea level. Difficult of access, and without any rich hinterland to support it, Jerusalem remained confined to her role as Holy City. Dominating all else was the Temple, a vast edifice which had recently — thanks to Augustus — been restored in most sumptuous style by Herod, King of Judaea.

What made the Jews remarkable — indeed, unique — in the Roman Empire was not their race (Semitic groups, including Phoenicians, Arabs and Syrians, abounded there) but their religion. They worshipped one God only, whose name they considered it blasphemous to utter. Nothing here to arouse hatred, it may be argued. But the Jews could not dissociate this God of theirs from a book ("the Law," as they called it, or the Bible, as it is known today) and one particular cult center, the Temple in Jerusalem. In addition, they actively despised all other gods, and abominated not only their cults but such persons as worshipped them — that is to say, all non-Jews, the pagans or *goyim*, whom they referred to as "dogs." Such contempt bred highly vocal hatred among the pagans themselves.

The Roman authorities had a very healthy respect for Jewish fanaticism, and as a result granted certain important privileges to the Jews. Their communities were exempt from any act of worship in honor of the municipal or Imperial gods. They had the right to abstain from work on Saturdays, to establish synagogues, and to levy a tax for the upkeep of the Temple in Jerusalem. Roman troops were debarred from entering the Temple precincts, and indeed all pagans were forbidden, on pain of death, to set foot in it.

But despite this official protection on the part of the Emperors, the Jewish quarters in various provincial cities were frequently invaded by bands of young pagan students who smashed up shops and synagogues. Sometimes the local authorities actually served an expulsion order on the Jews under their jurisdiction. Such customs as circumcision, the stringent taboos on food, the horror of all pagan cults and the laws governing the Sabbath tended to isolate Jewish communities. When they emigrated they usually stuck together, forming segregated groups organized along ghetto lines.

Nevertheless, they were, as always, profoundly divided among themselves. They split up into sects and clans, which opposed one another even on such matters as the interpretation of Holy Writ and the correct rules for a God-fearing life. The priestly aristocracy of Jerusalem was represented by the Sadducees, who derived their name from Sadok, High Priest of the Temple in Jerusalem under Solomon. This high religious body exercised its jurisdiction with Rome's approval: the Sadducees were embattled conservatives and loyal "collaborators" who would have had everything to lose from a change of regime. They had little time for the newfangled ideas which were gradually gaining ground among the Jews, in particular those to do with the idea of resurrection and the Kingdom of God. They sat in the Sanhedrin — the sovereign Council of State which governed Jerusalem's affairs — under the watchful eye of the Roman Procurator.

The deadliest enemies of the Roman occupying power in Palestine were the Zealots, a group of revolutionary terrorists who might be likened today to the Algerian *fellahin* or the Moslem Brotherhood in Egypt. They followed a policy of violence and sedition, continually fomenting popular uprisings against the military garrisons or the Imperial administration. When one of their raids failed, or the legions were in hot pursuit of them, they could always retreat into the desert, which reached almost to the gates of Jerusalem.

For over a century another sect, of ultra-pietistic leanings, had been increasingly active throughout Judaea. Its members advocated strict adherence to the Law: in the Gospels we find them described as Pharisees. Among themselves they were known as the "pious," the "pure," or the "elect."

Originally these "pure" sectarians had been fervent and sincere believers; but with the embittered mood brought about by the Roman occupation, they had very soon oriented themselves along political lines. They included those who were with the Resistance in spirit, but lacked the courage to use a dagger or take to the *maquis* as the Zealots did. Their hatred for Rome was demonstrated in more discreet ways: a wary hawking of saliva as a soldier passed by, assiduous attendance in the Temple or at their local synagogue.

But the strangest sect, beyond any doubt, was that of the Essenes, who described themselves as the Sons of the New Alliance, and who appear to have been divided into two main groups, lay and monastic. Some were scattered among various towns and villages in little communities of about a dozen persons; others flocked to the monastery by the Dead Sea, where they lived as hermits. But in either case they submitted to a rigorous, almost military discipline, and practiced the most rigid sort of asceticism. They had a rule, and leaders; they organized themselves in units corresponding to phalanx and cohort. They refused to acknowledge the reformed calendar; and they therefore persisted in celebrating feast days at a different time from anyone else. This meant that they could not worship in the Temple and caused them to be regarded as schismatics, rather like the Old Believers in Russia at the time of Peter the Great. They believed in the resurrection of the dead, awaited the coming of two Messiahs, practiced baptism by total immersion, and met for communal meals of bread and wine. Their ideal was purity, both physical and statutory (according to the Mosaic Law), and this ideal they pursued with quite fanatical intransigence. Not only did they execrate the pagans, but extended their contempt to the rest of Jewry as well, on the grounds that they themselves were the sole repositories of divine truth. They were excellent scholars, and part of their time was spent in copying out the Bible. In addition they wrote tracts outlining their own doctrines, in particular, the works of the order's anonymous founder, the Master of Justice, who lived in the middle of the second century B.C.

If Pharisees, Essenes, and Zealot terrorists all loathed the Romans, those Jews who were most deeply compromised with the occupying power — and most hated by their fellows in consequence — were the Samaritans and tax collectors (*publicani*). The Samaritans were regarded as traitors and schismatics, who fraternized with the enemy and worshipped God on Mount Gerizim, near Shechem.

As for the *publicani*, who made a rich living by collecting taxes and customs revenue, they were regarded as corrupt, both politically and financially — public sinners on the same level as the village whore, or, in our own times, the drug trafficker and the brothel owner. Their extortions were a crying scandal; they fleeced the Jews to pay the Romans but kept a sizable percentage of the takings for themselves. People envied them their wealth, begged them — secretly — to use their influence to get friends out of trouble, and hated them for their lack of patriotism, their pliant adaptability, their uncommitted attitude.

After the death of Herod the Great, in 4 B.C., Judaea lost its last vestige of independence. The Romans changed its status from protectorate to province — and an Imperial province at that, under the Emperor's direct administration. A procurator took up residence in Caesarea. Those familiar with the Jewish problem foresaw that sooner or later there was bound to be trouble.

2

THE DILEMMA OF THE JEWISH CONSCIENCE

FOR CENTURIES Israel had felt herself charged with a universal mission. The Jews were God's chosen people. In the Old Testament the lives of the Patriarchs, as there related, embodied the promise made to Abraham of a posterity "as the stars of the heaven, and as the sand which is upon the sea shore." The poems, both epic and lyrical, of the major prophets promised Israel a just king, a new Temple, the worldwide spread of her religion, and a radiant and universal glory. More recent writings had accepted this prophetic hope, and, indeed, exalted it. It was after the bloody struggle which Antiochus IV (Epiphanes), the Seleucid monarch, had in 165 B.C. unleashed against the Jews that the author of the Book of Daniel sketched out his systematic synthesis of universal history. He depicted Babylon as the capital of four successive world empires, each of which in turn collapsed. Then, through the dreams of his hero, he prophesied the unforeseen and supernatural advent of a new empire, incarnate in a Man.

This Man, being descended from Heaven, was by the purity and splendor of his origin in natural opposition to the old Adam, that creature of clay and earth. He symbolized Israel and her new King the Messiah — God's anointed Messenger, the recipient of divine unction. At his coming the dead would rise, and the earth, clothed in new radiance, would see a new race of supermen spring up, as glorious as the stars in heaven.

Many other writers elaborated similar prophecies, concealing their purport under the cloak of mystical and numerical revelations attributed to such persons as Adam, Enoch, Lamech, Noah, or Shem. It was now commonly held that Babylon, the ancient Eastern city, had been replaced by Rome, the evil

capital of the world, whose imminent fall was awaited with
trembling and joyful impatience.

But side by side with these secret apocalyptic dreams — what
might be termed the resistance movement's surrealistic literature — direct political action had its own part to play. In 162
B.C. it had scored a signal victory through the *maquisards*
commanded by Judas Maccabaeus, known as the Hammer. It
really looked as though the Hasmonean dynasty might have
fulfilled those promises and prophecies. But all that had in
fact been achieved was the independence of a state no larger
than modern Israel. In the area between Galilee and the Negeb
a few Samaritans had been slaughtered, one or two Greeks cir-
cumcised and naturalized. In the end the Hasmoneans had
given way to Herod, who was not even a Jew but, rather, was
descended from the abhorred Edomites. "He seized the throne
by devious means, like a fox," the French historian Capefigue
wrote; "he ruled like a tiger; and he died a dog's death."

He certainly built some formidable fortresses, besides en-
circling the Temple with vast protective walls, and decorating
it in the most showy and luxurious bad taste. But had Israel's
Messianic hopes sunk to so debased a level that they could be
embodied in this cruel and debauched old libertine, whom
even the Romans regarded with disgust? The Zealot guerrillas
nursed an ambition — as ruthless as it was insensate — to
attain political mastery of the world. The Essenes and the
Pharisees expected God himself to inaugurate this marvelous
era. Only the Sadducees kept their heads. As for the country
peasants, their concern for the whole affair was decidedly luke-
warm. Men toiled in their fields, and prayed God for a good
crop come harvest time.

One strange anomaly of the times was that the hope of a
new Golden Age was not exclusively restricted to the Jews. A
glimmering of the concept actually filtered through into Virgil's

Fourth Eclogue, where we find this mysterious prediction (lines 4-5):

> *Ultima Cumaei venit iam carminis aetas;*
> *magnus ab integro saeclorum nascitur ordo.*
>
> *Now the last age foretold by the Sibyl's prophecy*
> *Is here; now begins anew the centuries' great line.*

But only the Jews believed that the regeneration of the world was to be their exclusive prerogative. Renegades apart, none of them would for one moment have challenged the idea that this formed the Jewish people's *raison d'être*. But what shape would this universal renewal take, and what means would be employed to bring it about?

Herein lay a considerable dilemma. Did it imply world sovereignty for the Jews, or the liberation of all peoples whatsoever? Was the process to be evolutionary or catastrophic, peaceful or warlike? Would God's enemies be enslaved, massacred, or converted? Were the pagans God's enemies by definition, or to be excused on the grounds of ignorance? Would God intervene in human affairs directly, and without assistance, or would the Jews act as the instrument of his intervention? Lastly, was the end purpose of such action political supremacy or a spiritual rebirth?

The internal divisions among the Jews were accentuated by the fact that in a pinch each faction could find Biblical support for its views. Though the end chosen lay with God, the choice of means to that end appeared to depend on mankind; these divine promises contained, as it were, the framework within which Israel's freedom could operate. They both steered the national conscience and imposed a deliberate choice of destiny upon the Jewish people.

One factor, the decay and collapse of Roman civilization, seemed inevitable. Even the pagans themselves — the more estimable of them, at any rate — were aware of this. Poets, moralists and philosophers could not close their eyes to the blots on their society: slavery, the cruelties practiced in the amphitheater, the insolent reign of violence. Such things could not be camouflaged by mere civilized amenities — especially since the latter were available to only a small minority. Despite one or two shining exceptions — mostly among the Stoics and other philosophers with high moral standards — the Imperial aristocracy was, as a class, hopelessly corrupt. No one any longer believed in the traditional pagan gods: their feasts were kept up, but only as a sort of archaic device for reinforcing public conservatism. The Eastern cults of Adonis, Isis, Cybele, and above all (though he was a comparative latecomer) Mithras — these attracted many devotees precisely because of their mysterious and exotic ritual, though Romans of the old school found them repugnant. An echo of this contempt is to be found in Juvenal. Many pagans were willing to concede that the Jews had diagnosed the situation correctly — even though they might not look forward with any great enthusiasm to the prospect of world revolution. What no Gentile would have dreamed of admitting was that this revolution could conceivably be brought about by the Jews, of all people — the most arrogant and despised ethnic group in the entire Empire. As soon grant in our day that an African Negro could become President of the United States.

To ensure that the God of Israel would one day be worshipped in Rome, and that a Jew would sit on the supreme throne of the Caesars — this, at a fair estimate, would mean massacring something like three-quarters of all civilized people in the Mediterranean. The Jews of the Dispersion — those resident in Rome, Carthage, Corinth, Alexandria, or Antioch — had no illusions on this score: they were well aware of how their Greek and Roman fellow-citizens felt. The more intelligent Jews, such as Philo of Alexandria, did their best to reduce Judaism to a system of philosophy — the only possible way in which it could be made attractive to pagans. But in Jerusalem and Judaea no one bothered about such problems. Was not God infinitely more powerful than Caesar? Was He not absolute Master of the world? Did He not cherish the Jews above all other peoples? Did He not detest the pagans to the point of spewing them forth from His mouth? Had He not undertaken the most solemn and explicit promises to Israel? No one saw any possibility of distinguishing, much less dissociating, the Jewish religion from Jewish politics. They were waiting for the time when God would take Caesar's place, when His heavenly legions would score a resounding victory over the cohorts of Rome. Then Jerusalem would at last become the bright and glorious capital of the new world, a capital built on the ruins of that accursed modern Babylon, Rome.

3

THE BAPTISM OF JOHN

ABOUT A.D. 30 word began to spread abroad through the streets of Jerusalem concerning a new prophet named John, who was preaching beside the Jordan, not far from Jericho. Prophets were common in Israel, and one more was nothing out of the ordinary. But John — whose name meant "Jehovah is Merciful" — had every quality calculated to impress the multitude and intrigue public opinion. He made his first, solitary appearance dressed in the garb of the desert tribesmen, those known today as Bedouins.

The nomadic life was no more than a memory for the Jews, who read of it in the Old Testament when studying the lives of the early Patriarchs. But the desert itself lay close at hand. Its dunes gleamed brassily under the summer sun. It was strewn with

rocks and boulders, scored with deep-cut gorges and sheer
wadis, cave-haunted, scoured by burning, dust-laden winds
that drove the gray desert sand in men's eyes. Nomadic encamp-
ments were still to be found along the old trails; it was dangerous
to travel these routes by night, for fear of meeting some
Nabataean or Arab tribe, on the move from Sinai to the
Euphrates with their herds of black goats and camels. Sometimes the desolate bush country offered a convenient refuge to
outlaws. On its distant horizon there gleamed the sluggish
waters of the Lacus Asphaltites, which we know as the Dead
Sea.

Those who knew him claimed that John belonged to a
priestly clan; but he did not perform the functions of priesthood, and in the desert he was unable even to observe all the
requirements of the Mosaic law. Both his way of life and the
message he preached suggested a close link with the monastic
sect of the Essenes; and people may well have wondered whether
he had not, in late adolescence, undergone a lengthy novitiate
at the Essenian monastery on the northwest shore of the Dead
Sea. It is true, however, that his gray camel-hair loincloth was
more in the Bedouin style than anything else; it bore little
resemblance to the white-cowled robes worn by the brethren
of the New Alliance. His food consisted of flat loaves, barley or
rye bread, which he augmented with wild honey and roasted
locusts. Such a diet, though permissible to a Jew, was decidedly
austere.

John soon became an extremely popular figure. But he was not
content to live merely as a nazir, the equivalent of a modern
yogi in India. He held forth without stint to all those who
sought him out in the desert; and the message he preached
was one calculated to stir the crowds deeply. "The Kingdom
of Heaven is at hand," John declared: according to him it
appeared that Israel's old national dream might at last be ful-

filled. The corrupt and oppressive rule they had to endure was nearing its end.

But John went even further. Every kingdom presupposes a king. Was the king who was destined to rule the Kingdom of Heaven already alive? Yes, John declared, he was. But how, with the Kingdom so close at hand, was this future king to be recognized? And how could men worthily stand beside such a leader when battle was joined, and his triumphant forces advanced to conquer the entire world? Should they follow the example of the rabbis and strict sectarians, who claimed that meticulous observance of the Law was the one great essential? Or should they rather arm themselves and march out into the desert? Was it preferable to step up the guerrilla campaign against the Romans, or retreat into an Essenian monastery? To live a hermit's life, as John himself did, or conduct high diplomatic intrigue in the manner of the priestly caste? John's answer was always the same: Only by repentance and baptism could men enter the Kingdom of Heaven.

The sort of conversion he preached did not entail any break with one's ordinary day-to-day life. He did not ask soldiers to leave the army, or insist that tax collectors and excise officers abandon their dishonorable calling. It was enough that a man repented of the sins he had committed against God and righteousness. Thus John's position was different from that of the Essenes, and, *a fortiori*, in sharp contrast with the views held by strict Pharisees or Sadducee priests. Though his message was as old as the Bible — and indeed as prophecy itself — it nevertheless seemed both novel and original. John was not concerned with mere nationalism. Pointing to the rock-strewn desert, he exclaimed in his rough but vigorous way, "I say unto you, that God is able of these stones to raise up children unto Abraham."

Unlike the Essenes, John held out God's bounty and favor

to all men; and baptism was the outward token of this reconciliation, a sign that the Kingdom of God was at hand.

Water in the desert is always a miracle, life gushing from
the heart of death — limpid and gay, a bright, babbling harbinger
of flowers and palm trees in a dusty, burning wilderness. What
matter if the Jordan in summer is only a ribbon of greenish
mud, winding through reedbeds beneath high white shimmering banks? It is still a river; it is *water*.

Baptism — that is, total immersion in this water of Jordan —
was not a Biblically authorized practice. The Law, it is true,
prescribed certain ritual ablutions; but the Essenes appear to
have been the first people to introduce the rite of baptism into
Jewish custom; and even so, they performed it in tanks or
cisterns. John chose the river partly from necessity, and partly
by deliberate intent. This process of immersion symbolized rebirth rather than ritual purification. It is possible that prior
to being dipped in the Jordan the neophytes made a public
confession of their sins. Plunging beneath the surface of the
water symbolized death. What emerged was a new being —
just as Earth herself had emerged from Ocean at the creation of
the world. And from this virgin soil man himself had been
born, the issue, at several removes and by God's decree, of the
primeval sea of Chaos. Thus, to be worthy of the coming
Kingdom, one must be reborn of water.

John often spoke of the coming Kingdom. The old sinful
world would be consumed by divine fire — the baptism of fire,
as he called it. After this it was to be redeemed by the breath
of God: this was the baptism of the spirit. At His coming God
would sit in judgment on mankind, and winnow out the grain
from the chaff like a husbandman. John's concept of the future
king was so exalted that he said — thinking of the moment
when this Messiah should himself strip for baptism — "There

cometh one mightier than I after me, the latchet of whose shoes I am not worthy to stoop down and unloose."

People flocked out from the towns and cities to hear John. Some stayed on, and John soon had a core of disciples, in particular four Galilaeans, fishermen from Lake Gennesaret, who were attracted by his prophetic teachings — Simon and Andrew, James and John, two pairs of brothers.

The movement developing around the central figure of John the Baptist gave the Jewish authorities in Jerusalem legitimate cause for alarm. A priestly deputation was commissioned to make inquiries. They went and questioned John as to his identity. "Who art thou?" they asked.

"I am not the Christ," he declared.

A popular tradition, for which Biblical authority existed, held that Elijah (Elias) would return to earth at the coming of the Kingdom. "What then?" the priests asked him, perhaps with an ironic smile. "Art thou Elias?"

It was true that John did give a strange, almost savage impression — much the same as had been left in men's memories by the epic prophet of Mount Carmel, the fierce enemy of Ahab and Jezebel.

"I am not," he said.

They repeated the question. "Art thou that prophet?" they asked.

"No."

Then they said: "Who art thou?"

It was not John's identity in the ordinary sense that these envoys wished to ascertain; they knew that well enough already. What interested them was the precise role that John regarded himself as fulfilling. Did his message contain incitement to political revolt? John's reply, though on the face of it "correct," was most suggestive. He quoted from Isaiah: "I am the voice of one crying in the wilderness, 'Prepare ye the way of the Lord, make his paths straight.'" This text was crucial for the Essenes, who saw in it the very heart and substance of their Messianic expectations. An anonymous prophet of the Babylonian exile, whose writings had been interpolated into the Book of Isaiah, spoke of the expatriates returning to Israel and being obliged to cross the Syrian desert. God would accompany them on their journey, moving in front of their caravan just as he had once guided the Jews towards Canaan. Like some great Eastern prince, Jehovah desired his route through the desert made smooth in preparation for his triumphal entry into a new and splendidly refashioned Jerusalem. John was the messenger appointed to bid the people make ready this processional way.

The new prophet associated himself so emphatically with this text from Isaiah that in the end he became known among his followers simply as "the voice crying in the wilderness." But there were those who asked themselves whether the voice carried sufficiently far. If the Kingdom of God *was* at hand, the time had surely come to acquaint all men with the truth. Was it not imperative to proclaim such wonderful news — *evangelion* was the Greek term for it — to every village and city? John was relying on people's coming out to hear his good tidings in the desert. But not everyone could abandon his family and undertake a period of self-denial by the banks of the Jordan. Who was to bear the joyful news concerning the Kingdom to poor country peasants, to women in their villages, to all who were bowed down with toil and suffering, to the blind and the paralyzed, to the innumerable poverty-stricken, brutalized masses of the East, sunk so deep in sweat and squalor?

It was at this juncture that Jesus of Nazareth made his appearance on the banks of the Jordan.

4
JESUS OF NAZARETH

JESUS WAS about thirty when he joined John's desert entourage. Of his physical appearance — height, expression, mannerisms — we know nothing, much less any details concerning such things as his way of writing or how he looked when he smiled. From his capacity for lengthy fasts and journeys on foot, however, it has been deduced that he was probably tall, well built, and muscular.

Like many of his compatriots he was of royal descent* — that is, a little of David's blood ran in his veins; nowadays in the Near East there are similarly millions of men claiming descent from Mahomet, who recognize one another by their green turbans. But his circumstances were comparatively humble. He was from the village of Nazareth, a carpenter and cartwright who spoke Aramaic with a northern accent, and whose early education must have been restricted to the village school and the local synagogue. He knew Hebrew, and probably understood Greek too: people of many races passed through the villages of Galilee, and children brought up there tended to be as fluently multilingual as any little Greek or Bulgarian Jew is today.

Life as a rural artisan was in no way incompatible with high spiritual development: many rabbis also practiced manual crafts to earn their bread. In point of fact Jesus knew his Old Testament extremely well, and was passionately concerned about the religious future of his people. His Galilaean origin also equipped him with many traits characteristic of the better sort of northern provincial: hardheaded realism, broadminded-

* See St. Paul's Epistle to the Romans 1, 3.

ness, the common touch, a certain rather prickly defiance when dealing with scornfully superior Judaeans.

The religion which both he and his family followed was Orthodox Temple Judaism, modified in one or two respects by old-fashioned habits such as adherence to the old traditional calendar, and a marked weakness for certain specifically Essenian practices — ascetic self-denial, baptism, sharing property in common, communal meals of bread and wine, a contempt for money. On the other hand, he displayed little or no regard for the monastic ideal, with its strict discipline, blind obedience, and quasi-military organization.

Jesus had been brought up in a tradition of ideas very much akin to those held by good Pharisees. He believed firmly in the resurrection of the dead and intercession by angels in human affairs; yet there was much that he found to dislike about these strict sectarians: their ostentatious habits, their self-righteousness, their holier-than-thou attitude.

What sent him, a fully mature man, out into the desert was the warm sympathy with which John's message was received by devout Galilaeans everywhere. Jesus shared John's absolute conviction that the Kingdom of Heaven was at hand, and made up his mind to join the throng of those seeking baptism.

From his very first encounter with Jesus, the desert prophet got the impression that he had met the Master he sought. Jesus' insight into future events was so striking, his strength of character so self-evident, and his moral purity so absolute that when he asked John to baptize him the latter at first refused, though finally he capitulated and did as Jesus requested.

It seems possible that when the time came (perhaps just before his actual immersion) for Jesus to confess his sins, he instead — being without stain — declared his intention of taking upon himself the sins of all mankind. Not long afterward, John described him as "the Lamb of God, which taketh away the sin of the world" — that is to say, the suffering servant we read of in Isaiah,* the immolated Paschal Lamb whose blood is to be shed, the victim who will one day rise in triumph.

When Jesus emerged from the green-slimed, sluggish water of the river, he had a vision. The bright heavens were opened to the Infinite, the breath of God blew upon his face, and he heard a voice that said: "Thou art my beloved Son, in whom I am well pleased."

Like the very first man, whom God fashioned from clay in Paradise, he received the lifegiving spirit direct. He heard himself addressed as the Son of God, a title which in bygone days the kings of Israel had assumed. By means of this mystical vision, experienced in a state of ecstasy, Jesus was celebrating his own kingly consecration. The ancient kings, however, did not connect their divine adoption with the moment of consecration; they knew it applied from the very moment any one of them was conceived. So it was with Jesus. His baptism only confirmed that natural bond, existing between him and God, which lent such infinite richness to his inner life.

This ritual act of initiation into the New Kingdom — preached so fervently by John — made Jesus feel more closely bound to humankind than ever before.

After his baptism Jesus found himself eagerly sought out by the Baptist's disciples. But after a little while he slipped away from the group around John and vanished. He fled into the rock-strewn fastnesses of the Judaean desert, intending (as was the Essenian custom) to make a retreat there.

By receiving baptism in the Jordan, Jesus had become a member of John's community. But John did not maintain among his friends that iron discipline which flourished in an Essenian group: he thought of himself neither as a lawgiver

* See Isaiah 53.

nor as a Messiah. His spiritual family was a free association of those who awaited the imminent coming of God's Kingdom. By demanding baptism, Jesus had recognized the divine and inspired nature of the ceremony which John performed; and when he left the banks of the Jordan he did so with the same freedom the prophet allowed all his followers.

Never afterward was Jesus to waver in his admiration and respect for John. He went so far as to declare him the greatest of all the prophets, and to attribute to him the powers of a resurrected Elias. He was to make baptism the ritual which specifically symbolized entry into the Kingdom. The word of John was a condensed summing-up of what the prophets had declared; and John's rite of baptism embodied, indeed transcended, all the virtues contained in other Biblical ceremonies. Jesus saw more in it than a preparation for the Kingdom. It was indeed an act of enthronement, since in Jesus the Kingdom had found its King. As John had declared, this King was now living on earth. But how was he to make himself manifest? What laws would govern this new Kingdom of God? How were its ministers and their powers to be determined?

Faced with this Messianic mission — a mystical confirmation of what his own self-awareness told him — Jesus felt the need for a period of absolute solitude and retreat. The greatest mystic of all time would now, by prayer and contemplation, achieve a condition of union and communication with God. The desert was the ideal setting for his task. During the day its sands were seared and scorched by a heat so oppressive that it seemed to annihilate every flicker of life: in this empty wilderness a man could feel himself lost indeed. The nights, on the other hand, were often icy-cold there, and haunted by jackals prowling about in search of carrion. Under a full moon, the horizon was a faint silhouette of rock formations: the effect was uncanny, like the landscape of some dead star or deserted planet.

Jesus stayed there forty days and forty nights, fasting. Such an ordeal presupposes an iron constitution. By this act of self-deprivation — for God alone, with God alone to witness it — he proposed to test the absolute quality of his mastery over himself, the strength of his unconquerable will. So long a fast gives the mind supranormal clarity, frees the body from its enslavement to the things of this life, and draws forth the soul from that cloudy opacity which is its normal condition.

But for the great ascetics, fasting never remained *merely* a means of sharpening one's faculties to supranormal intensity; it was also an act of identification with the great mass of mankind who were suffering from chronic undernourishment. In the time of Jesus, as today, such unfortunates formed by far the greater part of the world. Slaves, chain-gang miners, peasants in poor districts, desert nomads, the urban proletariat — all these died like flies during the frequent famines, which were aggravated still further by the slowness of transport and communications. Besides, Jesus was anxious to share the great ordeals of his people. Each day he fasted represented a year of the Israelites' wanderings in the Sinai Desert. Each day also corresponded to a day in Moses' fast on Mount Horeb, or a day in the fearful pilgrimage of the prophet Elias to the same mountain. Moses and Elijah had both, ultimately, met God in the wilderness. These giants of Israel's sacred history had undergone their supreme ordeal there — an ordeal before which they had well-nigh succumbed.

The royal consecration by baptism was accomplished. But now a grim struggle awaited Jesus, to be fought out under a blazing sun, by the Jordan's chalky cliffs, in the stony lifeless world of the desert. What was this struggle?

5

The Temptations in the Wilderness

LONG AFTERWARD, Jesus himself was to describe for his friends the fantastic imagery which shaped his dreams in the desert. When we use the word "dream" we commonly assume the images under discussion to be *unreal* as well as impalpable. But dreams and visions do not stand in direct opposition to reality: they represent rather what we may call surreality. They may exist as truly and objectively as do the pebbles beneath our feet, but at a deeper and more spiritual level of truth. Jesus could not have explained himself in the language employed by psychoanalysts. The ineffable realities with which he saw himself at grips were not (as Pascal might have put it) of the same order as those which haunt invalids' troubled nights. What he had to deal with was, in a manner of speaking, the fate of the whole universe.

All the great mystics assume the existence of certain intangible forces which strive to prevent God's ultimate victory. Philosophers speak of a "natural inertia" inhibiting evolutionary development. The Jews had a name for this "adversary," this spiritual enemy of God: they called him Satan.

They knew no more than we do today of his origins, history, and power. Satan appeared to enslave certain men for his own purposes; but the true diabolical presence was more likely to be found in Tiberius' soul than in that of an epileptic. A whole mass of superstitious beliefs and nonsensical magic attributes clung about the figure of Satan in popular belief; he was widely regarded as a sort of wizard. The Satan that Jesus went out to confront, however, was altogether more redoubtable than this devil of folklore. For him Satan represented the dream of political power; he was the archetypal original of Dostoevsky's Grand Inquisitor in *The Brothers Karamazov*, with the difference that the Inquisitor was a mere figment of the romantic imagination, whereas this Satanic figure was all too real.

Jesus never told his disciples that he saw Satan in human guise; it was only a voice that tempted him. "If thou be the Son of God," it said, "command that these stones be made bread." Here was the lure of miraculous power, the dream of exercising a Faustian control over the created world. Today, when men can detonate such fiery comets as could reduce the whole world to cinders, we speak of "the miracles of science." But to know that you, and you alone, were endowed with the power of reproducing the miracle of the manna in the wilderness, and thus, by a word and a gesture, of bringing nourishment to starving millions — would not that be a greater miracle still? It would mean the immediate realization here on earth of those words in the Lord's Prayer: "Give us this day our daily bread." No need to wait for God's grudging bounty, harvest after slow harvest; all could now be had at will, and immediately. For Jesus himself this miraculous ability to transmute matter would mean the inauguration of the Kingdom, there and then, in the wilderness. With this bread, which one day would become the symbol of his Body and that Body's Presence, he could assuage his pressing hunger. Moreover, by transforming these loaf-shaped stones into real bread, he would cease to be the "Lamb of God," the Lamb whose blood must be spilt, who was doomed to be sacrificed and devoured. Instead he himself would become the devourer, the Lion of God, the Lion of Judah, the King whose coming every village awaited, the Messiah who would forge the Jews into a powerful, satisfied, well-fed, dominating nation — a horde, in other words, of splendid, and splendidly glutted, human animals.

Jesus countered this temptation with a text from Deuteronomy: "It is written, 'Man shall not live by bread alone, but
by every word that proceedeth out of the mouth of God.'"
The divine Word had created the world, and bread itself was no
more than one of the "creatures" conjured from nothingness
by this all-powerful Word. Further, this text furnished mankind with an insight into God's will concerning the Kingdom:
it was to be a kingdom of the spirit.

Jesus resumed his trancelike meditation, and once again the
voice of Evil assailed him, reinforced on this occasion by a most
grand and resplendent vision.

The Temple of Jerusalem was built on the ancient threshing
floor of Araunah. Its southeast ramparts rose high above the
Cedron Valley, a ravine used by the Jews as a burial ground. In
his dream Jesus saw himself standing on the topmost point
of these ramparts, the so-called Pinnacle of the Temple, which
rose nearly five hundred feet above the Cedron gorge. From here
he would have had a magnificent bird's-eye view of the crowded
outer court before the sanctuary. To the south he could see the
palace of the High Priests, and to the west that of the Hasmonean kings. Northward lay the Antonia fortress. "If thou be
the Son of God, cast thyself down: for it is written, 'He shall
give his angels charge concerning thee: and in their hands
they shall bear thee up, lest at any time thou dash thy foot
against a stone.'"

Satan's quotation from the Psalms was intended to make
Jesus fulfill the popular dream of a Messiah.

When the Messianic King appears [an ancient rabbinical legend
tells us], he will stand upright on the pinnacle of the Temple and
proclaim himself to the people of Israel: "All you who travail, your
redemption is at hand. If you believe, rejoice in my light." Then
they will come forward and bow their heads in the dust before the
feet of the Messianic King, as it is written. . . . And every

Israelite shall possess two thousand eight hundred slaves for his private use, as it is written.

If Jesus agreed to appear in this manner, as the heaven-sent leader, he would certainly be acclaimed by the crowds who haunted the streets of the Old City beneath the pinnacle; while the priests would acknowledge him as the Messiah, thus making their long-hoped-for revolt a fact. He would drive out the Romans. With his power behind it, the Jewish national army would wipe out the occupying legions. He would subdue Rome and rule from the throne of the Caesars.

But Jesus was ready with another Biblical quotation, once again from Deuteronomy. "It is written again," he declared, " 'Thou shalt not tempt the Lord thy God.' " God's hand was not to be forced, as the Israelites in the wilderness tried to do at the time of Moses. When the Messiah appeared for the last time there would be a sign from heaven. This Jesus knew, just as he knew that he would give out bread to the multitude — but when God willed it, and not before. For the present Jesus refused to announce his identity by means of such portents, and later on he was to disappoint the Pharisees by a similar refusal.

Then the vision slid into fantasy. Jesus saw himself on the summit of a lofty mountain (somewhat similar to the "high sacred places" of the Babylonians) from where he could see "all the kingdoms of the world, and the glory of them."

Attempts have been made to treat this account as a sober, objective narrative, firmly rooted in fact. Edersheim writes:

All the requirements of the text as we possess it would be satisfied if we assume Jesus to have stood on a high mountain, with Judaea to the south of him, Edom far off on the southeastern horizon, a range of mountainous plateaus stretching away eastward towards the Euphrates, and the snowy Lebanon ranges in the north. Here

were the cities of Herod, and there on the far western horizon the
pagan coastline of Philistia, with the vast, ship-dotted expanse of
the Mediterranean sparkling behind it. Such a panorama might well
have suggested "all the kingdoms of the world" to him. Under his
searching gaze they revealed themselves in all their grandeur, passing before him like some rich pageant that dazzles the beholder
with its wealth and the glitter of its beauty. From the far distance
came the gleam and clash of arms; his ear was caught by a subdued
oceanic murmur in which trumpet calls and human voices and the
deep impersonal roar of great cities could all be distinguished, while
the peaceful harmonies of thought, the music that is art, all com-
bined to ravish his senses and hold his judgment in abeyance.

This poeticizing description attempts to give Jesus' spiritual
ordeal a merely geographical location, and by so doing greatly
reduces its depth and intensity. Exhausted as he was by his
fast, Jesus could hardly have struggled up to the summit of
some mountain close to the Jordan; nor would he have needed
to do so in order to visualize all the kingdoms of the world in
their Satanic glory. The sight of Mount Hermon's snowy peak
could add nothing to his vision. He understood his people's
longing for world domination very well. It mattered little that
Jesus was not *au courant* with the secret maneuvers of Roman
politics, that he had never heard of the Germanic hordes or
the unknown civilizations of India, China, and Central America.
He only needed to recall the stories told in his own village
about Herod's sumptuous feasts, or the pomp and power that
attended a Roman general's retinue. He was well acquainted
with the true nature of political power, and slavery, and the
oppression of man by man.

All this inexhaustible power Satan now offered to place at
his disposal, for the benefit of the Jewish race as a whole —
on condition, naturally, that Jesus accepted the rules which
such authority implied. The moral standard he would hence-

forth have to recognize would no longer be divine charity, but human power, a ruler's might. He must bow down and worship force, obey the aggressive instincts by which all great expansionist empires had been carved out. Then he would know the grandiose destiny of a Sargon, an Alexander, a Caesar. War and diplomacy would become his instruments of government. His empire would not be eternal, but in after time children would learn his name as the most fabulous conqueror the world had ever seen, the unknown, lowly Jew who triumphantly overthrew Tiberius.

Confronted by this dream of Jewish Messianism, Jesus replied: "Get thee hence, Satan: for it is written, 'Thou shalt worship the Lord thy God, and him only shalt thou serve.'" To counter the temptation of political idolatry, Jesus once more referred to a text from Deuteronomy; and at once he was freed from his demonic obsession. A miraculous exorcism indeed! The divine words of Holy Writ had risen spontaneously to his lips as a defense against his people's mad dream of power — a dream in which he alone had perceived the Satanic motive that we call Caesarism. He had rejected the power that did not derive from God. The Kingdom now at hand would be a spiritual regime, nothing to do with politicians in Jerusalem or the Emperors of Rome. For this his people would never forgive him. Even today, after two millennia, the Jews still reproach Jesus for failing to set their country to rights.

When the good news of the Kingdom spread among the Greeks, and became known as the Evangelium, or Gospel, the story often began with an account of the temptations in the wilderness; this spiritual struggle was regarded as a crucial indication of the Kingdom's true nature. "In a similar fashion . . . certain Euripidean prologues bring on a divine personage who explains the plot of the tragedy in advance, and establishes its moral point." The Bible recorded that Adam, the first man, had been tempted in the Garden, and had succumbed. The second Adam, the first man of a new dispensation on earth, had been tempted in the wilderness — that Garden which had been blasted and made desert by the curse upon his predecessor — and had triumphed over temptation. His victory became that of all humanity, since all humanity was embodied in him, as earlier it had been embodied, to its own loss, in Adam, the first man.

But this was neither a simple nor a clear-cut victory. Jesus foresaw that everywhere, on the faces of princes and possessed idiots, rich and poor alike, he would find the same Satanic smile. As he made his way down the stony path that led to the Jordan, he knew he had a long and difficult struggle ahead of him; and this knowledge received prompt confirmation in the shape of some shattering news about John the Baptist.

two

The
News
of
the
Kingdom

1

The Return to Galilee

On his return to the Jordan, Jesus learned that the Baptist had been arrested by the police of Herod Antipas and incarcerated in the fortress of Machaerus. The Jewish historian Josephus offers the following account of the Tetrarch's action:

Crowds had gathered to hear John, and were passionately stirred by his words. Herod feared that such powers of oratory might kindle rebellion, especially since the people appeared ready to do whatever this man commanded them. So he secured the person of John before any trouble could arise on his account, with a view to preventing sedition and avoiding unnecessary danger at a later date: better safe than sorry. As a result of Herod's suspicions, John found himself consigned to Machaerus.

Rumors were flying round among John's disciples, and Josephus echoes the attitude of the politically minded. For them, Herod Antipas had been primarily concerned with keeping the peace in his domains, and had acted to that end. He had suspected John of being a revolutionary and an agitator. Others, including the Evangelists, attributed John's arrest to certain violent diatribes he had uttered against Herod himself. The desert prophet, it was said, had censured the prince's moral conduct in divorcing the daughter of the King of Arabia* so as to marry Herodias, the wife of his half-brother Herod-Philip (and thus his own sister-in-law) while her husband was still alive. It was whispered that Herod's action against John

* This monarch was Harith IV, King of Petra. [Tr.]

had been inspired by the lively hatred which Herodias felt for so outspoken a critic: left to himself, people argued, the Tetrarch would have felt for this desert prophet nothing but wonder and superstitious dread. After John's arrest, the rumor ran, Herod summoned him to hear what he had to say for himself. Certain people inferred from this, legitimately enough, that such "hearings" were in fact a form of trial.

The ruins of the Machaerus fortress still exist. They stand on a knoll, some little way inland from the eastern shore of the Dead Sea, in Moabite territory.

The northern flank of the hill contains several underground passages, their black and gaping mouths a notable landmark. To reach the summit one picks one's way up a series of footholds in the rock: these were originally chiseled out to form the foundations of a flight of steps. The summit itself is encircled by a leveling course of stones, the foundations of the fortress that was built by Herod's command. At the northern end of the flat plateau crowning the tell there is a large sunken cistern, sixty feet long and over twenty-five feet wide, built of dressed stone blocks, with here and there large patches of glazed cement still adhering to them. . . . On the southeast side, well back from the outermost fortifications, the remains of other walls can be observed, which possibly belonged to the royal palace. The sides and top of the tell are thick with shards of Roman pottery, and splinters from smashed antique glassware. At the base of the escarpment a sizable heap of dressed blocks indicates where (before its collapse) there stood one of those sixty-cubit corner towers described by Josephus.

At the time of John's imprisonment there the fortress was still brand-new, complete with a luxurious palace within its walls. Josephus refers to the size and splendor of the palace apartments. There were vast cisterns that fed the fountains in the courtyards. Towers and battlements ensured that Machaerus remained an impregnable stronghold. From its colonnades one could gaze out over the unique (and uniquely impressive) landscape of the Dead Sea and its surroundings.

John now lay captive in the subterranean vaults of this citadel. The great voice crying in the wilderness had been stilled. If the priestly caste in Jerusalem had wanted to save John, they could have done so by intervening on his behalf with Herod Antipas. But they stirred not a finger in support of the prophet, and for that Jesus never forgave them.

In this scandalous arrest Jesus perceived a sign, a portent. John had designated him as his successor. He must, there-fore, replace John; but it was too risky a step to take any-where near the Jordan. Besides, Jesus had worked out an al-together different plan of action. Like several other disciples of the Baptist, including Simon, James, John and Andrew, he thought it preferable to return to Galilee.

Here there was no desert, apart from a narrow strip on the northeast side of Lake Gennesaret. But Jesus did not propose to restrict himself to this area, much less to join some Essenian community. He was neither monk nor cenobite, nor yet an isolated prophet, and he had no intention of put-ting himself on show as an ascetic for the benefit of desert pilgrims. Instead of waiting for people to come to him, Jesus was determined to go and seek out the people himself. Like those itinerant preaching rabbis, the so-called Pilgrims of Galilee, he would go from village to village, spreading the good news that God's Kingdom was at hand.

There were two ways open to him to reach the mass of the people: speaking in the synagogues or speaking in the streets. Ever since the end of the Babylonian exile and the subsequent concentration of their religious ceremonial on the Second Temple in Jerusalem, the Jews had been obliged to establish a series of prayer centers throughout the land in which every local community could assemble for worship. Such a center they termed the *knesset* — a name used today for the National Assembly of the State of Israel. The Greeks translated this word as *synagōgē* — literally, meeting place.

Such "synagogues" existed not only throughout Palestine, but in any town whatsoever containing one or more Jewish communities. Each of these communities, which sometimes preserved private customs and spoke an idiosyncratic dialect, was furnished with its own separate synagogue. Every Friday evening, on the eve of the Sabbath, orthodox Jews would assemble there, and return once more on the Saturday morning. On other days of the week there might be various occasional ceremonies: otherwise the synagogue (like an Islamic mosque) was available for use as a meeting hall, discussion center, or lecture theater. The local council of elders would hold their deliberations there. The synagogue was not unlike the kind of modern Protestant church which can also be used as a village hall, whether for council business or a fête.

The service on the Sabbath began with prayers in praise of God, which were followed by readings from Scripture. Each book, or group of books, of the Old Testament was transcribed — without punctuation, in Hebrew — onto its own special roll of parchment, which was then slipped into a richly decorated cylindrical case and stored away in a cupboard. The Torah — the first five books of the Old Testament, known to us as the Pentateuch — was the object of quite extraordinary veneration. It was the sacred object *par excellence*, the Divine Book revealed and dictated by God to Moses; even the square characters in which it was written — though of recent origin and Aramaic provenance — were latterly supposed by the rabbis to have been traced by the divine hand of God. No one was permitted to alter its text even in the slightest detail. It was divided into one hundred and seventy-five sections, and these were read out one after the other, Sabbath by Sabbath, over a period of three and a half years — much as the New Testament is divided nowadays for Sunday reading in Christian churches. After a passage of the Law there followed various extracts from the Prophets. These "lessons" were declaimed from a lectern, by scribes with a perfect knowledge of Hebrew. "On the Sabbath day," Edersheim writes, "at least seven lectors were called upon in turn to read a portion of the Law, no portion ever being less than three versicles in length." These lectors were chosen in descending order of precedence. The first lesson was read by a priest who could claim direct descent from Aaron, or, failing such a one, by a Levite. Afterward it was the turn of the ordinary laity, according to their moral reputation and the extent of their scriptural knowledge.

During these readings in Hebrew it was the job of the meturgeman — interpreter — to give a verse-by-verse translation into Aramaic, Greek, or Latin, whichever happened to be the tongue spoken by the local Jewish community. In Galilee the language most commonly employed was Aramaic. This rendering could be improvised on the spot, which must have meant considerable latitude of interpretation at times — though often a set version was recited. The Greek translation of the Bible, known as the Septuagint, was composed for just such a purpose in the synagogues of Alexandria and Egypt. It corresponded roughly to the bilingual Roman Catholic missals in use today.

Synagogue ritual lent itself admirably to the type of teaching which Jesus intended to give. The readings for the day from the Law and the Prophets were expounded by a lay reader. After his address there often took place one of those open discussions, cast in dialectical form, to which the Jews were peculiarly addicted and which ranged over a variety of religious topics — the interpretation of the Law, the meaning of various oracular prophecies, cases affecting the individual conscience, all with concrete instances. These homilies and improvised glosses, even sober discussion of the most abstruse textual points, were frequently liable to turn into popular free-for-alls; and the constant comments and interjections of the congregation ensured that they were never less than lively. The majestic prayers of benediction were generally pronounced against a background of sharp Jewish disputation and rabbinical hairsplitting.

Thus, thanks to his detailed knowledge of the Old Testament, Jesus was in a position to intervene in the synagogue, and assume the role of scribe, or rabbi. But the unchanging social habits prevalent in the Near East (not to mention the routine of daily life that characterized every Galilaean township of the day) suggested another course of action — street-corner argument.

The races who populated the Mediterranean littoral enjoyed so sunny a climate for the greater part of the year that they lived more or less out of doors, seldom returning home except to sleep. Peasants and fishermen spent all their working hours in the open air. Most craftsmen, such as potters, wainwrights, and shoemakers, had booths that faced the street, unless they were tucked away down some narrow alley off the marketplace. The same applied to stallkeepers, butchers, and cooked-meat vendors. Any purchase, however trifling, involved endless discussion. People had time and to spare. While they argued and gesticulated, in the street outside donkeys went trotting by, and women plodded slowly along, bundles or water jars on their heads, or a child sitting astride their shoulders.

Four and a half centuries earlier Socrates had already realized that a Greek street offered the best possible setting for a moral and philosophical revolution. Jesus too, after his first brush with authority in the synagogues, went out and preached in streets and public squares, beside the nearby lake, in the fields. Here the scribes did not follow him — but the common people, the peasants and fishermen, were now able to hear him speak freely. They found themselves in communion with the spacious world of God's creation. This time the setting was not some cloistered Essene monastery, or the desert solitude of John the Baptist, but broad fields of asphodel, cool lakeside shade, and white tracks winding away into the low foothills.

The police did not disturb him; they were used to itinerant preaching rabbis. Besides, there were plenty of handy frontiers. A few hours' unhurried march on a clear night would take one from the Galilee of Herod Antipas into Gaulonitis, and thence to Batanaea or the Decapolis. If he had the fishermen on his side, a lakeside dweller could never be picked up; and Jesus had good friends among them in John's former disciples. While John himself lay in the dungeons of Machaerus, Jesus approached them with an invitation to join his own mission.

2

The Fishermen

IF YOU APPROACH Lake Gennesaret by the road from Cana and Mount Carmel, the view you get of it from the heights above Tiberias is, during the spring months, one of the loveliest in the world. Beyond the steel-blue mirror of water ancient Gadara lies silhouetted on its lofty hills. Those familiar with the area will recall the rocky beaches where hot springs gush out beside the fresh waters of the lake. Farther on, when the shore itself comes in sight, the traveler can see other distant landmarks — the clumps of trees outside Capernaum, the ford of Bethsaida, the heights of Chorazin, and, towards the west, the fertile Gennesar plain, dominated by the steep cliffs of the Wadi El Hammoud.

This panorama contains the entire background of Jesus' missionary activities: the traveler's eye can take it all in at a single glance. If to this picture he then adds the Arab villages in Upper and Lower Galilee which he has passed through on his journey, with their white flat-roofed houses and veiled women clustering round the single well to draw water, and the narrow alleys where shops stand open to the passer-by, and the cactus growing by the roadside, and the vines in stepped terraces, and the fields planted with gourds and watermelons, where wattle huts stand sentinel over their owners' property — then he will be able to visualize, against their original setting, all those historical scenes which the civilized Western world keeps so ineradicably graven upon its memory.

Galilee is a colorful, charming place. On palm and banana tree the fruit hangs ripe and plentiful. As dawn comes up, the pale waters of the lake are still warm to the touch, and you can hear the chuckling flow of the fresh springs by the shore. To a traveler coming from the deserts of the south, it must seem a veritable paradise.

Unfortunately, the dismal results achieved by man's political machinations have always tended to darken the horizons of this smiling garden. Today the village Arabs feel themselves in bondage to the Jews of the Israeli State. Two thousand years ago the Jews bore the yoke of Roman domination with equal impatience. Galilee was a haunt of Zealots and cutthroats. The insurrection of Judas of Gamala had been sparked off by a Galilaean, and other Galilaeans had recently attempted a revolt against the Procurator, Pontius Pilate. Behind that picturesque façade civil war was brewing.

Nevertheless, in Jesus' day Galilee was a prosperous region. Along the shores of the lake numerous rich townships flourished, one of which deserves special mention. This is Capernaum, originally known as Kefar Tehoumim, or the "frontier village." Capernaum was the center of the fishing industry, and in its market were sold the wheat and fruit produced by the rich Gennesar valley — famous then as now, and so rich, indeed, that the Jews took the word Gennesar to signify the "garden of princes." The close proximity of the frontier explained the need for customs officials and administrators in Capernaum: they were essential to control the flow of commerce along the route linking Damascus with Carmel and the Mediterranean ports.

Somewhere along the shore near Capernaum — perhaps on the beach known as Aïn Tabgha, or by the stretch of basalt rocks towards Magdala — Jesus met the friends he had made in John the Baptist's community: Simon and Andrew, James and John. Their Aramaic names were Shimeon, Nebzer, Yacob, and Jokanaan.

Like Jesus, they had fled from the region around Jordan, and had resumed their old occupation as lakeside fishermen. They owned their own boats and had other men working for them. All four were young, and well read; they had received John's baptism, lived in expectation of the Kingdom, and had only taken up their trade again after John's deviation from Essenism had got him into trouble. Had they also been involved in direct action of a political nature? It seems more than likely that they were members of the secret resistance movement against the Romans. Simon's surname was Bar-Jonah, which has generally been taken as a patronymic. Though Peter may have in fact been the "son of Jonah," there is also the possibility that *barjona* was an ancient word of Akkadian derivation, signifying "terrorist." The nickname Jesus gave to James and John, the sons of Zebedee, was Boanerges, the "sons

of thunder"; and here too a tendency towards political violence may be deduced. We would not, I suspect, be too far
from the truth if we assumed that Jesus' first friends and followers were ardent nationalists, who had seen John the Baptist
as their promised Messianic leader and were ready to turn
their hands to any sort of action.

So they met Jesus by the lakeside; and there they heard
the words they were never to forget as long as they lived.
With the faintest touch of irony Jesus said: "Come ye after
me, and I will make you to become fishers of men." And they
followed him. After all, they may have argued, why not spend a
week or two — perhaps even a few months — with so highly
regarded a comrade? Had not their master John sung his
praises in no uncertain fashion? He was going to spread John's
good tidings through the streets and synagogues and villages.
Why not help him in his task? In the hearts of all four of
them — Simon and Andrew, James and John — the hope of
political revolution was rekindled.

A strange life now began for the five friends. They trudged
on from village to village; on the eve of the Sabbath, Jesus
would go into a synagogue. As a pious and Orthodox Jew he
joined wholeheartedly in the prayers which the congregation
intoned in praise of God. When his turn came he would read
aloud some verses from the Law or the Prophets. Then he spoke
for himself, either discussing the text for the day or asking
some pertinent question of a scribe. Certain questions recurred
again and again, and made the congregation uneasy. What
was the greatest commandment of the Law? Suppose a man's
donkey had fallen into one of those unwalled wells to be
found throughout Palestine: was it permissible for him to haul
the beast out on the Sabbath, bearing in mind that by the
following day it would have died? Who was the Messiah? When

would he come? What was John the Baptist's function? Should
one do harm to one's Roman enemies? Was one obliged to
accept impositions ordered by the army of occupation? What
was the best form of resistance?

These questions Jesus asked, and listened attentively to the
answers the scribes propounded. Sometimes he raised an objection. His recurrent keynote was always the same: "The time is
fulfilled, and the kingdom of God is at hand; repent ye, and
believe the gospel." Everywhere he found confirmation of this
promise that God's Kingdom was nigh: in the Law, in the
oracular prophecies, even, one day soon, in the ripening harvest
and the budding of flowers.

A specific record of one occasion when Jesus intervened
in a synagogue has come down to us. The episode took place
in Nazareth, his own village: "And he came to Nazareth,
where he had been brought up: and, as his custom was, he
went into the synagogue on the sabbath day, and stood up
for to read. And there was delivered unto him the book of
the prophet Esaias. And when he had opened the book, he
found the place where it was written, 'The Spirit of the Lord
is upon me, because he hath anointed me to preach the gospel
to the poor; he hath sent me to heal the brokenhearted, to
preach deliverance to the captives, and recovering of sight to
the blind, to set at liberty them that are bruised. To preach
the acceptable year of the Lord.' And he closed the book, and
he gave it again to the minister, and sat down. And the eyes
of all them that were in the synagogue were fastened on him.
And he began to say unto them, 'This day is this scripture fulfilled in your ears.' And all bare him witness, and wondered
at the gracious words which proceeded out of his mouth."

Jesus was very careful not to put himself forward as the
prophetic hero described by Isaiah, but he made it clear that

the prophet's words had real and present applicability. In other words, he was carrying on John's teaching. The people of Nazareth were deeply stirred by his simple, moving eloquence. The scribes and Pharisees — those strict sectarians — congratulated themselves on acquiring so notable a recruit. They too believed in the advent of the Kingdom; and up till now there had been nothing to suggest the slightest difference of opinion between them and the new preacher in Galilee.

3

Teaching in the Synagogues

THERE ARE GROUNDS for supposing that Jesus' teaching in the synagogues of Galilee has not been lost altogether without trace. When we study his great inaugural discourse concerning the Kingdom, in the Gospel according to St. Matthew, we can distinguish certain moral maxims which contain no Messianic declaration, and may therefore date back to the very first stage in the dissemination of the Gospel — the period, that is, when despite his connections with John the Baptist, Jesus appeared the perfect Pharisee, a *jeune maître* applauded and honored in every synagogue.

The least exceptionable part of this teaching, which could hardly fail to command unanimous admiration, had to do with detachment from the wealth and the cares of this world.

In Galilee, Jesus found himself addressing very mixed audiences. It was a center of commerce, and local businessmen tended to amass vast fortunes. Money — as in every place and age — was a constant topic: perhaps more here than in Jerusalem. After the readings from the Law and the Prophets, Jesus would slip in some words of counsel concerning the Kingdom of God and the behavior propitious for those who looked to its coming: "Lay not up for yourselves treasures upon earth, where moth and rust doth corrupt, and where thieves break through and steal: but lay up for yourselves treasures in heaven, where neither moth nor rust doth corrupt, and where thieves do not break through nor steal: for where your treasure is, there will your heart be also."

The structure of this homily, so characteristically Aramaic and Semitic, is discernible even in translation. Jesus gives his words an antithetical rhythm, a strophic balance. The images — moth, rust, thieves — are sharp and striking. Heaven and earth stand in direct opposition. Then there comes the final clinching aphorism, unforgettable in its brevity and force: "Where your treasure is, there will your heart be also."

It was noticeable that Jesus spoke in a way that appealed at every level, to each member of his audience; he also showed a poetic grasp of metaphor that delighted those who loved verbal elegance. His tone was authoritative but never defiant; has matter brief and lucid, yet at the same time as moving as it was acute. "No man," he said, "can serve two masters: for either he will hate the one, and love the other; or else he will hold to the one, and despise the other. Ye cannot serve God and mammon."

The scribes dared not speak in so forthright a manner. Respect for success and wealth is a basic element of the Jewish temperament. Jesus was not, however, making an unqualified apologia for the condition of poverty; he was simply reminding his hearers that God and money were two sovereign masters of the human heart, that both strove for the world's allegiance, and that each individual had to choose between them.

For Jesus, money represented anxiety, the quest for comfort and an assured future, a safeguard against life's hazards, and possibly a weapon with which to challenge divine Providence: "I say unto you, take no thought for your life, what ye shall eat, or what ye shall drink; nor yet for your body, what ye shall put on. Is not the life more than meat, and the body than raiment?"

Jesus was very far from discouraging the idea of work as such. A man had to win his daily bread. But he ought not to occupy his mind with thoughts of food and clothing to the exclusion of all else. The people Jesus had in mind were the wealthy rather than the poor, those whose sole interests in life were their rich meals and luxurious garments. His image, when it came, was by no means devoid of irony: "Behold the fowls of the air: for they sow not, neither do they reap, nor gather into barns; yet your heavenly Father feedeth them. Are ye not much better than they?"

Jesus never suggested, here or elsewhere, that men should abstain from sowing and harvesting. Later he was to base his most striking image of the Kingdom on the sower's labors. He was merely observing that there are creatures in this world who feed themselves without difficulty, flourish and multiply, and nevertheless are considered singularly stupid. In proverbial wisdom the world over birds symbolize human witlessness; but they manage to survive.

"Which of you by taking thought can add one cubit unto his stature?" What Jesus was attacking through these questions was that worried preoccupation characteristic of the man who believes that he can master not only himself but the world by virtue of his anxiety. Later, it is true, he said that men *should* act responsibly, though in the last resort God was the one supreme master. Jesus was not preaching a doctrine of fatalism; but for wealth, success and power he felt nothing but contempt. To him they seemed not only out of all proportion but lacking in reality, and his irony on the subject has a Socratic quality about it: "Consider the lilies of the field, how they grow; they toil not, neither do they spin: and yet I say unto you, that even Solomon in all his glory was not arrayed like one of these." Jesus loved flowers. He had studied them and knew how frail they were: he admired the grace of their precarious and transient existence. He heard people worrying over next day's food, discussing the way prices had risen in the market, asking themselves how they were going to manage. The Kingdom was at hand, yet all people could think about was the cost of watermelons or a new pair of sandals! "Seek ye first the kingdom of God, and his righteousness; and all these things shall be added unto you."

He knew very well that poor folk were starving — but the reason for their plight was, precisely, that the rich did not look to the coming of the Kingdom, and had made no preparations for it. He knew from personal experience that the man who accepts a life of poverty, without material commitments, will never lack for basic essentials. He knew, too, that it is the rich who are always the first to worry about money. To all alike he said: "Take therefore no thought for the morrow: for the morrow shall take thought for the things of itself. Sufficient unto the day is the evil thereof."

The sort of life he wanted was peaceful, relaxed, with a hopeful eye to the future. But he did not discourage individual effort: "Ask, and it shall be given you; seek, and ye shall find; knock, and it shall be opened unto you: for every one that asketh receiveth; and he that seeketh findeth; and to him that knocketh it shall be opened." Here is radiant optimism indeed, full of confidence, crystal-clear. God is good. The created world is good. Labor is not in vain. Men must not be ashamed to ask of either God or their fellow-men. They must seek, knock, open the door of the world.

After the prayer the illustrative image: simple, striking, vivid: "What man is there of you, whom if his son ask bread, will he give him a stone? Or if he ask a fish, will he give him a serpent?" And then the swift general conclusion: "Therefore all things whatsoever ye would that men should do to you, do ye even so to them: for this is the law and the prophets."

In this way, at a single stroke, he concentrated all Biblical teaching into one unforgettable maxim. The six hundred and thirteen commandments enumerated by the rabbis were all reduced to the precept of charity. Henceforth humble illiterate folk would possess a rule of life that made them as wise as the most erudite scribe, since this summing up of the Law was something they could learn by heart and apply at will.

Before Jesus' time, Hillel the Elder had given the advice to his disciples: "Do not unto others what you would not they should do unto you." But Hillel had framed his golden rule in its *negative* form: to abstain from injuring one's neighbor was enough. But for Jesus the precept had *positive* force, and the charity it implied was of the active variety. He made no claim to originality; he had, he said, found everything he taught in the Law and the Prophets.

The most prominent characteristic of this early teaching of Jesus is, indeed, its close and obvious adherence to the Old Testament. Jesus spoke as an expounder of Holy Writ: his authority was the Bible, and he knew it thoroughly. As Klausner says: "The Pharisees themselves, we learn from a Jewish authority, could not challenge his scriptural knowledge. He could take them on in debate and confound them by textual citation, either from the Scriptures themselves or the laws subsequently based on them." But Jesus invested his Biblical discussions in the synagogue with an accent of authority that astonished the congregation, and this impression was strengthened as time went on. The people of Galilee began to realize that they were witnessing the dissemination of a doctrine whose roots lay far back in antiquity, but which had borne a wholly new sort of bud. It produced alarm and excitement in approximately equal quantities. It was a headier dose than the message of

John the Baptist, broader and more solidly based than the esoteric doctrine of the Essenes or the abstruse speculation of the apocalyptic writers.

When they left their village synagogue, these Galilaeans could remember some of the maxims they had just heard. *No man can serve two masters . . . Is not the life more than meat . . . Sufficient unto the day . . . Where your treasure is, there will your heart be also . . . All things whatsoever ye would that men should do to you, do ye even so to them . . .* Jesus, they told each other, was no ordinary man: such power, such lucidity! They were soon to have further proof of them.

4

INCIDENT AT CAPERNAUM

ONE SABBATH DAY, in the synagogue at Capernaum, a strange incident took place. After the reading of Scripture, Jesus was quietly discussing the text, in his usual manner. His authority and clarity of exposition held the congregation spellbound: people felt that the Word of God sprang to his lips spontaneously. The learned found nothing to criticize in what he said; while the poor, the sick, and even hard-worked housewives sensed such compassion for their lot in Jesus, so deep an insight into all they suffered during their weary and joyless lives, that it filled them with happiness.

These villages of Palestine swarmed with incurable cripples and invalids; much the same phenomenon can be seen today in the poverty-stricken, overcrowded streets of China or India. Lameness, blindness and paralysis were commonplace. Beggars in rags, lepers, hysterics and raving madmen roamed the streets. These latter were believed to be possessed by "unclean devils"; the crowd jeered at them, but gave them a wide berth. The wretched creatures were often left to fend for themselves, and lived from hand to mouth, begging for alms or picking up scraps in the gutter.

One such lunatic had slipped in with the crowd that filled the synagogue to hear Jesus. He listened, spellbound, but greatly excited by Jesus' discourse. When question time came he cried out: "Let us alone; what have we to do with thee, thou Jesus of Nazareth? art thou come to destroy us? I know thee who thou art, the Holy One of God."

For all its apparent lucidity, this was an enigmatic pronouncement; there was nothing about the madman's outburst which suggested any other emotion than scorn and anger. Here was some ill-disposed fellow accusing the new rabbi of leading the people to destruction, on the grounds that he risked sparking off a political revolt. Did he refer to Jesus as the Holy One of God in a mocking, sarcastic sense? It seems more than likely. Might he not have been picking up some part of Jesus' discussion, some allusion, apropos the prophetic books, to the Holy One of God, that is, the Messiah, and giving it an ironical application?

Whether he was inspired by hatred or by the strange mental clarity which sometimes occurs in the insane, there was danger here, and Jesus knew it. This hysterical ranter could easily work the crowd up. Whether knowingly or not, he was the instrument of another, that same powerful being who had tempted Jesus in the wilderness.

"Hold thy peace, and come out of him," Jesus said coldly. The madman howled and thrashed about, then collapsed, prostrate and silent, effectively calmed. The congregation in the synagogue were all struck by the way in which Jesus had won control over him with one brief command: in the ordinary way rabbis who practiced healing and exorcism went in for hypnotic passes, the laying on of hands, ritual spitting, and other such hocus-pocus. So brief, trenchant, and efficacious an intervention must have come as a great surprise to them.

Was this man a genuine lunatic, or consciously and willfully malicious while in his right mind? Did Jesus believe that Satan had usurped his personality, or did he merely detect Satan's influence operating through a deliberately hostile will? Jesus was to meet such madmen again in the village streets of Galilee — less often than is generally supposed, but on numerous occasions nevertheless. Today their treatment comes within the psychiatrist's province. Did Jesus honestly regard them as suffering from demoniacal possession, or was his apparent acceptance of this attitude a mere concession to the popular beliefs prevalent in his day?

Though we cannot avoid asking such questions today, they probably would have been meaningless to him. Some men were under the sway of evil. On occasion they were themselves morally responsible for the wicked acts they committed. They had trafficked with pure evil. At other times they were the victims of that occult power which has inspired several destructive geniuses — as we know to our cost — in this present day and age. Sometimes the patients Jesus treated were really mad, sometimes they were malingerers or hysterics, sometimes they were indeed possessed by the devil. In each case he varied his approach according to the circumstances.

A civilization such as our own (in which, despite all the advances made by psychoanalysis and psychiatry, millions of innocent persons are consigned, forcibly, to asylums, and die there unremembered) can scarcely boast that it has explained the root cause of this fearful scourge of humanity. Against his own wishes Jesus was compelled to face the evil incarnate in the world; and during such encounters he must often — though not invariably — have recognized the face of his tempter in the wilderness.

There was nothing mythical about Jesus' powers of healing.

One modern Jewish scholar, whose account of the matter is written from a non-Christian viewpoint, has the following to say about it:

Jesus obviously possessed quite extraodinary powers of influence and suggestion over people. If this had not been so, his disciples would never have held him in such veneration, remembering his every utterance by heart. Nor would the memory of him have survived so persistently, or made so dramatic an impact on their temporal and spiritual lives — and through them, by virtue of the power which he transmitted, on countless millions of men in after time. This power which Jesus possessed had some secret, mystical element about it: a quality which, though recognizable, is still very little understood by psychologists, medical experts, or scientists in general, whose knowledge scarcely extends beyond those natural laws revealed at any given time by their particular discipline. . . . Certain men, endowed with willpower far above the average and an inner life of exceptional strength, can modify the symptoms of most nervous disorders, even total insanity. This gift may be the result of the penetrating or compassionate expression they assume, or the profound faith they have in their own spiritual powers.

Whatever the validity of such an explanation may be, Jesus' miraculous powers do in fact account for the speedy authority which this young man acquired over his friends. John's disciples very soon got the feeling, without quite knowing why, that Jesus was dominating their lives. The reason for this Jesus himself acquainted them with at a later date. But the power shone forth of itself, long before anyone took it as a sign that the Kingdom was at hand.

5

Two Healings

AN APPARENTLY unimportant incident, which must date back
to this first period spent by Jesus in Galilee, shows him, as it
were, fighting his own healing gift. He shrank from the power
latent within him, and tried — not always successfully — to
shake off the crowd of desperate creatures who followed him
about. Among them none were more deserving of pity than
the lepers. At this period the term "leprosy" was used to cover
every sort of skin disease from dermatitis to elephantiasis and
cancer, as well as leprosy itself, which is the scourge of Africa
and the Middle East even today. Those tainted with it were not
only outcasts from all human society, exiled even from their own
families, but also under ban of excommunication, regarded as
"impure," cut off from every form of religious life, men stricken
and cursed by God. To lay hands on them was forbidden: they
were driven away with stones, and regarded as a species of living
filth, worse than wandering pigs or wild dogs. They aroused
feelings of horror that bordered on hatred.

One day, out in the countryside, Jesus happened to meet
one of these wretched creatures. Both of them, it seems certain,
were alone; and the leper had surely heard stories about this
young preacher. At all events, he made so bold as to supplicate
one who was regarded as a mighty rabbi. Falling on his knees
before Jesus, he exclaimed, as St. Mark tells us: " 'If thou wilt,
thou canst make me clean.' And Jesus, moved with compassion,
put forth his hand, and touched him, and saith unto him, 'I
will; be thou clean.' And as soon as he had spoken, immediately
the leprosy departed from him, and he was cleansed. And he
straitly charged him, and forthwith sent him away; and saith

unto him, 'See thou say nothing to any man: but go thy way, shew thyself to the priest, and offer for thy cleansing those things which Moses commanded, for a testimony unto them.' "

But hardly was the leper out of sight before he began to spread the news abroad and proclaim it openly. Jesus, as we learn from the Gospels, was seriously embarrassed by this publicity. He was afraid of trouble — not because he had contravened the law in laying hands on an unclean leper, but because his popularity was liable to increase beyond the limit of safety. Like John the Baptist, he might well be mistaken for a political agitator. This explains his near-angry attitude — not against the man who had wheedled a cure out of him, but because of the irksome consequences which that cure might entail. Let the healed leper, then, go with all speed and obtain a certificate from the appropriate source — as far away as possible for choice — maintaining a discreet silence as to the circumstances of his recovery. Unfortunately the leper talked, and what Jesus had feared might happen actually did so. It was now essential for him to avoid crowds.

This was not always possible. One day he was indoors, talking with his friends; it was a humble house, since the roof was flat, of beaten clay, like those of the poorest village houses in Galilee to this day. "It was noised that he was in the house. And straightway many were gathered together, insomuch that there was no room to receive them, no, not so much as about the door" (we should remember, however, that these houses are very small, consisting normally of a single room): "and he preached the word unto them. And they come unto him, bringing one sick of the palsy, which was borne of four. And when they could not come nigh unto him for the press, they uncovered the roof where he was: and when they had broken it up, they let down the bed wherein the sick of the palsy lay. When Jesus saw their faith, he said unto the sick of the palsy,

'Son, thy sins be forgiven thee.' But there were certain of the scribes sitting there, and reasoning in their hearts, 'Why doth this man thus speak blasphemies? who can forgive sins but God only?' And immediately when Jesus perceived in his spirit that they so reasoned within themselves, he said unto them, 'Why reason ye these things in your hearts? Whether is it easier to say to the sick of the palsy, Thy sins be forgiven thee; or to say, Arise, and take up thy bed, and walk? But that ye may know that the Son of man hath power on earth to forgive sins, (he saith to the sick of the palsy,) I say unto thee, Arise, and take up thy bed, and go thy way into thine house.' And immediately he arose, took up the bed, and went forth before them all; insomuch that they were all amazed, and glorified God, saying, 'We never saw it on this fashion.' "

If this time Jesus made no effort to withdraw, it was because he could not: he was standing, quite literally, with his back to the wall. Besides, his admiration for the unwavering faith of these people, who had without hesitation hauled an invalid up to the roof and let him down through a makeshift hole, was such that he could not but accede to their prayers. The crowd was elated at having among them so powerful a rabbi, a preacher so close to ordinary suffering humanity.

Would Jesus refrain from going any farther along this particular road, or would he continue to traffic with the poor and the sick? According to the beliefs of the time, a man suffering from paralysis had been stricken thus by God; either he was a sinner himself, or unhappily expiating the sins of his fathers. Sickness was always considered as a manifestation of divine punishment; despite Ezekiel's protestations, the Law of the Old Testament was quite explicit on this score. By healing invalids, by laying hands on a leper, Jesus appeared to be taking upon himself the sins of the world — as, indeed, he had done at the time of his baptism by John, in the waters of the Jordan.

So he had no cause to fear the taint of the "unclean ones." Would he now dare to approach those who, though less outwardly repugnant than the lepers, constituted a greater potential danger? How would he deal with a class that incurred the moral ostracism of all strict Pharisees and was regarded with contempt and disgust by "respectable folk" generally — the sick in mind?

6

PUBLICANS AND SINNERS

A SITUATION NOW AROSE which caused Jesus to place himself, voluntarily, in a somewhat compromising position. We do not know where it was he first met Mattatiya Levi ben Halphai: it may have been in his customs office at Capernaum, or while visiting a friend, or a chance encounter in the street. Matthew (as we know him) was a person of some consequence: educated, wealthy, influential, but by the very nature of his occupation prone to unscrupulousness. He was a *publicanus*, which meant that he farmed the customs duties Herod Antipas levied on his Galilaean subjects at the frontier with Gaulanitis. He fell into a more formidable category than that of the *gabbai*, who levied a one per cent tallage; he belonged with the *mokhes* or customs officers, whose extreme unpopularity was due to the fact that they had an absolutely free hand to collect on everything — livestock, cargo, ships. They were entitled to a two and a half per cent levy on all freight or cargo, and could raise this figure to twelve and a half per cent when dealing with "luxury goods." They controlled the main roads, the caravan trails, and the boats that plied on Lake Gennesaret; they made vast fortunes, and aroused the hatred of other lakeside dwellers, who regarded them as profiteers and pro-Roman collaborators.

As he walked down to the shore one day, Jesus paused outside the customs post and said to Matthew, "Follow me." The one thing Matthew had been hoping for was just such an invitation: he joined the group around Jesus without further delay. His joy at having won the rabbi's friendship and trust was so great that he invited Jesus to a meal in his house and assembled all his colleagues — customs officials, collaborators, self-made millionaires — to meet him. Jesus accepted the invitation, and came accompanied by his own friends. They all drank wine together. The scandal rocked Capernaum. Jesus had not yet reached the point where he let village girls kiss his feet, but this was even worse. To break bread with the filthy *publicani* — unheard-of!

As Jesus was a respected figure, the Pharisees did not dare to criticize him directly: they reserved their acidulous comments for those who passed as his disciples. "How can your Master eat in the company of these creatures?" they asked. But Jesus heard them, and replied: "They that are whole have no need of the physician, but they that are sick." This answer satisfied the Pharisees: Jesus, they argued, was admitting the corrupt nature of the *publicani*. Had he not compared them to the sick, and therefore by inference to those under God's curse? They themselves, of course, were the "whole." At this stage they still remained unaware of the irony in Jesus' words. Later he was to be more specific. In the eyes of God no one is "whole"; every honest man knows himself a *publicanus*, a sinner.

But though the Pharisees may have been satisfied, and dropped their complaints about Jesus' having eaten under Levi ben Halphai's roof, it looks as though John's own disciples reacted rather differently. They were ascetics, pledged, as was John himself, to abstain from wine. Their sense of outrage was exacerbated by Jesus' apparent lack of regard for the fasting practiced by the Baptist's followers. (It may be that this penance was self-imposed in an effort to obtain John's release from prison.) They still regarded Jesus as a disciple of John;

and not only did he ignore the prescribed fasts, but he habitually forgathered with notorious sinners, and drank wine in their company.

"Why do you not fast?" they asked him. Jesus replied with an image borrowed from the vintner's trade: it almost sounds like a deliberate snub. "No man putteth new wine into old bottles: else the new wine doth burst the bottles, and the wine is spilled, and the bottles will be marred: but new wine must be put into new bottles."

In the Western world today we preserve wine in casks; but in the Near East it is still stored in "bottles" made from goatskins that have been turned inside out and treated on their inner surface with pitch or resin. This is what gives Greek wine its faintly resinous flavor, so pleasant once one has acquired a taste for it.

How irritating Jesus' reply must have been! He was comparing his doctrine to a new wine, too raw, sparkling and effervescent for the old bottles of Judaism to contain without bursting. John's disciples were hurt by such a suggestion, and perhaps this was the beginning of the break which gradually came about between the growing community of Jesus' followers and John's own disciples.

Jesus had never visualized his mission in the same way as John. Despite his long fast in the wilderness, he had determined, from the moment he returned to Galilee, that he should live like any normal person, be at home among rich and poor alike. He was just as ready to break bread with a beggar as to grace some important official's banquet. He cheerfully drank wine and conversed with women. He would greet with a friendly embrace the *publicani*, whom strict Pharisees considered beyond the pale, Roman officers, who were loathed by the Zealots, or a village cobbler, whom the scribes regarded as beneath contempt. He was incapable of attributing any importance to distinctions of class, race, education, or income. Since he regarded no food as "unclean," *a fortiori* he applied the same criterion to his fellow-men.

He had little time for the various sects and labels which people thought up to emphasize the differences between them. Excessive asceticism he valued only as a temporary measure of self-discipline: it could not be the main purpose in life. The Pharisees had not yet perceived how profoundly his beliefs differed from theirs.

Rumors of what was going on in Galilee reached John's prison cell. Shortly afterward he sent two of his disciples to ask Jesus: "Art thou he that should come? or look we for another?" Perhaps John had hoped for swift and victorious political action from Jesus; perhaps, indeed, he expected the advent of the Kingdom while he himself was still in prison — which would release him from the unwelcome attentions of Herod Antipas and Herodias. He put his trust in certain specific Biblical prophecies and lived in expectation of God's triumph on earth. Now it had come to his notice that Jesus seemed interested in nothing except the physical and moral welfare of Galilaean villagers.

To this confidential but embarrassing question, Jesus gave no categorical answer; he simply said: "Go your way, and tell John what things ye have seen and heard." Then, either on this or some similar subsequent occasion, he quoted a text from Isaiah which described the healing of the sick, and concluded with a phrase he particularly liked: "To the poor the gospel is preached." Though Jesus may have diverged from John in his teaching and his way of life, he was never to repudiate the Baptist or say anything which might diminish his glory; and when John's steadfastness in the spirit led him to a martyr's death, Jesus was to pay him the highest tribute.

Nevertheless, Jesus felt himself at the crossroads. The common people adored him; he also had the respect of scholars and other important members of the community. Could he really afford to appeal to the outcast element, whom everyone despised? Dare he fly in the face of "respectable" opinion, or openly criticize certain established Jewish traditions? And if he followed this course, would his friends stand by him? Before doing anything else, he felt, it was vital to expound his views on the Kingdom. If he was to become involved in such a conflict, people must know the reason for it. So now he spoke less often in the synagogues: when evening came he would sit down at the edge of a field, or beside the lake, and talk to the people who gathered round him. It was springtime, and the Kingdom figured in these discussions with ever-increasing frequency.

7

The First Parables of the Kingdom

It would be a mistake to suppose that in Jesus' day the Kingdom of God could be discussed publicly without certain precautions being observed. The Romans, it is true, together with the collaborating police officials of Herod Antipas, left the rabbis free to give religious instruction. But any overbold views expressed on such a topic might well be given a political interpretation by those who heard them. If *that* happened, it would be rather like speaking on the liberation of France during the German occupation. To make quite sure there was no trouble, Jesus had to use semi-clandestine phraseology, an oblique approach — all the more so since the Jews remained profoundly divided among themselves. Some of Jesus' followers were partisans of the Resistance, while others, such as Matthew, were regarded as collaborators. Jesus was therefore obliged to tread warily, even where his own friends were concerned.

The parable (or fable, as we should call it today) was a device sometimes employed by the rabbis; it offered him an admirable means of self-expression. To begin with, it possessed a certain innate charm of its own. Jesus delighted in telling a story — not the kind of fantasy represented by the tales in *The Thousand and One Nights*, nor yet frankly incredible fables of the sort that originated in Babylonia and were collected by Aesop, but simple stories depicting the ordinary day-to-day life of Galilaean peasants and fishermen. He observed such folk with a keenly attentive eye, listening to their talk, relishing their natural wisdom and frank good humor. His village upbringing had left him with a wide knowledge of trees and birds and plant life, the multifarious complexity of which never ceased to astonish him. Rain and wind and clouds, the flicker of fish through water — such things he found perennially enchanting.

He had discovered models for such use of imagery in the Bible. Jotham, Nathan the prophet, Isaiah and Jeremiah, the author of the Book of Job, and several Psalmists had composed excellent verse parables, their rhythm as well defined as that of the long wailing chant which some Arab storyteller will intone as he squats in the shade beside a mosque.

On the face of it anyone, even a child or an illiterate woman, should be capable of understanding a parable. But appearances are deceptive, and that limpid simplicity not quite what it seems. The imagery carries significance beyond the bare sense expressed by the words; it can carry any meaning one cares to read into it. The poet is more richly endowed than the philosopher, and Jesus had chosen poetry for his vehicle. He knew that as his hearers meditated on the parables he told they would constantly discover fresh and deeper layers of meaning in them.

One day he was sitting in a boat moored just offshore, while his audience sat in groups along the beach, wherever it was shady. "Hearken," he told them; "behold, there went out a sower to sow: and it came to pass, as he sowed, some fell by the way side, and the fowls of the air came and devoured it up. And some fell on stony ground, where it had not much earth . . . But when the sun was up, it was scorched; and because it had no root, it withered away. And some fell among thorns, and the thorns grew up, and choked it, and it yielded no fruit. And other fell on good ground, and did yield fruit that sprang up and increased; and brought forth, some thirty, and some sixty, and some an hundred. . . . He that hath ears to hear, let him hear!"

This final phrase was an exhortation to pay close attention, the equivalent of "Keep your ears open." It seems plain that in this parable of the sower Jesus was drawing on his own experience. When he invited the rich Jews in the synagogues to think a little less about their money and a little more about God, some were so inattentive that they did not even hear what he said; others heard but failed to understand; while others again were charmed by his words, but very soon forgot them. But besides these there were others, who listened and pondered, and in whose minds the words they had heard sprang up like a tree, to bear rich fruit. Such an interpretation, though fairly close to the mark, imposes too detailed a load of allegory on this little story: we must not assume that wayside, stony ground, birds and thorns are each to be equated with some specific category of hearer. The main point about the parable of the sower is much simpler: the harvest is certain, the lost grain unimportant. The news of the Kingdom's imminence — like sowing time — is no sudden, unfamiliar bolt from the blue,

but a divine gift to mankind: unobtrusive, omnipresent, regarded as naturally as the changing seasons and the cycle of
labor in the fields. The Kingdom's advent is as near, and as
inevitable, as the end of spring and the quickening of grain in
the furrow that comes after. The sower never despairs. His
victory is assured.

Jesus took the same parable and explored it from a fresh
angle: "So is the Kingdom of God, as if a man should cast seed
into the ground; and should sleep, and rise night and day, and
the seed should spring and grow up, he knoweth not how.
For the earth bringeth forth fruit of herself; first the blade,
then the ear, after that the full corn in the ear. But when the
fruit is brought forth, immediately he putteth in the sickle, because the harvest is come."

The Kingdom, then, has nothing of the apocalyptic catastrophe about it: it does not burst upon the world, sudden and
stunning, like a thunderclap, but rather resembles the cumula-
tive, superhuman, infallible growth of grain in the earth. Jesus
laid great stress on images which presented the Kingdom in
terms of organic evolution. We observe him pondering the
matter before his audience: "Whereunto shall we liken the
Kingdom of God? or with what comparison shall we compare it?
It is like a grain of mustard seed, which, when it is sown in
the earth, is less than all the seeds that be in the earth: but
when it is sown, it groweth up, and becometh greater than all
herbs, and shooteth out great branches; so that the fowls of
the air may lodge under the shadow of it." This time Jesus was
contrasting the small beginnings of the Kingdom with its
greatness after it had grown and spread.

While he was sitting in that boat by the shore of the lake, did
his eyes, perhaps, once more turn to the distant horizon, to the
wilderness where he had seen a vision of all the kingdoms of
the world? And did he, now, foresee a time when the vast

branches of God's Kingdom — that grain of mustard seed — would with their spreading foliage obliterate so fantastic a spectacle?

People listened as he spoke. How different this Kingdom was from what people so often described to them — fire blazing from heaven, wild celestial wheeling and charging, shouts of victory, all the carnage and triumph! Even less did it bear any resemblance to the bloody vengeance promised by the Zealot guerrillas. Why, not even the Romans were to be killed under this dispensation!

Jesus produced another, still more prosaic image: "Whereunto shall I liken the Kingdom of God? It is like leaven, which a woman took and hid in three measures of meal, till the whole was leavened." There was nothing noble or elevated about leaven: it caused fermentation, and it was an "impure" substance, strictly prohibited during the Feast of Unleavened Bread. But this mattered little to Jesus. The Kingdom would leaven the bread of the world, and transform it utterly.

These early parables presented the Kingdom in a new and completely original light. Clearly Jesus was moving right away from John and the Essenes, from the apocalyptic writers, from the poets and prophets who dreamed of cataclysmic disaster. But it was equally plain that he had not yet expounded his concept of the Kingdom *in toto*; he had been concentrating on one aspect only of it. He had demonstrated the laws governing its growth in the world. But what did it really consist of? On this point the early parables had nothing to say.

One day Jesus referred, emphatically, to the incomparable value of the Kingdom, and the sacrifices that were necessary to gain it. The imagery he employed was even simpler than before: cautious almost to the point of furtiveness. He compared the truth of the Kingdom to the flame of a lamp: "Is a candle

brought to be put under a bushel, or under a bed? and not to
be set on a candlestick?" The Kingdom is pure Light, and not
to be hidden from men: they must all see it. But to enter that
Kingdom requires much toil, and sacrifices willingly undertaken, though he who acts thus may be thought to have taken
leave of his senses. "The kingdom of heaven is like unto
treasure hid in a field; the which when a man hath found, he
hideth, and for joy thereof goeth and selleth all that he hath,
and buyeth that field. Again, the kingdom of heaven is like
unto a merchant man, seeking goodly pearls: who, when he had
found one pearl of great price, went and sold all that he had,
and bought it."

These two parables should be taken together. The Kingdom
is in truth the heart of the world. Beside it all else is as nothing. Some of those present, as they heard Jesus making up his
parables, must have gradually begun to understand why he took
so strong a line against worldly cares and enslavement to money.
He was a man in possession of hidden treasures, which sooner
or later he would reveal to them. Intrigued and curious, but
with complete confidence, his friends watched him, awaiting
the moment.

8

THE TWELVE DISCIPLES

BOTH JOHN's disciples and a certain section of the Pharisees
were stirred to resentment by the attitude Jesus was now taking.
This may have been the reason why he decided to establish a
clearly defined inner group of intimates. He chose twelve of
them: a symbolic number. Jacob had begotten twelve sons, the
Patriarchs, who had in turn given their names to the twelve
tribes of Israel. There were twelve minor prophets listed in the
Old Testament canon.

The twelve were all Galilaeans. Simon Bar-Jonah, Andrew, James and John are known to have been disciples of the Baptist. According to the Fourth Gospel, Jesus met another disciple of John's called Nathanael, who is possibly identical with the Bartholomew listed in the Synoptic tradition. Philip, whose name, like Andrew's, is Greek, also figures in the Fourth Gospel. "Thomas" must be a surname: he was also known as Didymus, or the Twin. It is possible that James the son of Alpheus was brother to Matthew the *publicanus*. Thaddeus is a shorter form of Theodosius or Theodore. Simon, known as Simon the Zealot to distinguish him from Simon Bar-Jonah, belonged to a terrorist group — as did Judas Iscariot. Some scholars interpret the name of this unhappily notorious disciple as the "man of Kerioth," a small town in the northern part of Judaea; and the presence, among all these Galilaeans, of one isolated Judaean has given rise to some puzzlement. But as Cullmann remarks, "We may well wonder whether "Iscariot" is not, perhaps, a Semitic transcription of the Latin word *sicarius*. Philologically this derivation is quite possible."

The information we possess concerning Jesus' twelve disciples is both uncertain and curious; but at least it tells us something about their antecedents. They came from three groups: John's disciples; the so-called Zealots; and collaborators — at least Matthew, and James the son of Alpheus if he was Matthew's brother. Possibly Jesus brought these disparate elements together on purpose.

None of the Twelve was a Pharisee or an Essene; nor did any disciple belong to the aristocratic caste of the Sadducees. Jesus was to make friends in all these sects, but his disciples came from elsewhere. They have often been represented as working-class men, coarse, illiterate, and uncouth of manner. This is not accurate — though in itself it would have made no difference to Jesus. He might well have selected the Twelve from among the beggars, and other such pariahs; but all those whom he chose belonged to a fairly comfortable stratum of society. Simon and his comrades owned several boats. Matthew, it is certain, was a rich man. From the recollections later gathered together as the Acts of the Apostles, one gets the impression that the Twelve were young men — some of them, including Simon, already married — who followed a trade and had a smattering at least of higher education. They knew their Bible well, took a close interest in politics and local affairs, and belonged to the same social class Jesus did.

Jesus had not brought them together simply to establish a "group" like those we find among young people today. Even less did he mean to make them the nucleus of a toughly disciplined monastic community run on Essene lines. The purpose of these disciples was to visit such villages as Jesus himself could not get to in person. He had a well-defined missionary task for them: they were to proclaim the advent of God's Kingdom throughout Israel. The parables had revealed that this Kingdom was now in process of germination. Jesus was the King — the clandestine King — of his people. Who, under his guidance, would gather in the harvest? The Twelve. It was to them, and them alone, that Jesus later revealed his true identity.

The Twelve were to be the pillars of the Kingdom; they would lead its tribes and reap its fruits. But at present their role was that of heralds, envoys charged with the task of broadcasting the portentous news concerning the Kingdom's inauguration.

In the ancient world all dispatches were carried by messenger, either on foot or on horseback. The runner who brought the news of Marathon is still remembered today: having reached Athens, and broken the good tidings of victory over the Persians, he collapsed and died as a result of his superhuman efforts. The

Twelve would act as such messengers on Jesus' behalf, bearing news of the Kingdom. The Hebrew name for them was *sheluhim*; to the Greeks they were *apostoloi*, apostles.

Later, it is true, this role of apostle — that is, proclaimer of good tidings, spreader of the *evangelion* concerning the Kingdom — was to be performed by many other men besides the Twelve. From St. Paul's letters we can see just how numerous the apostles were in the various Christian communities. But the Twelve remain the first apostles, the pioneers.

Jesus attached so great an importance to their selection that we find him spending the whole of the previous night alone in prayer, as he was wont to do on occasions of grave importance. He wanted God Himself to choose the names of the Twelve. When morning came, he gathered his followers together on a little hill: this may conceivably have been Tell Kinnereth, which overlooks the northeast side of the lake and slopes down to the water in an avalanche of tumbled rocks, flanked by palms and pine trees. For Jesus' friends this eminence was, then and in after years, known as the Mountain, because they regarded it as the Sinai of the New Testament. Moses had toiled six thousand feet to the summit of that red rock in the wilderness. He had dragged Israel's chieftains after him to receive, amid the storm, the fearful revelation of the nomads' Torah. Now, at dawn, after a still night, Jesus climbed the rocks above the lake to nominate his lifelong companions, those who were to hold high office in the Kingdom of God. To them would be revealed the new Torah of Galilee — not to replace that given on Sinai, but to supplement and complete it, as God's wrath is followed by His smile.

It is possible that the rabbis of Jerusalem were profoundly shocked by the idea of comparing Jesus with Moses, and the hill of the apostles with Mount Sinai. If they found such a concept ridiculous, however, they were making a great mistake, because the day was not far off when mankind would find the Torah of Galilee instrumental in their conversion to the revelation made upon Mount Sinai. It was by climbing that lakeside knoll that humanity would discover the lofty peak in the desert. The Twelve were to become more renowned throughout the world than the Hebrew Patriarchs or the Seven Sages of Greece; yet so humble were they in their glory that save for three or four of them we know little more than their names.

His choice now made, Jesus was at last in a position to give a clear and unambiguous account of his mission. It seems very likely that he unfolded the plan of the Kingdom there on the hill where he had named his apostles.

9

THE CHARTER OF THE KINGDOM

THE KINGDOM, representing as it does God's infinite triumph, is not *per se* capable of definition. Jesus had told the populace that this Kingdom was quickening secretly, like sown corn in the furrow. But for the Twelve he was now obliged to clarify the code which would govern the Kingdom after its ultimate victory. He sat down on a rock, with the waters of the lake stretching away to the hazy blue horizon beyond him, and began to outline the nature of happiness. The Commandments laid down on Mount Sinai were now completed by the proclamation of the Beatitudes, which ultimately changed the face of the world. The Jews, the Romans, and indeed the inhabitants of every empire hitherto had exalted the wealthy, the powerful, the brave, the victorious. But Jesus said:

"Blessed are the poor: for their's is the kingdom of heaven. Blessed are they that mourn: for they shall be comforted. Blessed are the meek: for they shall inherit the earth. Blessed are [the hungry]: for they shall be filled. Blessed are the merciful: for they shall obtain mercy. Blessed are the pure in heart: for they shall see God. Blessed are the peacemakers: for they shall be called the children of God. Blessed are they which are persecuted: for their's is the kingdom of heaven.

"Blessed are ye, when men shall revile you, and persecute you, and shall say all manner of evil against you falsely, for my sake. Rejoice, and be exceeding glad: for great is your reward in heaven: for so persecuted they the prophets which were before you."*

For two thousand years now these ultra-simple words have provoked an endless flood of written interpretation and comment. Yet Jesus never committed his sayings to paper himself, any more than Socrates had done before him; he thought it sufficient to entrust them to the faithful memory of his disciples, who set them down with certain minor discrepancies. Yet they remain clear enough in essence; and the fact that one maxim may have been interpolated, or another given too specifically spiritual an application, makes very little difference to the main issue.

Jesus carefully avoids laying down any new commandments. The "men of old time" are always good, and God has nothing to add to the Decalogue. What he does is to use the "hymn of praise" as a vehicle to proclaim a series of *berakōt*, or Beatitudes. He does not say that the poor *will* possess the Kingdom of God, but that it *is* theirs, now. It is true that in the Greek text of St. Matthew the other promises are in the future tense; but we should remember that Jesus was *speaking* Aramaic, and therefore would have employed the imperfect, as the only tense which could convey the sense of a *continuing* present. Everything is to begin at once — the conquest of the

* This version of the Beatitudes is based mainly on Matthew 5, 3-12, but modified here and there from the more uncompromising account given in Luke 6, 20-23. [Tr.]

Kingdom by the poor, the meek inheriting the earth, the consolation of the afflicted, the filling of the hungry, the manifestation of God to the pure in heart. Jesus is not describing a regime under which present sufferings are to be compensated for by a blissful afterlife; his purpose is to convey the *immediate* happiness of those who henceforth are the heirs of the suprahuman reality. Jesus enjoys suffering and poverty no more than the next man; there is no taint of that puritan morality in him which equates misery with virtue. The poverty he regards as blessed is not wretchedness or starvation, but freedom from the tyranny of cash — and indeed, Matthew was later to gloss this as "Blessed are the poor *in spirit*." Similarly with the Beatitude of the hungry, whom he made to "hunger and thirst *after righteousness*." Poverty, affliction, pity, pureness of heart — they are all methods of reaching God through the liberation of the spirit, or soul.

The happiness which God bestows is, in Jesus' eyes, so overwhelmingly real and actual and *there* that he predicts instantaneous joy, like a bolt from heaven, for those persecuted on his account. The recompense they will obtain from God is great indeed. Already they feel in their hearts that perfect joy which was later to be experienced by St. Francis of Assisi — the man who most nearly lived out his life in accordance with the Beatitudes.

Jesus foresaw that his friends *would* be persecuted. When he placed this somber but, ultimately, triumphant prospect before the Twelve, he did so only after long and careful thought. He had anticipated the first rifts in his popularity in Galilee, and foresaw the storm that was bound to follow. His teachings on the Kingdom would force him to undertake a terrible purging of official Judaism, a process of spiritual regeneration. He would have to break the iron restrictions of the Sabbath, throw off the yoke of tradition and exclusive shibboleth that was paralyzing true religious faith. Such a struggle would be bitterly fought. But Jesus had spent much time meditating on the lives and writings of the Prophets: he knew how cruelly Israel had persecuted them. Long ago the people had risen in revolt against Moses; Elijah had been harried by Ahab and Jezebel; Isaiah, it was said, had died a martyr's death, while Jeremiah's life had been one long torment.

The blessed state of the poor in spirit led on to the happiness of the persecuted, who were at long last to reign triumphant. Jesus, in other words, applied the lesson of his own temptation to these Beatitudes. His refusal to gain world power through political action carried an implicit acceptance of the challenge he faced from the princes of this world. His followers would have to do likewise. Yet he knew that through his seeming failure God would triumph. Strange, the way in which God's victory is achieved by defeat.

Jewish society was so shattered by the Roman occupation that even these Beatitudes of Jesus could be taken as a kind of political program, a refusal to take sides between revolutionary assassins and the collaborators, who worked in with Rome. But Jesus himself refused to consider the Kingdom in political terms. He rejected the programs envisaged by these opposing parties, who were already lining up their forces for the savage and ruthless civil war that broke out in Palestine some forty years later. Power politics, whether employed by last-ditch nationalists or profiteering collaborators, Jesus regarded as uniformly rotten.

Jesus was anxious to make a clear exposition of the links between his doctrine and that held by the official custodians of Judaism. "Think not," he said, "that I am come to destroy the law, or the prophets [the Bible]: I am not come to destroy, but to fulfil. For verily I say unto you, Till heaven and earth pass [as long as the world endures], one jot or one tittle shall in no wise pass from the law, till all be fulfilled." Jesus recognized the fact that the Bible was permanent and unalterable, down to the last comma, as we would say nowadays. It was the Word of God, and as such sacrosanct. Nevertheless, some parts of it — such as the laws embodied in the Code of the Covenant and various other regulations — had now accomplished their purpose and been superseded. Life was no longer lived as it had been in the days of Mount Sinai. Jesus had accomplished and brought to completion what the Old Testament had left still unformulated. For this he had the authority of the Supreme Legislator of the Kingdom.

"For I say unto you, That except your righteousness shall exceed the righteousness of the scribes and Pharisees, ye shall in no case enter into the kingdom of heaven. Ye have heard that it was said by them of old time, Thou shalt not kill; and whosoever shall kill shall be in danger of the judgment: but I say unto you, That whosoever is angry with his brother without a cause shall be in danger of the judgment: and whosoever shall say to his brother, Raca, shall be in danger of the council: but whosoever shall say, Thou fool, shall be in danger of hell fire. . . . Ye have heard that it was said by them of old time, Thou shalt not commit adultery: but I say unto you, That whosoever looketh on a woman to lust after her hath committed adultery with her already in his heart. . . . Again, ye have heard that it hath been said by them of old time, Thou shalt not forswear thyself, but shalt perform unto the Lord thine oaths: but I say unto you, Swear not at all; neither by heaven; for it is God's throne: nor by the earth; for it is his footstool: neither by Jerusalem; for it is the city of the great King. Neither shalt thou swear by thy head, because thou canst not make one hair white or black. But let your communication be, Yea, yea; Nay nay: for whatsoever is more than these cometh of evil. Ye have heard that it hath been said, An eye for an eye, and a tooth for a tooth: but I say unto you, That ye resist not evil: but whosoever shall smite thee on thy right cheek, turn to him the other also. And if any man will sue thee at the law, and take away thy coat, let him have thy cloke also. And whosoever shall compel thee to go a mile, go with him twain. . . . Ye have heard that it hath been said, Thou shalt love thy neighbour, and hate thine enemy. But I say unto you, Love your enemies, bless them that curse you, do good to them that hate you, and pray for them which despitefully use you, and persecute you; that ye may be the children of your Father which is in heaven: for he maketh his sun to rise on the evil and on the good, and sendeth rain on the just and on the unjust. For if ye love them which love you, what reward have ye? do not even the publicans the same? And if ye salute your brethren only, what do ye more than others? do not even the publicans so? Be ye therefore perfect, even as your Father which is in heaven is perfect." That last lapidary aphorism is highly characteristic of Jesus' technique.

In this way, for the benefit of the Twelve, Jesus summed up his interpretation of Scripture, with particular reference to the Decalogue. His task now was to take the application of the Law beyond what the scribes and Pharisees envisaged. It was not by modifying the Commandments that this would be achieved, but by giving them depth. Jesus got right through to human *intentions*: he codified the morality of the heart, which in this context has nothing to do with sentiment. (Semitic languages do not admit such a meaning for the word.) What it refers to here is the *mind*, and its special attributes of intelligence and free will.

What attitude were the disciples expected to adopt in the face of persecution — the hatred of the terrorists, perhaps, or the burdensome impositions (forced labor, for instance) liable

to be laid upon them by the occupation authorities? Jesus required them to conduct themselves in a manner which reflected
the infinite compassion and mercy of God. It is not by force
that men triumph over brutality, but with patience and cheer-
fulness.

This moral attitude advocated by Jesus has been called a code
fit only for slaves and weaklings. But the natural instinct of
slaves the world over is for revolt; Spartacus, not Jesus, is their
spiritual leader. When it comes to the point of action, we find
it is, precisely, weaklings who most often employ sadism,
violence and brutality as their weapons. Peace of mind and self-
control are qualities that call for inner strength. Jesus wanted
his followers to have absolute mastery over their anger, and
indeed over all the passions.

Jesus loved the life bestowed upon mankind by their heavenly
Father, who had created all natural things — sun, rain, changing
seasons, the animal kingdom, man himself. He wanted men to
become conscious of their status as children of God. What was
absolutely without precedent in his Gospel of the Kingdom was
the creation of a race of men who would strive to model themselves after divine perfection.

If after two thousand years humanity has *still* only managed
to attain such an ideal on the rare and exceptional occasion,
these Galilaean Jews assembled by the lakeside can have had
only the dimmest inkling of just how profound and far-reach-
ing a moral-*cum*-religious revolution they had on their hands.
What rabbi of the day would have dared to dream that Israel
might expand till she embraced the world, or that the
Decalogue would become the charter for God's adoption of all
mankind? Or, indeed, conceived so radical and penetrating an
interpretation of the Bible as Jesus had?

In some vague way the Twelve still expected fantastic achieve-
ments on Jesus' part. The contrast between his spiritual King-

dom and that on which their own deluded hopes and nationalist ambitions rested did not worry them.

10

INNER JUSTICE

STILL JESUS reiterated his requirements: now he seemed to be
aiming at nothing short of perfection. One day he dealt with
the vital matter of those who were to constitute the Kingdom
of God on earth, and what conduct their sanctity demanded
of them.

In religious matters Galilee was subservient to the theocracy
of Jerusalem, which meant (as the man in the street saw it)
that middle-class respectability and piety called the tune. In
these small villages, as in small villages the world over, everyone's private life was public property; and it is not hard to
imagine the sort of tyrannical sanctions that could be imposed
under such conditions by the forces of moral conformity. An
ostentatious outward parade of fidelity to religious law became
the yardstick dividing "respectable folk" from the rest. The
rich had to "set a good example." Their lavish almsgiving
aroused the admiration of the poor and added to their already
high reputations: the prestige afforded by wealth was enhanced
by that attaching to good works. Jesus had a horror of such
showy religiosity: it seemed to him the canker at the heart of
Judaism. He was determined to root out any such tendencies
among his followers, and addressed them on the subject without
reservations; what he said constituted a relentless flaying of
fashionable observances.

"Take heed," he told them, "that ye do not your alms before
men, to be seen of them: otherwise ye have no reward of your
Father which is in heaven.

"Therefore when thou doest thine alms, do not sound a

trumpet before thee, as the hypocrites do in the synagogues and in the streets, that they may have glory of men. Verily I say unto you, They have their reward. But when thou doest alms, let not thy left hand know what thy right hand doeth: that thine alms may be in secret: and thy Father which seeth in secret himself shall reward thee openly."

Jesus had seen many of these rich and pious Jews, who arranged for the village crier to proclaim their distribution of goods on feast days, or publicly announce the sums they offered in the synagogues. Against them he let fly one of those biting phrases which he had such a genius for producing. With an illustrative gesture of his right hand he told his listeners not to let their left hand know what their right hand was doing. "And when thou prayest," he continued, "thou shalt not be as the hypocrites are: for they love to pray standing in the synagogues and in the corners of the streets, that they may be seen of men. Verily I say unto you, They have their reward. But thou, when thou prayest, enter into thy closet, and when thou hast shut thy door, pray to thy Father which is in secret; and thy Father which seeth in secret shall reward thee openly."

Jesus is not here condemning public and collective prayer as such — he scrupulously attended these meetings himself. What he objects to is *ostentation*, a built-in danger when a religion is official and prayer can be used to enhance individual reputations. "Moreover when ye fast," Jesus added, "be not, as the hypocrites, of a sad countenance: for they disfigure their faces, that they may appear unto men to fast. Verily I say unto you, They have their reward. But thou, when thou fastest, anoint thine head, and wash thy face; that thou appear not unto men to fast, but unto thy Father which is in secret: and thy Father, which seeth in secret, shall reward thee openly."

Here is a side of Jesus which both corrects and supplements the picture we have of him drinking wine at Matthew's banquet. He has no objection to fasting *per se*, but only to those who fast in an ostentatious manner. He clearly loathes long faces and sour, killjoy expressions. Nothing could be further from his ideal than that of the dirt-encrusted, fanatical ascetic, who sets up in men's minds a distorted caricature of their loving, compassionate, self-effacing Father in heaven. "Anoint thine head, and wash thy face," Jesus said; and indeed, he went further. He impugned the religious sincerity of those who presumed to criticize other men's conduct; those self-regarding paragons of all the virtues who, dazzled by their own perfection, appointed themselves judges of public morality: "Judge not, that ye be not judged. For with what judgment ye judge, ye shall be judged: and with what measure ye mete, it shall be measured to you again. And why beholdest thou the mote that is in thy brother's eye, but considerest not the beam that is in thine own eye? Or how wilt thou say to thy brother, 'Let me pull out the mote out of thine eye'; and, behold, a beam is in thine own eye? Thou hypocrite, first cast out the beam out of thine own eye; and then shalt thou see clearly to cast out the mote out of thy brother's eye. . . ."

"Beware of false prophets, which come to you in sheep's clothing, but inwardly they are ravening wolves. Ye shall know them by their fruits. Do men gather grapes of thorns, or figs of thistles? . . . A good tree cannot bring forth evil fruit, neither can a corrupt tree bring forth good fruit. . . . Wherefore by their fruits ye shall know them." He concluded by comparing the man who followed his advice to one who built his house upon a rock.

In such a spontaneous manner did his speech — so immediately intelligible, so loaded with vivid touches of realism for all its strong poetic rhythms — flow into the mold and pattern of parable. His followers would never be able to forget the image of the mote and the beam, or the false prophets as wolves masquerading in sheep's clothing, or the question "Do men gather grapes of thorns?" They were put on their guard against excesses of bigotry, hasty or ill-considered judgments, and rabbinical narrow-mindedness; yet Jesus had not attacked or injured any individual person.

Would he always keep silent, if questioned in public on the correct interpretation of certain laws which at present weighed so heavily upon the poor? If the Kingdom was to free men, and bring them to a faith whose God cared for each individual heart, could Jesus and his followers still avoid an eventual clash with the official religious authorities, who were only waiting for the triumph of Judaism before they made the Law a yet severer burden upon the shoulders of workers and humble folk everywhere?

11

THE PROBLEM OF THE SABBATH

AN EARLY DISPUTE broke out over something quite unimportant. "And it came to pass," we read, "that he went through the corn fields on the sabbath day; and his disciples began, as they went, to pluck the ears of corn." This was during the spring, and Jesus must have been taking only a short country stroll, since on the Sabbath walks of over a mile were forbidden. Nor could a hot meal be obtained anywhere. Since his companions felt hungry, Jesus allowed them to pluck a few ears of corn from a field as they passed by — a practice sanctioned by tradition and the Law. But some Pharisees had observed them, and said to Jesus: "Behold, why do they on the sabbath day that which is not lawful?"

While one had the right to pluck and eat ears of corn on a weekday, such an action on the Sabbath was regarded as "harvesters' work," and therefore forbidden. Jesus, in his reply, made no attempt to question this prohibition, or to deny that his followers had infringed it. "Have ye never read," he said, "what David did, when he had need, and was an hungred, he, and they that were with him? How he went into the house of God . . . and did eat the shewbread, which is not lawful to eat but for the priests, and gave also to them that were with him?"

The example Jesus chose was an admirable one. The Bible portrayed David as violating a law pertaining to the Sanctuary — a far more heinous offence than Sabbath-breaking. The scribes could have argued that David had certain special privileges; to which Jesus might well have replied that precisely because he *was* so great a man one could safely follow his example when dealing with a far less important law. In point of fact either the discussion broke off at this point, or, if it continued, we are told nothing of what was said.

Was it then, or at some later date, that Jesus formulated his general principle: "The sabbath was made for man, and not man for the sabbath." There is no doubt that the rabbis wrote: "The sabbath has been given unto you; you have not been given unto the sabbath"; but unfortunately they were far from putting such a principle into practice. To realize this we need only spend a Sabbath in the modern State of Israel, which practices Judaism today. Life comes to a complete standstill. Not only do people abstain from work, which is normal enough; it is also strictly forbidden to light a fire, or even a cigarette, or indeed to drive a car. Israeli hospitals employ a skeleton staff of Christians or Moslems to keep essential services going.

Such an interpretation of the law which decreed that man should rest on the seventh day brought in its wake the most stupefying amount of scholarly casuistry. The Talmud cites the case of one rabbi who spent a full two and a half years studying a single chapter of the twenty-four which it devotes to the

Sabbath. This Sabbatical law, though mentioned in the Decalogue, did not develop to its full extent till after the Exile; and there is scarcely a single reference to it dating from the time of the Prophets. Gradually it encroached further and further. As a Jewish historian has put it: "For the Pharisees in Jesus' lifetime, as for orthodox Jews today, Sabbath-breaking and the oppression of the poor were both crimes that deserved the death penalty, without distinction; and to Jews throughout history the first of the two has always been, and still remains, the greater offense."

These words by a contemporary writer help to explain Jesus' reaction. He could not but resent so serious a perversion of the religious life. Unless the Sabbath once more — and as soon as possible — became a day whose rituals were joyfully observed rather than this intolerable burden of taboos which made life impossible, it would remain a hateful and detested institution. The Pharisees had interpreted the law in a manner as ridiculous as it was oppressive, and Jesus took every opportunity of challenging their attitude.

"And he entered again into the synagogue; and there was a man there which had a withered hand. And they watched him, whether he would heal him on the sabbath day; that they might accuse him. And he saith unto the man which had the withered hand, 'Stand forth.' And he saith unto them, 'Is it lawful to do good on the sabbath days, or to do evil? to save life, or to kill?' But they held their peace."

The rabbis were agreed that one could, even on the Sabbath, save a man in danger of death. Jesus wanted to take this line further. If a sick man was left an extra day by a person capable of curing him, did this not do him actual harm? Have I not the right (he implied) to heal such a one on the spot, and is God not more honored by such a healing than by my abstention? They should all have cried "Yes!" but they preferred to keep silent. "And when he had looked round about on them with anger, being grieved for the hardness of their hearts, he saith unto the man, 'Stretch forth thy hand.' And he stretched it out: and his hand was restored whole as the other. And the Pharisees went forth, and straightway took counsel with the Herodians against him, how they might destroy him."

This was a serious incident. For once Jesus had not only made no effort to conceal his healing powers, but had demonstrated them in direct defiance of the Pharisees. Unable even to conceal his anger, he had snubbed the Pharisees publicly. He had glimpsed the hatred these strict sectarians felt for him, and now accepted their challenge. The establishment of the Kingdom would necessitate a struggle against the most faithful adherents of that true religion in which Jesus himself believed with all his heart. He would be obliged to oppose the spiritual leaders of his own people.

The Sabbath, however, was not to be the only bone of contention. Jesus and his disciples pointedly ignored the Jewish custom of washing one's hands before meals. This custom had not been established out of any sense of hygiene but as a ritual purification: one might, for instance, have earlier shaken hands with a peasant. "Why walk not thy disciples according to the tradition of the elders," the Pharisees asked Jesus, "but eat bread with unwashen hands?"

Instead of answering the question — as he would have done a month or so earlier — Jesus counterattacked fiercely: "Well hath Esaias prophesied of you hypocrites, as it is written, 'This people honoureth me with their lips, but their heart is far from me. Howbeit in vain do they worship me, teaching for doctrines the commandments of men.' For laying aside the commandment of God, ye hold the tradition of men."

Jesus was to repeat the same charge again and again. Outworn traditionalism had ended by stifling the spirit of the Bible and its great Commandments. Jesus attacked, item by item, the whole casuistical edifice erected by the Pharisees, from dietary taboos to the system whereby a man could, at the price of certain votive offerings, escape the obligation to support his own kith and kin. "Blind guides," he called them, with mocking contempt, "which strain at a gnat, and swallow a camel." The flesh of the camel was proscribed to the Jews, and as repugnant in their eyes as pork or hare. It is also true that they were forbidden to swallow gnats, and kept on the alert in case any appeared.

Jesus said: "There is nothing from without a man, that entering into him can defile him: but the things which come out of him, those are they that defile the man." But above all he kept harking back to the subject of the Sabbath. It exasperated him to see poor people treated with contempt because of their inability to observe every absurd detail of the Sabbath law. One day, when he was dining with a Pharisee, there was a man present suffering from dropsy. On his behalf Jesus renewed the challenge he had previously flung at the Pharisees over the man with a withered hand. He asked the same question: "Is it lawful to heal on the sabbath day?" and once again they said nothing. "Which of you," he persisted, "shall have an ass or an ox fallen into a pit, and will not straightway pull him out on the sabbath day?"

According to one manuscript of St. Luke, we are told that Jesus once met a man who was working on the Sabbath and said to him: "Blessed art thou, if thou knowest what thou dost; but if thou knowest not, thou art accursed, and dost sin against the law."* In other words, to do work on the Sabbath

---

* This passage is added after Luke 6, 5: see critical editions and A. Huck and H. Lietzmann, *Synopsis of the First Three Gospels*, page 56. Tübingen: J. C. B. Mohr (Paul Siebeck) 1936.

from necessity, or for the greater glory of God — even when the Pharisees prohibit it — is to act well, and in conformity with the spirit of the Law.

Thus, as regards the Sabbath, Jesus was learning to reckon with his enemies. From now on the Pharisees attacked him relentlessly and did everything in their power to destroy him. The more fanatical among them did not hesistate to make common cause with their enemies, the collaborating officials of Herod Antipas. The latter, too, had their own reasons for keeping a watchful eye on Jesus' activities. John had been imprisoned by the Tetrarch; Jesus was one of John's disciples. From now on the secret police began to take an interest in Jesus. As a suspicious character he must have had a dossier opened on him, even though for the present he did not merit the honor of being arrested.

12

THE MISSION OF THE TWELVE

IF THE PHARISEES were uneasy, and communicating their suspicions to Herod Antipas, Jesus himself was by no means inactive. Having nominated his twelve disciples, he now intended to send them round Galilee preaching the Kingdom. Before parting from them for a few days, he gave them their marching orders: "Go not into the way of the Gentiles, and into any city of the Samaritans enter ye not: but go rather to the lost sheep of the house of Israel. And as ye go, preach, saying, 'The kingdom of heaven is at hand.' "

For the time being Jesus had decided to ignore the Greek communities of Syria and the Decapolis, with their predominantly pagan populations. He was also keeping clear of Samaria. The news of the Kingdom must first be spread among the Jews, preferably those whose contact with the faith was somewhat remote. Jesus picked up one of those pastoral metaphors which had been applied to the Prophets and on which, a little later, he was to place such emphasis. He sent forth the Twelve to preach among the poor, to publicans and sinners. This meant a quick tour round various by no means remote villages; and the phrase "the hospitality of the East," as generally taken, is no exaggeration. Jesus was anxious for his disciples to regard themselves as ambassadors of freedom and poverty; he bade them: "Provide neither gold, nor silver, nor brass in your purses, nor scrip for your journey," and to travel "shod with sandals; and not put on two coats."

This program is not designed for beggars or turnpike tramps, but for travelers without luggage who rely on the hospitality of their hosts. Such are the rules of the Kingdom: one gives and takes freely, easily, naturally. There should be no hoarding. One trusts in God's providence and the kindness of one's fellow-men, in the joy of bright sunlight and the unrolling countryside through which one passes. Sandals, indeed, are a semi-luxury: poor men and laborers went barefoot. But the emissaries of Jesus did not affect indigence, either. They remained their own natural selves.

"The labourer," Jesus said on occasion, "is worthy of his hire." And the Twelve were laborers for the Kingdom. He told them to accept every invitation they received, cheerfully and without hesitation, from rich and poor alike, without distinction. Did he not do the same himself?

When the Twelve returned from their tour of Galilee, they had nothing but good news to report. Overwhelmed with joy, Jesus gave thanks to God: "I thank thee, O Father, Lord of heaven and earth, because thou hast hid these things from the wise and prudent, and hast revealed them unto babes.

Even so, Father: for so it seemed good in thy sight." And he outlined the program of the Kingdom: "Come unto me, all ye that labour and are heavy laden, and I will give you rest. Take my yoke upon you, and learn of me; for I am meek and lowly in heart: and ye shall find rest unto your souls. For my yoke is easy, and my burden is light."

Once again Jesus had recourse to a parable in order to demonstrate the nature of this freedom he brought for the world by liberating the Jewish faith from the shackles, the heavy yoke laid upon it by strict and literal-minded sectarians. His imagery was, as always, highly Oriental: it will come home with special force to anyone who recalls meeting porters in the alleys of Jerusalem or Istanbul doubled up beneath the weight of vast loads held in place with straps passed over the head and shoulders. They resemble beasts of burden.

Now, Jesus was the Prince of a Kingdom in which the crushed underdog would stand up straight once more, and no longer bend beneath the burden of inhuman laws. Jesus was no sentimentalist; his actions were ruled by his head rather than his heart, though in all humility, for Jesus had an instinctive understanding of the weak and the poverty-stricken. He gave comfort to their souls — that is, to their life, their breath. He allowed them to breathe freely once more. He was no repressive tyrant but a liberator, come to unlock every dungeon and bring all prisoners out again into the sunlight.

This ideal — so radically opposed to the aims of those in political authority — was something the Twelve found it difficult to get clear in their own minds: they were still expecting God's victory to be temporal and military. Jesus accordingly used every opportunity to drive the point home. One such occasion had a special significance.

The Twelve had joined him near Bethsaida, where the

Jordan flows into Lake Tiberias. He told them: "Come ye yourselves apart into a desert place, and rest a while." And so, as St. Mark tells us, "they departed into a desert place by ship privately." But people were determined to follow Jesus; and large numbers of them, some on foot, others in boats, succeeded in catching up with him, drawn by this wonderful Kingdom he proclaimed and his doctrine of a God who looked to the poor and humble.

When they were assembled on the northern shore of the lake — a barren, deserted region — Jesus once more began to preach to them. But when dusk was closing in, his disciples told him: "This is a desert place, and now the time is far passed: send them away, that they may go into the country round about, and into the villages, and buy themselves bread: for they have nothing to eat."

Jesus replied: "Give ye them to eat."

"Shall we go and buy two hundred pennyworth of bread, and give them to eat?" they inquired. (Two hundred *denarii* would be the equivalent of a hundred dollars in modern currency.)

"How many loaves have ye?" Jesus asked them. "Go and see."

They checked and reported: "Five, and two fishes."

Jesus ordered them to distribute what there was. He made the people sit down and recited a blessing. The crowd set about their frugal repast, and all had as much as they could eat. Later, Christians everywhere were to equate this meal with the gift of manna in the wilderness during Moses' lifetime; they also regarded it as a symbol of the Last Supper and a preparation for the Messianic feast that would celebrate the triumph of God's Kingdom.

Jesus attributed great importance to the communal meal: to the act of breaking bread together, then sitting down on the ground, with a piece of fish from the lake clapped between two slices of that bread, and eating it with one's fingers. The grain which was husked and milled to bake the loaf had already, in its germination, furnished Jesus with the most striking image of the Kingdom's growth. The fruit of the harvest gave nourishment to mankind. When we pray we must beg God to "give us this day our daily bread."

But the Twelve could not see that the Kingdom was, precisely, men gathered together in brotherly love, breaking bread that the King ordained by God had himself distributed among them. Such a notion seemed too prosaic for their liking, too crudely countrified, too far a cry from that great Caesarian triumph. When they were back in the house at Capernaum, Jesus asked them: "What was it that ye disputed among yourselves by the way?"

They made no answer, since as they walked along they had been arguing as to which of them took highest precedence. Then Jesus sat down and gathered them about him and said: "'If any man desire to be first, the same shall be last of all, and servant of all.' And he took a child, and set him the midst of them: and when he had taken him in his arms, he said unto them: 'Whosoever shall receive one of such children in my name, receiveth me: and whosoever shall receive me, receiveth not me, but him that sent me.' "

The low opinion which the ancient world had of children is well known. Jesus picked up one of these street urchins and embraced him. He presented him in the guise of the "little Prince" of God's Kingdom. The Twelve could not comprehend the revolution that was taking place there on earth, among men, at that moment in time, before their very eyes. When Jesus spoke, the gloomy tyrant Tiberius still ruled the Empire from Capri; while he who later would be acknowledged King of the world, the Pantocrator of the Byzantine mosaics, took a little Jewish boy in his arms and presented him as an emblem, an ideal, the chosen favorite of the Kingdom's supreme Lord. To welcome such a child was to welcome the Master of all mankind. It was truly a new humanity that Jesus had created by the lakeside.

13

THE GADARENE SWINE
AND THE HEALING OF JAIRUS' DAUGHTER

THE HOSTILITY OF the Pharisees did not keep Jesus from moving freely about Galilee. One evening he boarded a boat in order to cross the lake. During the night a severe storm blew up. Jesus lay asleep in the stern of the boat, head resting on the cushion that was commonly provided there. His disciples, somewhat alarmed, woke him up. Jesus arose, and rebuked the sea. It was a bold gesture. The wind dropped and the sea became calm: Jesus' followers were deeply impressed. About dawn they landed on the eastern shore of the lake, probably at a place known today as Kersa, which then formed part of the Greek territory of the Decapolis. The inhabitants were pagans.

"And when he was come out of the ship," Mark tells us, "immediately there met him out of the tombs a man with an unclean spirit, who had his dwelling among the tombs; and no man could bind him, no, not with chains: because that he had been often bound with fetters and chains, and the chains had been plucked asunder by him, and the fetters broken in pieces: neither could any man tame him. And always, night and day, he was in the mountains, and in the tombs, crying, and cutting himself with stones." This naked man, wandering about howling, throwing stones, and inflicting injuries on himself, was, to judge from the evidence, in the grip of total dementia. That he chose to sleep among the tombs, however, is not (as might be the case in our society) a sign of necrophilia. In modern as in ancient Palestine, tombs are hollowed out of the ubiquitous rock outcroppings. Such artificial caves are frequently to be found just outside villages. They are of considerable dimensions, and the outermost chambers sometimes remain empty, with abandoned mortuary niches at the back of them. But in antiquity the dead, being sacred, were also impure, and no one but a madman would ever have dreamed of passing the night in a cave sepulcher.

"But when he saw Jesus afar off," Mark relates, "he ran and worshipped him, and cried with a loud voice, and said, 'What have I to do with thee, Jesus, thou Son of the most high God? I adjure thee by God, that thou torment me not.'" The lunatic was not a Jew, it is clear, since he called God "the most high," an expression popular among the pagans. He also identified himself with the demons he believed were tormenting him — a common symptom of split personality. Jesus asked him, " 'What is thy name?' And he answered, saying, 'My name is Legion: for we are many.' "

A Roman legion numbered six thousand men, and the lunatic was plainly alluding to his own brutish, uncontrollable, contradictory impulses — suicidal and murderous by turns, and always violent, primitive, bestial. He besought Jesus not to send his legion "away out of the country." Now, a little way off there was grazing a herd of those black pigs which one so often sees roaming in Mediterranean countries. "Send us into the swine," the madman howled, "that we may enter into them." Jesus agreed; and at once — to the stupefied astonishment of the swineherds — the pigs rushed headlong into the lake. Cured and calmed by the divine power and virtue of Jesus, the possessed man first asked for some clothes, then quietly sat down.

This incident has often, mistakenly, been taken as a mere popular legend. It is far too vivid and circumstantial to have been invented: the joke is altogether too monstrous, too embarrassing. In fact it is a parable translated into action. For the Jews the pig was the unclean animal *par excellence*. Jesus found it amusing to give his followers an object lesson by transferring the man's demonic madness into a herd of unclean animals. At times one begins to wonder just where he drew the line with a joke. This aspect of his life, so disconcerting for a rational-minded Westerner, is something any born Jew will relish; for overseriousness is the bane of all naturally melancholy peoples.

On his return to Capernaum, Jesus still found himself drawing continual crowds. "And behold, there cometh one of the rulers of the synagogue, Jairus by name; and when he saw him, he fell at his feet, and besought him greatly, saying, 'My little daughter lieth at the point of death: I pray thee, come and lay thy hands on her, that she may be healed; and she shall live.' And Jesus went with him; and much people followed him, and thronged him." Jairus was a rich and influential citizen of Capernaum, whom Jesus must have known. Despite the public nature of his request, Jesus agreed to go and see the child.

"And a certain woman, which had an issue of blood twelve years, and had suffered many things of many physicians, and had spent all that she had, and was nothing bettered, but rather grew worse, when she had heard of Jesus, came in the press behind, and touched his garment. For she said, 'If I may touch but his clothes, I shall be whole.' And straightway the fountain of her blood was dried up; and she felt in her body that she was healed of that plague. And Jesus, immediately knowing in himself that virtue had gone out of him, turned

him about in the press, and said, 'Who touched my clothes?'
And his disciples said unto him, 'Thou seest the multitude
thronging thee, and sayest thou, Who touched me?' And he
looked round about to see her that had done this thing. But
the woman fearing and trembling, knowing what was done in
her, came and fell down before him, and told him all the truth.
And he said unto her, 'Daughter, thy faith hath made thee
whole; go in peace, and be whole of thy plague.'" The phrase
"go in peace" corresponds to the salutation *Shalom!* still in
use among the Jews. It is a form of farewell.

There are few anecdotes about Jesus which retain such
vivid immediacy as this woman's gesture. Since she had become
ritually unclean as a result of her infirmity, she knew that by
asking Jesus to lay hands on her and heal her she would transmit
this uncleanness to him. Accordingly she did no more than
touch the hem, or fringe, of his garment with one finger,
taking advantage of the crowd that pressed about him. At once
she felt herself cured; and Jesus sensed that his healing powers
had acted upon *somebody*, though the person's identity remained unknown to him. According to Mark's account, his
disciples showed some impatience with his inquiry. But when
he knew the truth, he felt moved, as always, by the absolute
unreasoning faith which suffering engenders.

"While he yet spake, there came from the ruler of the
synagogue's house certain which said, 'Thy daughter is dead:
why troublest thou the Master any further?' As soon as Jesus
heard the word that was spoken, he saith unto the ruler of the
synagogue, 'Be not afraid, only believe.' And he suffered no
man to follow him, save Peter, and James, and John the
brother of James. And he cometh to the house of the ruler of
the synagogue, and seeth the tumult, and them that wept and
wailed greatly. And when he was come in, he saith unto them,
'Why make ye this ado, and weep? the damsel is not dead, but

sleepeth.' And they laughed him to scorn. But when he had put them all out, he taketh the father and the mother of the damsel, and them that were with him, and entereth in where the damsel was lying. And he took the damsel by the hand, and said unto her, 'Talitha cumi'; which is, being interpreted, Damsel, I say unto thee, arise. And straightway the damsel arose, and walked; for she was of the age of twelve years. And they were astonished with a great astonishment. And he charged them straitly that no man should know it; and commanded that something should be given her to eat."

Jesus, it should be noted, would not act before an audience. He drove out the hired women mourners, who had only been waiting for the death of this rich man's child before setting about their dismal professional duties. In their presence he claimed that the girl was no more than unconscious. He aroused her by taking her hand, and told them to give her something to eat — thus displaying cool common sense in the midst of general disorganized hysteria.

Another account* tells us that the child was already dead when Jairus went in search of Jesus; but this version is called in question by Mark's narrative, which contains echoes of Simon's eyewitness testimony. When Jesus arrived at the house, the girl cannot have been dead for more than a few moments.

Jesus bound those involved to absolute secrecy. Simon described the incident only long afterward; at the time he kept silent in accordance with Jesus' wishes. It looks very much as though Jairus and his fellow-witnesses did the same, and that their own version of events was substantially identical with Mark's. The Rabbi had waked the little girl from her tragic sleep and restored her to her parents.

* Matthew 9, 18.

14
THE PRINCE OF EVIL

THE PHARISEES had not given up. Since they could hardly deny the Master's marvelous powers of healing, they had to find some way of discrediting him. They appealed to Jerusalem, and various erudite scholars arrived hotfoot, producing the simple explanation that Jesus was possessed by Beelzebub. This was the name of the ancient Phoenician deity against whose idol the prophet Elijah had exerted his powers. "By the prince of the devils," they declared, "casteth he out devils." In other words, Jesus was deemed to derive his powers of exorcism from Satan himself. This was tantamount to accusing him of magical practices; it rendered him liable to charges of sorcery which, if upheld in court, might well result in the death sentence.

When these rumors were brought to Jesus' notice, his reply was both unexpected and scathing: "If a kingdom be divided against itself, that kingdom cannot stand. And if a house be divided against itself, that house cannot stand. And if Satan rise up against himself, and be divided, he cannot stand, but hath an end." The implication was at once clear to everybody. The end of Satan meant the inauguration of God's Kingdom. So long as Satan's opposition to God continues, the world remains divided. The day of Satan's fall is also that of God's triumph.

What reply could the scribes from Jerusalem make to this? But Jesus had not yet finished. He wanted to prove that he was stronger than Satan, that he had the mastery over him. Again, he resorted to a parable: "No man can enter into a strong man's house, and spoil his goods, except he will first bind the strong man; and then he will spoil his house." To spoil *this* house, Jesus had first needed to overcome Satan.

Despite the way he had dealt with their charges, the scribes' slanderous accusations against Jesus spread through the townships of Galilee until they reached Nazareth. Till recently Jesus had been welcomed there with open arms: people were proud of him. But now a swing in public opinion began to take place.

Like most Eastern people, Jesus had a sizable collection of relatives: uncles, aunts, nephews, nieces, cousins. He was connected one way or another with almost everyone in the village. Though he was over thirty he was obliged — his mother now being a widow — to accept the authority of the head of his clan: probably one of his uncles. A family council was held, and it was decided to send a delegation to Capernaum and persuade Jesus to return home with them.

On the day of their arrival Jesus was talking with a group of his friends in a house that reputedly belonged to him, though the actual owner was probably Simon. Someone said: " 'Behold, thy mother and thy brethren without seek for thee.' And he answered them, saying, 'Who is my mother, or my brethren?' And he looked round about on them which sat about him, and said, 'Behold my mother and my brethren! For whosoever shall do the will of God, the same is my brother, and my sister, and mother.' " In his eyes the Kingdom of those who do God's will was a new family, superseding all previous ties. Through his physical nature man is born with attachments to race and clan, just as ants and termites have inborn allegiances to one particular anthill. But over and above this predetermined ethnic status, spiritual affinities can still be freely decided by the individual will. Jesus felt himself more closely bound to the Twelve than to his cousins and nieces, even to his immediate family.

The action taken by his relations in Nazareth caused his opinion of the family as an institution to deteriorate. He never actually declared that he hated family loyalties; but in the strong bonds linking members of all Eastern clans he perceived a dangerous obstacle to the spread of the Kingdom. "He that loveth father or mother more than me is not worthy of me: and he that loveth son or daughter more than me is not worthy of me." He was to go even further than this. One day he would see the Kingdom as a bloody reality, come to dismember other men's families as it had dismembered his own.

Having shown his relatives the door, he was anxious to gauge the mood of the Nazarenes himself; so he traveled to his village for a firsthand appraisal of the situation. Once again, when the Sabbath came round, he rose and spoke in the synagogue. But far from arousing admiration, as he had done on his previous visit,* he now felt a mounting tide of skepticism and jealousy. "Whence hath this man this wisdom, and these mighty works?" people asked. "Is not this the carpenter's son? is not his mother called Mary? and his brethren, James, and Joses, and Simon, and Judas? And his sisters, are they not all with us? Whence then hath this man all these things?" "A prophet," Jesus retorted, "is not without honour, save in his own country, and in his own house." And, as St. Matthew says, "he did not many mighty works there because of their unbelief."

Despite the growing hostility of the Pharisees, Jesus did not hesitate, when occasion offered, to accept their invitations; and he never passed up a chance to engage in argument with them. One day, in a Galilaean township which was certainly

* See Luke 4, 16.

neither Nazareth nor Capernaum, he found himself the guest
of a certain Pharisee called Simon. St. Luke relates the incident
as follows:

"And one of the Pharisees desired him that he would eat with
him. And he went into the Pharisee's house, and sat down to
meat. And, behold, a woman in the city, which was a sinner,
when she knew that Jesus sat at meat in the Pharisee's house,
brought an alabaster box of ointment, and stood at his feet
behind him weeping, and began to wash his feet with tears,
and did wipe them with the hairs of her head, and kissed his
feet, and anointed them with the ointment. Now when the
Pharisee which had bidden him saw it, he spake within himself, saying, 'This man, if he were a prophet, would have
known who and what manner of woman this is that toucheth
him: for she is a sinner.' And Jesus answering said unto him,
'Simon, I have somewhat to say unto thee.' And he saith,
'Master, say on.' 'There was a certain creditor which had two
debtors: the one owed five hundred pence, and the other fifty.
And when they had nothing to pay, he frankly forgave them
both. Tell me therefore, which of them will love him most?'
Simon answered and said, 'I suppose that he, to whom he forgave most.' And he said unto him, 'Thou hast rightly judged.'
And he turned to the woman, and said unto Simon, 'Seest
thou this woman? I entered into thine house, thou gavest me
no water for my feet: but she hath washed my feet with tears,
and wiped them with the hairs of her head. Thou gavest me
no kiss: but this woman since the time I came in hath not
ceased to kiss my feet. My head with oil thou didst not anoint:
but this woman hath anointed my feet with ointment. Wherefore I say unto thee, Her sins, which are many, are forgiven;
for she loved much: but to whom little is forgiven, the same
loveth little.' And he said unto her, 'Thy sins are forgiven.'
And they that sat at meat with him began to say within them-

selves, 'Who is this that forgiveth sins also?' And he said to the woman, 'Thy faith hath saved thee; go in peace.' "

If we are acquainted with certain daily customs prevalent in Jesus' day, we can appreciate the scene a little more clearly. It was common practice for slaves to wash the feet of the guests after formal dinner parties; and whatever the meal, those at table did not sit, but reclined on couches in the Roman fashion, barefooted, supporting themselves on one elbow. Jesus must have been placed with his feet towards the door, and thus unable to see the woman standing behind him; while Simon, on the opposite side of the table, had them both in view.

It has been supposed that this woman was Mary from the village of Magdala, whom we know as Mary Magdalene; but the two have nothing in common. Still less does she resemble Mary of Bethany, Martha's sister, whose family were on friendly terms with Jesus. But her anonymity detracts no whit from this woman's touching moment of repentance. She came from somewhere in Galilee; let that suffice. What was the nature of her sin? Was she some prostitute or adulteress, or merely the wife of a *publicanus*, and as such a social outcast? Perhaps she had heard Jesus preaching of God's mercy in the synagogue, and had come to thank him. The parable Jesus told Simon is crystal-clear; and he underlined the principle of forgiveness by applying it to this woman, an act which must have stirred his fellow-guests to considerable suppressed resentment. Jesus not only drove out devils but freed men from their sins. Little by little he was revealing to his followers a new aspect of the Kingdom — the amnesty which God bestows on those whom public opinion regards as unclean.

The further Jesus diverged from the Pharisees, the closer he moved to the *publicani*, to prostitutes, to Samaritans and pagans. His short life reveals a striking swing in this direction.

By the end he had completely reversed one idea at least concerning the Kingdom. Instead of being restricted to just and "respectable" Jews, this Kingdom of God's mercy opened its gates, first and foremost, to the "others"; and finally Jesus was to declare: "The publicans and the harlots go into the kingdom of God before you" — a claim which was indeed liable to provoke furious resentment.

Jesus' break with his family was not complete. His mother, Mary, held out against the general clan decision and decided to join her son permanently. She found herself in a group of several women who provided the Twelve with material support: they included "Mary called Magdalene . . . and Joanna the wife of Chuza Herod's steward, and Susanna, and many others." These wealthy middle-class women gave Jesus much unobtrusive help. In the darkest hours we find them silently waiting there, close beside him, a reminder of feminine courage and affection.

15

THE SIGN FROM HEAVEN

To PRESENT THE Kingdom in the guise of a magnanimous divine pardon for all shady financiers, collaborating officials, and prostitutes — this, surely, was an untenable paradox if one compared it with the ideas advanced by the apocalyptic writers. The latter expected some storm-racked cosmic upheaval. God, or at the very least the victorious Messiah, would be seen amid the clouds of heaven. The majority of the Pharisees, too, lived in hope of some such divine manifestation. They did not scruple, therefore, to demand some sign from heaven of Jesus, tempting him. Jesus, sighing "deeply in his spirit," said: "When it is evening, ye say, 'It will be fair weather: for the sky is red.' And in the morning, 'It will be foul weather today: for the sky is red and lowring.' O ye hypocrites, ye can discern the face of the sky; but can ye not discern the signs of the times? . . . Verily I say unto you, There shall no sign be given unto this generation." According to St. Matthew, he concluded: ". . . there shall no sign be given . . . but the sign of the prophet Jonas."

Jesus considered the Pharisees perfectly competent to read the weather signs in the sky and from them deduce rain or fine weather. If they studied the world with equal attention, they would also be able to foretell the advent of the Kingdom. The "sign of Jonas" is simply the summons to repentance: "The men of Nineveh shall rise in judgment with this generation, and shall condemn it: because they repented at the preaching of Jonas." Thanks to the Old Testament prophet, the pagans were converted; but in Jesus' day the most important citizens spent their time interpreting his actions as the work of the Devil and setting traps for him. If Jesus for the time being refused to grant them a sign from heaven, this did not imply that he repudiated the revelations of the great apocalyptic writers concerning the heavenly Kingdom to come. Rather was he in the process of establishing this Kingdom on earth — only to find the Jews in opposition to him.

Jesus expounded all this to the Twelve in several new parables. Here, for the first time, images of evil and the enemy make their appearance. "The kingdom of heaven," he said, "is likened unto a man which sowed good seed in his field: but while men slept, his enemy came and sowed tares among the wheat, and went his way. But when the blade was sprung up, and brought forth fruit, then appeared the tares also. So the servants of the householder came and said unto him, 'Sir, didst not thou sow good seed in thy field? from whence then hath it tares?' He said unto them, 'An enemy hath done this.' The servants said unto him, 'Wilt thou then that we go and gather them up?' But he said, 'Nay; lest while ye gather up the tares, ye root up also the wheat with them. Let both grow together until the harvest: and in the time of harvest I will say to the reapers, Gather ye together first the tares, and bind them in bundles to burn them: but gather the wheat into my barn.' "

This parable has the same fundamental meaning as that of the sower, but its setting is slightly different. The sower was a solitary peasant, a small landholder. Here we are dealing with a big farmer, a slaveowner. The size of his property, the amount of labor he employs — these explain the revenge taken upon him, even if they do not excuse it. The "tares" sown in his fields by night are nothing but poor seed: that is why it is impossible to tell them from good healthy grain. As for the malicious individual responsible, his presence is by no means allegorical; he is there to point the conclusion. What matters to Jesus is the blending of the two crops, and the need to wait till harvest time before they can be separated. Till the Kingdom reaches full maturity, good and evil are inextricably mingled in every human breast, and any attempt to sort them out would be mistaken. Both the Essenes and the Pharisees are, therefore, on the wrong track. Not only is Jesus criticizing the exclusiveness of those strict sectarians who claim to isolate good grain from bad *ab initio*; the thought has clearly crossed his mind that such persons run a distinct risk of themselves becoming the bad grain of the parable.

Another parable, that of the fishnet, has on the surface a seemingly identical meaning. In fact, it is quite different. Though we must await the coming of harvest time in the Kingdom before we can judge our fellow-men, we must nevertheless be able to sum them up immediately as regards their ability to build the Kingdom itself. To the first disciples, who were lakeside fishermen, Jesus had said: "I will make you fishers of men." Now he showed them how to sort the haul the moment they got it ashore. "The kingdom of heaven," he told them, "is like unto a net, that was cast into the sea, and gathered of every kind: which, when it was full, they drew to shore, and sat down, and gathered the good into vessels, but cast the bad away." In other words, the appeals made by Jesus and the Twelve would bring in plenty of people. Among these there would be some who were unfitted for the apostolic mission and must be rejected. The rest would remain.

Thus the two parables complement one another. Good and bad seed cannot be distinguished at first sight, and the Pharisees are wrong to label men good or evil. But with fishermen it is different. The moment they haul up their nets they can tell the genuine fish from pebbles, shells, seaweed. Their work, unlike that of a field laborer, does not involve long periods of patient expectation. Though Jesus may wait for the harvest, and God Almighty let the grain sprout at its own leisurely pace, the news of the Kingdom, on the other hand, will brook no delay. It requires immediate dissemination, and the nature of the work means that one must be exacting.

It was not to be long before Jesus told his disciples the full truth about himself. The crisis he saw gathering ahead perhaps tended to stiffen the conditions he laid down for those who wanted to follow him; and an unforeseen catastrophe was to precipitate that crisis.

16

The Death of John the Baptist

NEWS SUDDENLY REACHED Galilee that John the Baptist had
been condemned to death by Herod Antipas and executed in
the prison of Machaerus. The prophet's end made a dramatic
story, which lost nothing in the telling. Popular rumor surrounded it with the most grandiose and romantic details: the
version preserved is as highly colored as something from the
Book of Esther:

"And when a convenient day was come, that Herod on his
birthday made a supper to his lords, high captains, and chief
estates of Galilee; and when the daughter of the said Herodias
came in, and danced, and pleased Herod and them that sat
with him, the king said unto the damsel, 'Ask of me whatsoever thou wilt, and I will give it thee.' And he sware unto
her, 'Whatsoever thou shalt ask of me, I will give it thee,
unto the half of my kingdom.' And she went forth, and said
unto her mother, 'What shall I ask?' And she said, 'The head
of John the Baptist.' And she came in straightway with haste
unto the king, and asked, saying, 'I will that thou give me by
and by in a charger the head of John the Baptist.' And the
king was exceeding sorry; yet for his oath's sake, and for their
sakes which sat with him, he would not reject her. And immediately the king sent an executioner, and commanded his
head to be brought: and he went and beheaded him in the
prison, and brought his head in a charger, and gave it to the
damsel: and the damsel gave it to her mother. And when
his disciples heard of it, they came and took up his corpse,
and laid it in a tomb."

There is nothing *prima facie* implausible in the idea that
Herod Antipas would grant a woman the desert prophet's head.

He was a petty Eastern tyrant, the son of a man whose excesses even the Romans had found disgusting. It may be surmised, however, that John's execution was not solely occasioned by an oath Herod swore in his cups: there were political motives afoot also. The Tetrarch wanted to give Pharisees and the Resistance alike a sharp warning. Just as Alexander Jannaeus before him had crucified Pharisees by the hundred, so Herod was now taking similar action to check the terrorism and revolutionary activity which formed a constant threat in Galilee.

John's disciples were stupefied by the news. Right to the end they had trusted in their prophet-leader's ultimate victory over the Tetrarch. Now it appeared that John's prediction of imminent triumph for the Kingdom had been mistaken. But Jesus could not share their opinion. John, he was convinced, had spoken the truth; his death must have been foreordained. Only a short while before he had reaffirmed his faith in John's message: "What went ye out into the wilderness for to see?" he asked. "A reed shaken with the wind? But what went ye out for to see? A man clothed in soft raiment? Behold, they which are gorgeously apparelled, and live delicately, are in kings' courts. But what went ye out for to see? A prophet? Yea, I say unto you, and much more than a prophet." And then he quoted two lines from Malachi, which John had employed to define his role as God's messenger.

Now that John was dead, Jesus in no way modified his high opinion of the man: "Among those that are born of women," he declared, "there is not a greater prophet than John the Baptist." However, after a moment's reflection he added: "But he that is least in the Kingdom of God is greater than he." Humanity, in other words, was now divided by the watershed of the Kingdom. There was mankind as it had been before the Kingdom's advent; there were those who belonged to the Kingdom itself, a kind of suprahuman elite. John was a man from the past, who had died on the very threshold of the new world. His death heralded a period of violence and murder, a conflict. "And from the days of John the Baptist until now," Jesus proclaimed, "the Kingdom of heaven suffereth violence, and the violent take it by force."

The politicians were trying to suppress the Kingdom, but the Kingdom had its own reserves of strength. Jesus no longer made any secret of the fact that John had, indirectly, fallen a victim to the Pharisees, who had not hesitated to accuse him — as they did Jesus himself — of being possessed by the Devil. "But whereunto shall I liken this generation? It is like unto children sitting in the markets, and calling unto their fellows, and saying, 'We have piped unto you, and ye have not danced; we have mourned unto you, and ye have not lamented.' For John came neither eating nor drinking, and they say, 'He hath a devil.' The Son of man came eating and drinking, and they say, 'Behold a man gluttonous, and a winebibber, a friend of publicans and sinners.'" The implication was plain. You have to make up your mind. A desert ascetic or a man who lives like other men: which do you prefer?

Jesus soon realized that Herod had been informed about him; certain Pharisees had briefed the Tetrarch's police. It was suggested to Herod — with more than a touch of skepticism — that Jesus was John the Baptist risen from the dead. Herod Antipas was not so naïve as to believe this literally: what the phrase meant was that Jesus had taken John's place, and therefore constituted a similar potential danger. The Tetrarch would be well advised to have this new prophet placed under arrest and disposed of in the same way as John.

Jesus was not wholly without friends in Herod's entourage, however: certain Pharisees, and people such as Chuza the steward, Joanna's husband. These now came to Jesus and

warned him: " 'Get thee out, and depart hence,' " they said,
" 'for Herod will kill thee.' And he said unto them, 'Go ye, and
tell that fox, Behold, I cast out devils, and I do cures today and
tomorrow, and the third day I shall be perfected. Nevertheless I
must walk today, and tomorrow, and the day following: for it
cannot be that a prophet perish out of Jerusalem.' "

Jesus regarded Herod as a mere stinking animal; and his
allusion to Jerusalem carries a somewhat macabre joke at the
expense of the official priesthood resident there. What he said,
in effect, was: *Tell him to leave me alone — but if he has to
finish me off, he should let the authorities in Jerusalem do the
job for him. They will prove far more efficient at it than he
could ever be.*

But Jesus was now on his guard. One day, just before he and
his disciples boarded a boat to cross the lake, he asked them if
they had enough bread with them. Only one loaf, they said.
"Take heed," he told them, "beware of the leaven of the
Pharisees, and of the leaven of Herod." They puzzled at this
among themselves. "It is because we have no bread," they said.
Jesus heard them, and a gust of impatience swept over him.
How thick-witted his disciples were! What he had been alluding
to was the fermentation, the corruption which the Pharisees, no
less than Herod's police, represented. As for the loaves, he
reminded them, had not the multitude in the wilderness been
fed? Would the Twelve understand, ever? Yes, without a doubt.
And it was at this point in his recollections that Simon placed
one particular healing — of a blind man. He saw in this miracle
a symbol of hope, the end of the disciples' blindness.

"And he cometh to Bethsaida; and they bring a blind man
unto him, and besought him to touch him. And he took the
blind man by the hand, and led him out of the town; and
when he had spit on his eyes, and put his hands upon him,

he asked him if he saw ought. And he looked up and said, 'I see men as trees, walking.' After that he put his hands again upon his eyes, and made him look up: and he was restored, and saw every man clearly. And he sent him away to his house, saying, 'Neither go into the town, nor tell it to any in the town.' "

This is the only healing performed by Jesus which was both difficult and non-instantaneous. It was also, of course, the first time he had been confronted with one of those blind beggars so common in Eastern countries. He began by employing a method of treatment borrowed from popular medicine: the Jews at that time believed saliva to have a therapeutic effect on ocular disorders. But this did not suffice, and Jesus was obliged to lay his hands a second time on the man's partially restored eyes. Once again he told the healed person to hold his tongue and stay out of the public eye. There were many good reasons for this. Bethsaida lay outside the territories and jurisdiction of Herod Antipas. Nevertheless, Jesus felt that the least act of imprudence on his part might well prove fatal.

17

The Cursing of Galilee

IF JESUS INTENDED leaving Galilee to escape the attentions of Herod's police, he had no choice but to disperse his followers. The Twelve had now been joined by about a hundred more disciples: St. Luke, symbolically, isolates seventy-two of the latter, a figure which — according to the tenth chapter of Genesis — corresponds with the total number of nations in the world, and perhaps also matched the titular membership of the Great Sanhedrin in Jerusalem.

Before Jesus took temporary leave of his disciples, he gave them some parting advice and instructions. "The harvest truly is great," he said, "but the labourers are few: pray ye therefore the Lord of the harvest, that he would send forth labourers into his harvest." As we know, many parables compared the Kingdom to a harvest field. "Behold, I send you forth as lambs among wolves," he told them, and in the circumstances it was a well-justified remark. Hence the following advice: "Be ye therefore wise as serpents, and harmless as doves . . . The disciple is not above his master, nor the servant above his Lord. It is enough for the disciple that he be as his master, and the servant as his lord. If they have called the master of the house Beelzebub, how much more shall they call them of his household? Fear them not therefore: for there is nothing covered, that shall not be revealed; and hid, that shall not be known. What I tell you in darkness, that speak ye in light: and what ye hear in the ear, that preach ye upon the housetops."

Jesus wanted neither discretion nor secrecy. Let the news of the Kingdom be openly proclaimed: "And fear not them which kill the body, but are not able to kill the soul: but rather fear him which is able to destroy both soul and body in hell. Are not two sparrows sold for a farthing? and one of them shall not fall on the ground without your Father. But the very hairs of your head are all numbered. Fear ye not therefore, ye are of more value than many sparrows."

Jesus was still, through the medium of these striking metaphors and brief parables for which he had so marked a taste, in the process of developing the lesson contained in the Sermon on the Mount. One should fear no man.

With an abrupt change of tone he went on: "Think not that I am come to send peace on earth: I come not to send peace, but a sword. For I am come to set a man at variance against his father, and the daughter against her mother, and the daughter-in-law against her mother-in-law. And a man's foes shall be they of his own household." His quotation from the prophet Micah was designed to show just what a policy of violence meant. Victory would, indeed, have its brutal, bloody side; but this violence could not come from the Kingdom's evangelists. It would be the work of those who persecuted Jesus' disciples.

Never before had Jesus drawn in public so harsh a picture of the future. He was expecting a bitter struggle before the triumph of the Kingdom. Keeping with him only his four original disciples, Simon, Andrew, James and John, he made what seems, in all probability, his last journey to Nazareth.

As was his custom, he went to the synagogue and addressed the congregation there. What was the specific excuse for his intervention? Had he been reading some incident from the life of Elijah in the First Book of Kings, or had someone asked him a question on this particular point? All we know is his reply: "But I tell you of a truth, many widows were in Israel in the days of Elias [Elijah], when the heaven was shut up three years and six months, when great famine was throughout all the land; but unto none of them was Elias sent, save unto Sarepta, a city of Sidon, unto a woman that was a widow. And many lepers were in Israel in the time of Eliseus the prophet; and none of them was cleansed, saving Naaman the Syrian."

These words at once stirred up his hearers into an angry frenzy: "And all they in the synagogue, when they heard these things, were filled with wrath, and rose up, and thrust him out of the city, and led him unto the brow of the hill whereon their city was built, that they might cast him down headlong. But he passing through the midst of them went his way." Jesus had narrowly escaped being lynched in his own home town. For the first time he had been attacked by a furious mob. All he could do was to flee, and his bitterness found memorable expression: "Woe unto thee, Chorazin! woe unto thee, Bethsaida! for if the mighty works, which were done in you, had been done in Tyre and Sidon, they would have repented long ago in sackcloth and ashes. But I say unto you, It shall be more tolerable for Tyre and Sidon at the day of judgment, than for you. And thou, Capernaum, which art exalted unto heaven, shalt be brought down to hell: for if the mighty works, which have been done in thee, had been done in Sodom, it would have remained until this day. But I say unto you, that it shall be more tolerable for the land of Sodom in the day of judgment, than for thee."

This commination, so characteristically Semitic in its cadenced antitheses, is an impressive outburst — though the towns in question were three modest enough settlements, clustering close together on the shore of Lake Gennesaret. At the time they were flourishing, wealthy communities where for months on end Jesus had conducted his mission, preaching and healing the sick. Today the pilgrim who lingers on the site of Capernaum can see nothing but a barren coastal strip, strewn with basalt rocks and planted with eucalyptus. It is as though Jesus' curse still reverberates over the area.

If he had not possessed an absolute conviction of his ability to triumph over every obstacle, Jesus might well have felt deeply discouraged at the turn events had taken. For the first time the propagation of the Kingdom had met with a setback. So now he was resolved to leave his country, the towns and villages of his beloved Galilee. The villages were destined to imperishable fame as a result of the events they had lately witnessed, but their inhabitants remained indifferent. They continued to busy themselves with their private affairs and the making of money. They were quite happy to hear Jesus preach in the synagogue — provided he did not upset their religious ideas too violently.

Jesus had now come to the conclusion that these people, far from following him, would not even rally in his defense. As far as they were concerned, the Gospel of the Kingdom remained a problematical and uncertain prospect. Homosexuality had flourished in Sodom, and the guilty city had been purged by fire from heaven. Tyre and Sidon were bywords for corruption. Yet if Jesus had preached in these pagan cities, he felt, he would have made numerous conversions and have brought many to faith in the Kingdom. We may note that he did not bring any accusation of vicious moral practices against the cities of Galilee: and this hints at their more negative fault, the stagnating mediocrity of their inhabitants' lives, the contempt and indifference with which they greeted Jesus' message.

Perhaps when he cursed the cities of Galilee, Jesus really had Judaism as a whole in mind. He still had a chance to win the day in Jerusalem itself, however: to convert the Holy City for the Kingdom of God. This was a risk that must be taken, though the possibility of his people's siding as a whole against God was something he clearly foresaw and was the reason why he made no attempt to conceal his deep distress. The anger he displayed was the consequence of this rebuff to his great love.

But Israel was not the whole world. If Tyre, Sidon, and above all Sodom — the image and embodiment of all those vast pagan cities under the Empire — were amenable to conversion, should he not make the effort to reach them? More and more Jesus' thoughts were turning to the prophet Elijah. Herod Antipas and Herodias were repeating the cycle of persecution and hatred directed against Elijah by Ahab and Jezebel. Was it not right that Jesus, like Elijah, should now take refuge in the region of Tyre and Sidon, and find out what reception the pagans would give to the Gospel of the Kingdom?

When he quit Galilee, Jesus had reached a decisive turning point in his life. The inaugural phase of his mission was now over. Gone forever was that atmosphere of peace and joy which seemed so quintessentially Galilaean, and which Jesus absorbed so naturally as he moved about his small native district, surrounded by faithful friends, feted and admired in the synagogues where he preached. Henceforth the Gospel message was to be harder, more demanding, and at the same time to appeal still more clearly to all social outcasts. Official Judaism was moving towards its rejection. John's violent death had been one portent; the expulsion of Jesus from the synagogue by an angry mob was another. This was why Jesus went into exile.

three

The
Hunted
Messiah

1

Among the Pagans

A FEW HOURS' JOURNEY on foot would take Jesus across the
frontier between Galilee and Phoenicia. The southern border
of the Roman province of Syria had made considerable en-
croachments upon territory which once formed part of Palestine.
It had annexed the western half of the Carmel range, together
with the coastal approach to the Plain of Esdraelon; it had
swallowed up such towns as Dora, Ptolemais, and Oedippa. The
frontier line ran a bare fifteen miles west of Sephoris and
Nazareth.

The southern extremity of this country was still haunted by
the tremendous memory of the prophet Elijah. On the slopes
of Mount Carmel — now in pagan hands — Jehovah's redoubtable old warrior had faced and slaughtered the priests of
Baal, that same Baal whose servant (or so his enemies declared)
Jesus himself was. Now, Elijah stood in the Messianic tradition:
men believed he would rise again in the fullness of time. It was
not so long since the Jews had been asking John the Baptist
whether perhaps he was Elijah reincarnate. By turning his face
towards Phoenicia, Jesus was following in the footsteps of the
prophet of old.

We know nothing of his life while he remained in this pagan
enclave. Did he restrict his movements to the immediate vicinity
of Mount Carmel, and what we know today as the Bay of
Haifa? Did he go into solitary seclusion? or may he not rather
have welcomed this first opportunity of observing pagan *mores*
at first hand? We cannot tell, though he appears not to have had

any noteworthy discussions with any of them. He did not feel contempt for the Gentiles, but he had nothing to say to them. He may have hesitated for a moment, but now he was certain he had been sent to the Jews, and felt himself drawn towards Jerusalem.

Only one incident from the period he spent among the pagans is on record. St. Mark tells us that he "entered into an house, and would have no man know it: but he could not be hid. For a certain woman, whose young daughter had an un-clean spirit, heard of him, and came and fell at his feet: the woman was a Greek, a Syro-phenician by nation; and she be-sought him that he would cast forth the devil out of her daughter. But Jesus said unto her, 'Let the children first be filled: for it is not meet to take the children's bread, and to cast it unto the dogs.' And she answered and said unto him, 'Yes, Lord: yet the dogs under the table eat of the children's crumbs.' And he said unto her, 'For this saying go thy way; the devil is gone out of thy daughter.' And when she was come to her house, she found the devil gone out, and her daughter laid upon the bed."

For the first time — if we are to rely on Simon Peter's recol-lections as collated by Mark — Jesus had performed a healing miracle *from a distance*. He was aware of what was going on elsewhere, and could influence a sick person's condition without actually being present at the bedside.

This healing of a pagan woman's child was more or less forced out of him by the mother's quick-witted retort. Jesus admired her humility, her faith, and, not least, her presence of mind. Expressing himself in characteristically Jewish fashion, he had rejected her claim upon him: the Messianic feast was, as he saw it, a privilege open only to the chosen race, the chil-dren of God, and not (he added harshly) to mere dogs of pagans. But nothing will daunt a desperate mother. Far from showing resentment at the insult, the woman swallowed it with good grace, and, indeed, contrived to crown it with one of the most satisfying ripostes in the New Testament. Since she was a dog, let her be treated as such, and given the scraps that were her due.

It is not surprising to find this woman regarded by later generations as a symbol of *all* pagans who welcomed that evangelical sustenance which the Jews scorned and rejected.

Authentic testimony for this Phoenician interlude is almost nonexistent. Apart from the moving account of Jesus and the Syro-phenician woman, all we hear of is the healing of a deaf stutterer which took place in the Decapolis region, after Jesus' return. Employing the same procedure as he had done for the blind man, Jesus touched this person's ears, and dabbed his tongue with spittle, saying as he did so *"Ephphatha,"* an Aramaic word meaning "Be opened."

We next (the precise date cannot be determined) find Jesus in the northern region of Philip's tetrarchy, near one of the major sources of the Jordan. It was here that a most momentous act of identification took place.

2

FAITH IN CAESAREA PHILIPPI

CAESAREA PHILIPPI was a pagan city, built on the lower slopes of Mount Hermon. Jesus did not take up residence within its walls but kept moving around the neighborhood, from one town to the next. All his time was devoted to discussions with his disciples. It was now that he made up his mind to take a step the crucial importance of which was as great for the Twelve as it was for him. He would persuade them, each one of them, to give a personal, unaided opinion concerning *him*, Jesus, and the role he was destined to play in the Kingdom of God.

A more delicate, irksome, and momentous question could scarcely be conceived. It was bound up with the whole of Israel's past history and with the future of the Jewish people. It affected the entire meaning of Jesus' past labors and of all that would come in his wake.

He had publicly proclaimed the advent of God's Kingdom. His words and deeds alike had presupposed this Kingdom's inauguration and operative existence. He had laid down a charter for it in the Beatitudes. Through his parables he had demonstrated that the Kingdom's germination had already begun and could not fail. He had appointed the Twelve as servants and couriers to this new community. They had broken bread together beside the lake. But one question still insistently posed itself, a question to which John the Baptist had recently attempted to provide the answer: Who was the King of this Kingdom?

According to beliefs current among the Jews of Jesus' day, this King could not be God Himself, since the Kingdom had an earthly basis, being composed of living men. Thus its leader was of necessity a man himself; though one destined, perhaps, to become manifest riding upon the clouds of heaven rather than to be born of normal terrestrial stock. The apocalyptic writers, in particular the earliest among them, the author of the Book of Daniel, certainly predicted the future along these lines. A "new man" would descend from heaven, one furnished with all the divine powers necessary to subjugate earth's bestial dynasties. People repeated the old Aramaic verses to one another:

"I saw in the night visions, and, behold, one like the Son of man came with the clouds of heaven, and came to the Ancient of days, and they brought him near before him. And there was given him dominion, and glory, and a kingdom, that all people, nations, and languages, should serve him: his dominion is an everlasting dominion, which shall not pass away, and his kingdom that which shall not be destroyed."

But beside this heavenly vision there stood still more ancient prophecies, which spoke of one born of the house of David, who should reign over the Kingdom. He would bear the Hebrew title bestowed on all those who were anointed kings: he would be the Messiah. Those Jews of the Dispersion who spoke Greek translated this term into their adopted tongue and referred to the Messiah as the *Christos*. This King would enjoy one prerogative which the harsh monotheism of the Jews had tended to suppress in the past: he would be the Son of God. In the far-off days of the Israelite monarchy, Egyptian beliefs concerning kingship (especially the notion of the Pharaoh as Son of Amon) had penetrated as far as Palestine. Though David and Solomon had never been regarded in Jerusalem as genuine "sons of Jehovah," both these rulers assumed the filial relationship by adoption. This explains why they were high priests of their people. Confirmation comes from the Psalms:

"I will declare the decree [i.e. the oracle of Jehovah]: the Lord hath said unto me, 'Thou art my son; this day have I begotten thee.' "

And again:

"The Lord hath sworn, and will not repent, 'Thou art a priest for ever after the order of Melchizedek.' "

Priest, that is, in a royal and sacerdotal tradition going back to the time when a prince of Canaan ruled over Jerusalem.

This royal Messiah, who was both the son of Jehovah and a consecrated priest, nevertheless remained a man like other men, and would faithfully re-establish the line of earthly kings in Israel. Now Jesus had never made it clear which of the two rival concepts of the King God would choose to rule over His Kingdom he himself favored. Hitherto he had not so much as mentioned the matter; and his disciples might well ask themselves whether truth lay with the heavenly and spiritual concept of Kingship, or that which rested on an earthly, political basis. All Jesus had done was to outline the program of a Kingdom which seemed a far cry both from that aimed at by the terrorists and from the cosmic catastrophe predicted by apocalyptic writers. (As regards the latter, he refused to give a sign from heaven; and the Kingdom he described was *earthbound* — rooted in the soil like a crop.) Lastly, and most important, his Kingdom had very little in common with the Divine Covenant as interpreted by the legalistic, sectarian minds of Pharisees and Essenes. The throne of this elusive and mysterious realm remained vacant; and no one knew whether it was set in heaven or below on earth.

It was at this juncture that Jesus asked his disciples the crucial question: "Whom do men say that I am?" They answered: "John the Baptist: but some say, Elias [Elijah]; and others, one of the prophets." These notions were understandable enough. That Jesus was John the Baptist may have been the view circulated, tongue in cheek, by Herod's police agents; it was also, very probably, a genuine belief current among simpleminded and credulous folk throughout Galilee. John, they argued, could not have been mistaken. The authorities *thought* they had beheaded him, but he had, miraculously, escaped. Others, possibly, thought his death genuine enough, but assumed he had risen from the grave immediately afterward and was now traveling around Galilee under the name of Jesus. Obviously those who spread these absurd yet rather touching rumors had never themselves *seen* either John or Jesus. Such ideas must have been the merest bazaar gossip.

Those who took Jesus to be Elijah reincarnate did at least give evidence of some scriptural knowledge. The Bible told how Elijah had been taken up to heaven in a fiery chariot while yet alive; and his return in aftertime was foretold by the

prophetic Book of Malachi.* For much the same reasons people sometimes suggested Moses as a candidate. To be sure, the
Old Testament recorded Moses' death; but it also laid stress
on the fact that his place of burial remained unknown. Building
on this, one popular theory proclaimed that Moses, too, had not
really died, and was now risen again at God's command, to
make further intercession on Sinai for the children of Israel.

For the Jewish man in the street, then, Jesus' personality was
to be explained by reference to one of the most important and
revered figures in the Old Testament. He was regarded as a
Biblical character; but the characters chosen were invariably
those associated with the Messianic era, whose reappearance was
to herald the advent of the Kingdom. No one suggested he was
Abraham, or David, or Solomon; the chosen candidates were
John the Baptist, Elijah, and, possibly, Jeremiah. "And he
saith unto them, 'But whom say ye that I am?' And Peter
answereth and saith unto him, 'Thou art the Christ.'" St.
Mark adds: "And he charged them that they should tell no
man of him."

The account given by St. Matthew is somewhat fuller and
more circumstantial. Perhaps the declaration of Jesus which
it records was made later, and in a different context, but it remains absolutely crucial. Date and provenance cannot affect
its weight or authenticity: "Blessed art thou, Simon Bar-jona:
for flesh and blood hath not revealed it unto thee, but my
Father which is in heaven. And I say also unto thee, That thou
art Peter, and upon this rock I will build my church; and the
gates of hell shall not prevail against it."

In Simon's phrase "Thou art the Christ" Jesus saw, not the
result of human speculation, but a God-sent enlightenment,
the discovery of a mysterious, indeed a divine truth. Through
Simon's lips humanity was greeting its King; and at the same

*Malachi 4, 5.

moment this King, by virtue of the powers God had granted him, bestowed upon Simon a new name. He was to be called Peter; and, with a play upon words common at Eastern naming ceremonies, this appellation would also signify the rock (*petros*), the granite-hard foundation upon which, like a palace, the new fellowship of the Kingdom would be built. To this fellowship the Greeks gave the name used for their national assembly by the citizens of Athens: they called it the *ekklēsia*, from which derives the French word *église*.* Over this fellowship, Jesus at once declared, the gates of hell would not prevail.

He was thinking of the future. Hell, for him, was not the ancient Babylonian realm of the dead, with its successive barred doors through which the goddess Ishtar passed. Hell was rather the power of evil operating here on earth: the diabolical possession which held imperial Rome in its grip, the specter of political domination, the same Satan who had, in the wilderness, offered Jesus all the kingdoms of the earth if he would bow down and worship the principle of violence. He had resisted triumphantly; and his fellowship, his Church, would resist too. But it was essential that the Church should, right from the beginning, stand out against the idea of a *temporal* triumph for the Messiah. This is why Jesus at first bound Peter and his companions to strict secrecy. Under the seal of this secrecy he began to formulate the astonishing program which his princely dominion — now acknowledged by these disciples — would henceforth entail.

* Our English word "church" derives from the Greek *kyriakon*, meaning the Lord's House. [Tr.]

3

THE SON OF MAN

IN SHARP AND deliberate contrast with Simon Peter's recognition
of him as the Messiah, the Son of God, Jesus at once began to
speak of himself as the Son of Man. The Aramaic phrase *bar
nāsha* carries no other meaning *per se* than "of man," although
its use in modern parlance has special poetic overtones. But in
Jesus' day the words "Son of Man" awoke the most extraordinary echoes and associations.

To begin with, there were the visions of Daniel. It is true
that the apparition of "one like the Son of man" — the image
of a perfect man, enthroned on the clouds of heaven — was
here set in contrast to the beastliness of earthly dynasties, as
represented by the lion, the bear, and the leopard. But this
Son of Man — symbol of the new Jewish world-wide dominion,
in which man would be restored by God to his true natural
dignity — was associated by Daniel with the end of the world.
His advent was to be strictly celestial. Just as the creation of
Adam, the first man, had marked the beginning of time, so
this "new man" would write *Finis* to history and be coeval with
the resurrection of the dead.

It is not only in the Book of Daniel that reference is made to
the Son of Man. He is also a central figure in the apocalyptic
Book of Enoch; a being with human form yet of heavenly substance, hidden by God until his revelation at the Last Judgment.
Created, yet existing before the world itself was made, he
predates the very sun and stars. He is the Chosen One of God,
the Saviour of the world, the sole embodiment of perfect
justice, the supreme judge and mediator, the triumphant victor
who, at his coming, will reveal all the secret wisdom of the
universe:

"In this place mine eyes beheld the Chosen One, in whom justice and faith abide. I beheld where he abode beneath the wings of the Lord of Hosts. . . . All the just and the chosen shine before him like fire. Their mouths show forth praises and blessings, and their lips glorify the name of the Lord of Hosts."*

The Son of Man, then, presides over the community of the just, those who have risen again in glory; he is King of the age that is to come, the promised ruler of a renewed, transfigured, supraterrestrial world.

Where did the Jews get hold of an eschatological doctrine so alien to that embodied in the Old Testament? The Biblical Messiah whose coming various prophets foretold was always an *earthly* King. Perhaps it was simply the reappearance of a very ancient concept, which we can detect lurking behind the account of the Creation in Genesis: the primitive, archetypal human figure, the "anthropos ideal" that was a common subject of discussion in Eastern countries. A glorious and flawless man, he had been created before all things, and in him the pattern of the macrocosm was made manifest: he was the new, radiant Adam, the Lord of Paradise. His soul was the soul of the world, his destiny set an example which his innumerable descendants would imitate. Among the Persians and, latterly, the Gnostics — even for groups as remote in time as Freemasons and the Illuminati — he came to represent ultimate victory over the powers of evil, in the last days. Already he was endowed with all those marvelous attributes which Nietzsche bestowed upon his Superman, and which Marxists — by translating them from a religious to a political context — assume in future generations of mankind. What we have here is man's fundamental dream of the millennium; and like all dreams, its deeper truth is easily discernible beneath that mythical top dressing. Men need to

*Book of Enoch 39, 3-7.

project their ideal vision. They may turn to the past and conjure up a Golden Age; or to the future, when their vision will show mankind, at last, in that final stage of development which embodies the perfection to which human beings continually aspire.

The rabbis of Jesus' day could find little evidence of such a concept in the Old Testament Prophets. Yet there were one or two allusions to it, especially in Ezekiel's poem on the King of Tyre:

"Thou sealest up the sum, full of wisdom, and perfect in beauty. Thou hast been in Eden the garden of God; every precious stone was thy covering . . . the workmanship of thy tabrets and of thy pipes was prepared in thee in the day that thou wast created. Thou art the anointed cherub that covereth; and I have set thee so: thou wast upon the holy mountain of God; thou hast walked up and down in the midst of the stones of fire. Thou wast perfect in thy ways from the day that thou wast created . . ."

But it was the account of Adam's creation in the earthly Paradise which best lent itself to speculation of this sort. Mowinckel writes:

There can be no doubt that later Jewish Adamic mythology was influenced by the concept of the "archetypal man." In it Adam appears as an unambiguously divine being whose existence precedes the Creation: he is the *fons et origo* of all cosmogonies, the primordial world-soul, the original embodiment of piety and dispenser of justice, one of those who are to be reincarnate at the end of time, men clad in divinity.

But though he referred to himself as the Son of Man, Jesus was very far from sharing the muddled or contradictory beliefs which such a title might arouse in the minds of his disciples.

Even supposing he regarded the whole idea of the Son of Man as something to be developed piecemeal, according to the dictates of Providence — and as permitting him to reveal certain of the Kingdom's mysteries — nevertheless he was determined to break with the unreal and artificial ideal of superhuman perfection. He wanted the Son of Man to be fully reintegrated with humanity at large. He must restore to this glorious title its etymological meaning: Son of Mankind. And in order to make his disciples realize that the Son of Man was truly man, he must needs experience those terrible sufferings to which the human condition is at times subject. This was his appalling secret.

4

THE TEMPTATION OF THE SON OF MAN

"AND HE BEGAN to teach them, that the Son of man must suffer many things, and be rejected of the elders, and of the chief priests, and scribes, and be killed, and after three days rise again." The tragic private dilemma facing Jesus was this: How, having adopted for his own purposes the glorious title of Son of Man, could he then develop a program so flatly opposed to the radiant visions conjured up by Daniel or the Book of Enoch? If he accepted the role of God's Messiah, how could he then reject the Messianic prophecies, or appear to turn them upside down in support of a harsh and unpalatable paradox?

There was, however, a series of Old Testament prophecies which the rabbis had never thought of connecting with the Messiah's fate, and which similarly the apocalyptic writers had never applied to the Son of Man. It was in these prophecies that Jesus saw the dark pattern of his own future mission. The songs of Jehovah's servant, in the Book of Isaiah, are strange poems, written by some unknown author during the Babylonian exile, which extol the sufferings and glory of a heroic Redeemer. Jesus could hear their arresting, cadenced antitheses surge through his memory:

"'I was not rebellious, neither turned away back. I gave my back to the smiters, and my cheeks to them that plucked off the hair: I hid not my face from shame and spitting."

And again:

"Surely he hath borne our griefs, and carried our sorrows: yet we did esteem him stricken, smitten of God, and afflicted. But he was wounded for our transgressions, he was bruised for our iniquities: the chastisement of our peace was upon him; and with his stripes we are healed. . . . And the Lord hath laid on him the iniquity of us all. He was oppressed, and he was afflicted, yet he opened not his mouth . . . For he was cut off out of the land of the living: for the transgression of my people was he stricken."

This terrible imagery was a far cry from the vision of the Son of Man in his glory. But Jesus, as we know from his dream in the wilderness, when he saw himself on the pinnacle of the Temple, had refused to manifest himself to the Jews against a background of celestial portents. It followed, logically, that he must take upon himself the full burden of men's miseries, must endure to be spat at contemptuously by those who would not acknowledge him the Kingdom's royal Master. His rejection of a political triumph was bound to mean that his own people would in turn reject him; he was doomed to die a reviled outcast. Could this be what God desired, this strange and complete reversal of tradition?

It could be; it was. God's incomparable grandeur was such that only one who appeared the lowest and most wretched among men could stand, a King, at his right hand. Suddenly Jesus began to see the whole of the Bible in a new light: it was shot through with a mystique of suffering which no one hitherto had clearly discerned. Jesus linked the songs of the suffering servant with the oracular prophecies of glory. It was through the most degrading and repugnant suffering that God's triumph would reach fulfillment. Jesus recalled the great prophets such as Moses, Elijah, Jeremiah and Ezekiel: how *they* had suffered, and mostly without understanding the reason why. And what of the nation as a whole, those millions who had died in battle or on the long road towards exile, prisoners impaled alive and dying of thirst, disemboweled women, the martyrs who suffered under Antiochus IV (Epiphanes)? While Jesus knelt in prayer, all over the Empire countless human beings endured the yoke of slavery. Some were condemned to labor camps, others sweated in the Sicilian silver mines. In the arenas gladiators writhed dying before bloodthirsty audiences. Starvation and prostitution went hand in hand. Everywhere, to a greater or lesser extent, human beings were hunted down like animals. Could Jesus hope to heal *their* wounds unless his own sufferings equaled, indeed surpassed what they endured?

But Peter could not stomach this. He "took him, and began to rebuke him. But when he had turned about and looked on his disciples, he rebuked Peter, saying, 'Get thee behind me, Satan: thou art an offence unto me; for thou savourest not the things that be of God, but the things that be of men.' " Even if Peter did not actually quote Jesus those splendid verses from the Book of Enoch, he must at least have reminded him of his sovereign powers as Messiah and world Emperor. A king is created to rule, not to let himself be condemned to death. So Peter would have argued: he completely failed to understand Jesus' paradoxical position, and attributed it either to failure of nerve or acute pessimism. He had not grasped the fundamental principle behind this new Kingdom of God. But before we accuse him of obtuseness, we should ask ourselves whether we would have acted otherwise in his position.

As Simon Peter spoke, Jesus was carried back, in a flash, to his desert vision. His dearest friends were now abetting those same forces of evil as had already, among the lonely, scattered rocks beyond the Jordan, offered him the kingdoms of the world on condition that he would acknowledge the principle of force. Simon Peter was taking on the lineaments of his old enemy. With brutal abruptness, Jesus dismissed him. This was one occasion which called for absolute firmness, and enabled Jesus to express both his beliefs and his rigorous personal demands in their most extreme form. "And when he had called the people unto him with his disciples also, he said unto them, 'Whosoever will come after me, let him deny himself, and take up his cross, and follow me.'"

This was the first time in his life that Jesus had referred to the instrument of torture employed by the Roman army. He was not making a direct prophecy of his own death so much as presenting a generalized image of cruelty which all those present would readily comprehend. During this period, both in Palestine and throughout the Empire, crucifixions were as commonplace as bullfights are in Spain to this day. Deserters, recaptured fugitive slaves, terrorists, and the brigands who swarmed in the Trachonitis hinterland — all these were crucified by the hundred. Everywhere one came across little clumps of crosses, on which, day after slow day, naked bleeding wretches coughed away their lives, tortured by attacks of tetanus, their flesh torn from them by night-prowling jackals. Crosses were as ubiquitous in this period as gibbets at road junctions in the Middle Ages. Corpses were left nailed to them till they rotted away. A condemned man was forced to carry the heavy upright to his place of punishment, together with the crossbeam affixed to it. Everyone had seen such wretches stagger past, lashed on by their military escort.

Are you, Jesus was asking in effect, *strong enough to face even the risk of crucifixion?* The Resistance terrorists were, and did. Jesus required an equal standard of courage from his disciples; he was also, on this occasion, emphasizing the gulf of incompatibility that lay between God's Kingdom and the Empire of men who crucified their fellows.

In this connection other maxims of his were recalled by the Evangelists, such as: "Whosoever will save his life shall lose it; but whosoever shall lose his life for my sake and the gospel's, the same shall save it." There could have been no clearer possible statement, nor one that threw the paradox of Jesus' "good tidings" into such sharp relief. He also said: "Whosoever hath, to him shall be given, and he shall have more abundance: but whosoever hath not, from him shall be taken away even that he hath." And again: "For what shall it profit a man, if he shall gain the whole world, and lose his own soul? Or what shall a man give in exchange for his soul?"

All these aphorisms, with which he from time to time adorned his discourse, could easily have sprung from the central idea he was now evolving, that of a Son of Man who was to know persecution, abject humiliation, and death. To follow him meant risking one's life; but he promised that those who did would at once discover the true life of the Kingdom, the only life that mattered.

He had said to Peter: "Thou art an offence unto me." At some later date he was to repeat and crystallize, in a few telling words, his fierce intransigence where obstacles hindering one's entry into the Kingdom were concerned: "If thy hand offend thee, cut if off: it is better for thee to enter into life maimed, than having two hands to go into hell, into the fire that never shall be quenched . . . And if thy foot offend thee, cut it off: it is better for thee to enter halt into life, than having two feet to be cast into hell . . . And if thine eye offend thee, pluck it out: it is better for thee to enter into the kingdom of

God with one eye, than having two eyes to be cast into hell fire."

The word Jesus used for hell was Gehenna, originally used to designate the western valley of Jerusalem, where kings of Judah once sacrificed their children in the flames. Jesus took this Biblical image to convey the idea of perdition, of being shut out from the Kingdom.

Thus by revealing to his disciples the sufferings of Jehovah's Servant, Jesus linked his fate to that of all those who were persecuted for the Kingdom's sake. They too would have to overcome every obstacle. The kind of "force" which this community demanded was gradually being made clear. To achieve the Kingdom was a task for the toughest, a stark and indeed brutal business. Hence the balance struck by Jesus between the joyful lot of martyrs (as foreshadowed in the relevant Beatitudes) and his pronouncements against family ties. The forebodings he had felt concerning his disruptive effect on society grew daily stronger and more definite. The Kingdom was a prize to be grasped by force, with raw and bleeding hands, through submission to the nails and the cross. It meant a bloody struggle: the fearful agonies of the Messiah were bound up with those of his people, became inseparable from them. In that, at least, the Zealots were right. The conquest of the Kingdom had nothing pious or idyllic about it. The image of the harvest was now drowned in blood, and the sword usurped the reaping hook. Jesus was preparing to carry his disciples with him on a venture which well might have scared the stoutest heart.

But would he continue to lead them through this vale of tears and suffering without first giving them some sort of respite, a haven of peace? He was, in fact, anxious for them to have a foretaste of the Kingdom's glory; and so when he underwent his mystical Transfiguration on the mountain, they were there at his side.

5

THE TRANSFIGURATION

ENOCH HAD SEEN the Son of Man in his glory upon a high mountain. Jesus, too, took his disciples "up into an high mountain": its identity has provoked much discussion. Mount Tabor, which lies midway between Upper and Lower Galilee, its rounded summit dominating the Plain of Esdraelon, is an obvious candidate: but at this period it was crowned by a Herodian fortress, which at once eliminates it as the scene of the Transfiguration. No one contemplating a condition of mystical ecstasy would choose a barrack yard for the purpose.

As the episode occurred about a week after Jesus' declaration at Caesarea Philippi, some writers have identified its mountainous setting with the nearby slopes of Mount Hermon. But it is possible that Jesus' meditation did not in fact take place till somewhat later, when he had reached the southern part of Peraea. If this is so, it must have happened on Mount Nebo. It was here that Moses had died, and hereabouts that Elijah (Elias) had been taken up to heaven in a fiery chariot — which would explain their unexpected appearance during the Transfiguration.

"And after six days Jesus taketh with him Peter, and James, and John, and leadeth them up into an high mountain apart by themselves: and he was transfigured before them. And his raiment became shining, exceeding white as snow; so as no fuller on earth can white them. And there appeared unto them Elias with Moses: and they were talking with Jesus. And Peter answered and said to Jesus, 'Master, it is good for us to be here: and let us make three tabernacles; one for thee, and one for Moses, and one for Elias.' For he wist not what to say; for they were sore afraid. And there was a cloud that overshadowed them: and a voice came out of the cloud, saying, 'This is my beloved Son: hear him.' And suddenly, when they had looked round about, they saw no man any more, save Jesus only with themselves."

We have to do here with the kind of ecstatic experience that frequently figures in the lives of the great mystics, Christian and non-Christian alike. Characteristic details include the shining brightness of Jesus' face and garments, the two apparitions, and the fear engendered in those who witnessed the incident. This was not, however, a mystical vision which Jesus alone experienced, and afterward communicated to his disciples; unlike the episode of his baptism, it is (on the face of our evidence) incompatible with such a theory. On the other hand, it seems by no means impossible that Simon Peter was the only other person who actually *saw* the vision. In comparable cases, such as St. Paul's experience on the road to Damascus, it often happens that those present are aware of the visionary's ecstatic condition but do not themselves see what is revealed to him.

The metamorphosis or transfiguration which Jesus underwent was the result of his ecstatic union with God: it prefigured the glory to which the Son of Man would attain, and allowed Peter to glimpse the person of the resurrected Christ. It also translated Jesus' inner spiritual condition into a visible image. He was not only engaged in solitary prayer; he also conversed with Moses and Elijah. Their presence need cause no surprise. The Jews of Jesus' day believed that God had already raised Moses from the dead; the apocryphal book known as the Assumption of Moses portrayed this heroic servant of the Lord in constant prayer upon Mount Nebo, making intercession on Israel's behalf. Elijah was supposed to have escaped death, and men looked to his second coming in the days of the Messiah. If Jesus was on that selfsame high mountain where

Moses lay awaiting his hour and whence Elijah had been carried up to heaven in a fiery chariot, his encounter with these two personages — their nature a compound of human and divine, of the living and the risen — need cause us no surprise. Between them, moreover, they embodied the whole canon of the Old Testament. For the Jews of this era, Moses was the only begetter of the Law, the Torah; and even if Elijah had written nothing — since rabbinical opinion held that all doctrine whatsoever was contained in the Law — he still remained the heroic *fons et origo* of the prophetic tradition. So, when Jesus interrogated them, he was in a very literal sense addressing the Law and the Prophets — that is, the whole Bible, this being the title then applied to it. He was not scrutinizing a dead text but conversing with living persons. Moreover, he had the mastery over these giants of Judaism. Here, at the very fountainhead of the Law and Prophets, he could devote his spoken meditations to a new, creative, and authoritative interpretation of Holy Writ. If he received from Moses and Elijah secret truths concerning God's past actions, he could in turn reveal to them the future fulfillment of the Scriptures.

Peter believed himself on Sinai. When he offered to put up the tents that they had brought with them on their journey, his intention was that they should be used as "tabernacles," or sanctuaries where the Elect of God could converse. Indeed he was, as it turned out, on a mountain no less awesome and holy than Sinai. The cloud that had hidden God from the Israelites in the desert descended upon the vision confronting Peter, and a divine voice was heard to utter the words: "This" — that is, Jesus, as opposed to Moses or Elijah — "is my beloved Son." Moses and Elijah vanished: from now on God was to express His purpose through His Son. Now Peter received divine confirmation of the words he himself had addressed to Jesus: "Thou art the Christ, the Son of the living God." The voice from heaven also fulfilled Jesus' reply: "Flesh and blood hath not revealed it unto thee, but my Father which is in heaven." Once again the royal rite of baptism was being enacted, but this time in Peter's presence and for his special benefit. Surely, too, the Transfiguration had another purpose — to authenticate the new gospel of the suffering Messiah which Jesus had revealed to his disciples, and which he was to embody before their eyes. A new gospel was beginning: the Gospel of the Passion.

Henceforth the person of Jesus was to occupy a central position in the gospel message: it embraced not only his sayings, but also what he did, what he was. The royal Master's function was not to eclipse the Kingdom but to enhance it with his presence and mediation.

Throughout the account of this ecstatic vision there can be detected echoes from the magnificent ceremonial with which all Eastern monarchs were enthroned. To look upon the face of the King, whether in Egypt or at Babylon or Susa, was the supreme favor lesser mortals could enjoy. This court etiquette had left its mark on Biblical phraseology: the Old Testament often portrayed the cult of the Temple in terms more appropriate to royal protocol. By revealing himself to Peter in the sumptuous splendor of a king, Jesus was making a concession to his disciples' wish to behold his Messianic glory; he was also giving them a lesson which completed what the parables had begun, by translating his spiritual primacy in terms of Biblical metaphor and Eastern symbolism. From this episode Peter would learn that Jesus was not repudiating the glorious appellation Son of Man absolutely, but merely refusing to realize its human and political aspects. He aimed at achieving a balance between men's faith in some supernatural, apocalyptic manifestation, and the servitude imposed by his own human status. He was, indeed, to achieve glory: but not yet. First he must endure persecution. All he could do now was to offer some earnest of his future victory.

"And as they came down from the mountain, he charged them that they should tell no man what things they had seen, till the Son of man were risen from the dead. And they kept that saying with themselves, questioning one with another what the rising from the dead should mean. And they asked him, saying, 'Why say the scribes that Elias must first come?' And he answered and told them, 'Elias verily cometh first, and restoreth all things; and how it is written of the Son of man, that he must suffer many things, and be set at nought. But I say unto you, that Elias is indeed come, and they have done unto him whatsoever they listed, as it is written of him.'" The enjoinment of absolute silence which Jesus imposed upon his disciples conforms in all respects to his general attitude at this period.

The disciples questioned him on the subject of Elias [Elijah]. Was he to come again? Yes, Jesus replied. But there was something of greater importance they should consider when they looked to the future: the sufferings of the Son of Man. Besides, Elijah was come again already, in the person of John the Baptist. This identification looks odd on the face of it, since John had replied in the negative when asked the same question; and indeed Jesus knew quite well that John was not a reincarnation of Elijah, but had simply performed that particular prophetic role in the Kingdom's advent which Malachi had attributed to Elijah.

This emphasis on the sufferings of the Messiah brought John the Baptist to mind; and appropriately enough, since he was the first martyr for the Kingdom.

If Jesus' friends supposed — when they came down from the mountain after this mystical experience — that henceforth they

would have no more to do with the miseries of the world and
the flesh, they were soon rudely disabused of such a notion.
"And when he came to his disciples," St. Mark tells us, "he
saw a great multitude about them, and the scribes questioning
with them. And straightway all the people, when they beheld
him, were greatly amazed, and running to him saluted him.
And he asked the scribes, 'What question ye with them?' And
one of the multitude answered and said, 'Master, I have brought
unto thee my son, which hath a dumb spirit; and wheresoever
he taketh him, he teareth him: and he foameth, and gnasheth
with his teeth, and pineth away: and I spake to thy disciples
that they should cast him out; and they could not.'"

The child, obviously, was an epileptic. After hearing the
father's account of what had happened, Jesus became very
angry: not with his disciples, but because the crowd lacked faith
in his powers and the scribes were once more trying to catch
him out. "O faithless generation," he cried, "how long shall I
be with you? how long shall I suffer you?" He was weary of this
endless struggle against dishonesty and skepticism. But in the
end he took up the challenge. "Bring him unto me," he said,
and they did so. Not surprisingly, the boy at once went into a
fit: "And when he saw him, straightway the spirit tare him;
and he fell on the ground, and wallowed foaming. And he asked
his father, 'How long is it ago since this came unto him?' And
he said, 'Of a child. And ofttimes it hath cast him into the fire,
and into the waters, to destroy him: but if thou canst do any
thing, have compassion on us, and help us.' Jesus said unto him,
'If thou canst believe, all things are possible to him that be-
lieveth.'" This is an astonishing remark. Jesus was not speaking
of rare, exceptional powers, but of something normal, something which anybody endowed with faith possessed.

"And straightway the father of the child cried out, and said
with tears, 'Lord, I believe; help thou mine unbelief.' When

Jesus saw that the people came running together, he rebuked the foul spirit, saying unto him, 'Thou dumb and deaf spirit, I charge thee, come out of him, and enter no more into him.' And the spirit cried, and rent him sore, and came out of him: and he was as one dead; insomuch that many said, 'He is dead.' But Jesus took him by the hand, and lifted him up; and he arose. And when he was come into the house, his disciples asked him privately, 'Why could not we cast him out?' And he said unto them, 'This kind can come forth by nothing, but by prayer and fasting.' "

This response may sound rather strange to modern ears, since nowadays we take it for granted that epilepsy is a disease requiring medical treatment. But in Jesus' times medicine as we know it did not exist. Biblical psalms were often employed as prayers to cure the sick. But Jesus did not resort to prayer in order to heal the epileptic boy: he exerted his own innate power and authority. Yet he was weary of such interventions.

6

OUR FATHER

JESUS' JOURNEY TOOK HIM from Caesarea Philippi, in the northernmost part of Palestine, down to a point on the eastern bank of the Jordan, just opposite Jericho. He must have hurried through parts of Galilee enroute: and in Samaria he was received with active hostility: "He stedfastly set his face to go to Jerusalem, and sent messengers before his face: and they went, and entered into a village of the Samaritans, to make ready for him. And they did not receive him, because his face was as though he would go to Jerusalem. And when his disciples James and John saw this, they said, 'Lord, wilt thou that we command fire to come down from heaven, and consume them, even as Elias did?' But he turned and rebuked them . . . And they went to another village."

Jesus still repudiated the use of force, and refused to command a "sign from heaven." It was perhaps on this occasion that he ironically nicknamed James and John Boanerges, the Sons of Thunder — a title which, unlike that of Peter, did not stick. He also acquired a few new disciples along the way. Sometimes he welcomed these would-be members of his community; on occasion he recognized a merely frivolous impulse, and was discouraging. "And it came to pass, that, as they went in the way, a certain man said unto him, 'Lord, I will follow thee withersoever thou goest.' And Jesus said unto him, 'Foxes have holes, and birds of the air have nests; but the Son of man hath not where to lay his head.' And he said unto another, 'Follow me.' But he said, 'Lord, suffer me first to go and bury my father.' Jesus said unto him, 'Let the dead bury their dead: but go thou and preach the kingdom of God.' And another also said, 'Lord, I will follow thee; but let me first go bid them farewell, which are at home at my house.' And Jesus said unto him, 'No man, having put his hand to the plow, and looking back, is fit for the kingdom of God.' "

These aphoristic replies, so swift and vivid for all their melancholy harshness, enable us to catch Jesus' spontaneous reactions in the very moment of utterance. To enter the Kingdom, the disciples learned with some dismay, was a long and wearisome business; and this Kingdom was no otherworldly domain, like a dream of the Fortunate Isles, but a mission, to be tackled here and now. Like all great undertakings, it held out magnificent prospects, but also involved much thankless and demanding toil.

It may have been at some time during this journey that the disciples asked Jesus how they should pray to God. "Lord," they said, "teach us to pray, as John also taught his disciples."

Jesus replied: "When ye pray, say, 'Our Father which art in heaven, Hallowed be thy name. Thy kingdom come. Thy will be done, as in heaven, so in earth. Give us day by day our daily bread. And forgive us our sins; for we also forgive every one that is indebted to us. And lead us not into temptation; but deliver us from evil.' " These words crystallize the entire Gospel of the Kingdom. They are an expression of Jesus' innermost beliefs, and demonstrate his supreme originality in comparison not only with the Old Testament but with all other religious aspirations of mankind.

The first affirmation in the Lord's Prayer is that of divine paternity. In the Old Testament, it is true, God was already represented as the Father of His people. But in those days the relationship was both primitive and harsh, laying considerable stress on punishment. It followed that God exercised a similar function in relation to the community as a whole. From his earliest synagogue preaching in Galilee, Jesus had emphasized God's paternal character, and he continually reverted to the point. God was a compassionate father, full of kindness, moved by the plight of his children whom he loved. Here we can discern a strong intuitive feeling for what was later to be known as the Christian spirit, something that changed men's religious sensibilities for all time by giving them trust, and pity, and love: what men afterward called charity.

God's true name, Jehovah or Jahweh, had become taboo among the Jews, never to be uttered. Though Jesus may have respected this prohibition, he did not give it the positive sanction of his authority. What mattered to him was that people should be reminded of the sanctity attaching to the name. In the East to a far greater extent than amongst Westerners, all names are an active extension of their owner's personality, a verbal double of the living self. By uttering a man's name, you could influence the man himself. The name of God *was* God.

Jesus' greatest longing was, naturally, for the Kingdom, already begun but not yet accomplished: and in what did it consist, if not in bestowing upon all mankind that heavenly bliss which ensued from their fulfillment of the divine Will? Moreover, this Will was plain enough in its intentions. God wished all men to receive their daily bread, their sustenance; to release one another from such debts as they might owe, in a species of perpetual jubilee, or amnesty; and to escape the wiles of the Evil One, the Lord of all powers of dominion and oppression, even of death itself.

It has been claimed that all the basic elements embodied in the prayer which Jesus made up derive from rabbinical teaching. This is true insofar as Jesus had no intention of adding to Biblical doctrine, and made no reference to his own role, but addressed himself exclusively to God. But three things the rabbis lacked: that direct and confident tone which is the hallmark of all Jesus' sayings; the unity into which he fused both praise of one's Maker and those simple, commonplace petitions which go up to God the world over; and, lastly, his gift for expounding and interpreting what he taught.

He explained the Lord's Prayer by means of three illustrative parables. St. Matthew tells us: "Then came Peter to him, and said, 'Lord, how oft shall my brother sin against me, and I forgive him? till seven times?' Jesus saith unto him, 'I say not unto thee, Until seven times: but, Until seventy times seven. Therefore is the kingdom of heaven likened unto a certain king, which would take account of his servants. And when he had begun to reckon, one was brought unto him, which owed him ten thousand talents.* But forasmuch as he had

* A fantastic sum, equivalent to about twelve million dollars today.

not to pay, his lord commanded him to be sold, and his wife, and children, and all that he had, and payment to be made. The servant therefore fell down, and worshipped him, saying, Lord, have patience with me, and I will pay thee all. Then the lord of that servant was moved with compassion, and loosed him, and forgave him the debt. But the same servant went out, and found one of his fellowservants, which owed him an hundred pence: and he laid hands on him, and took him by the throat, saying, Pay me that thou owest. And his fellowservant fell down at his feet, and besought him, saying, Have patience with me, and I will pay thee all. And he would not: but went and cast him into prison, till he should pay the debt. So when his fellowservants saw what was done, they were very sorry, and came and told unto their lord all that was done. Then his lord, after that he had called him, said unto him, O thou wicked servant, I forgave thee all that debt, because thou desiredst me: shouldest not thou also have had compassion on thy fellowservant, even as I had pity on thee? And his lord was wroth, and delivered him to the tormentors, till he should pay all that was due unto him. So likewise shall my heavenly Father do also unto you, if ye from your hearts forgive not every one his brother their trespasses.' "

The piquancy of this little tale lies in a series of contrasts: the enormous disproportion between the two debts, the different attitude adopted by the creditor in each case, the transformation of the original debtor from humble suppliant into harsh, demanding man of property. All these details are there for the sole purpose of driving home the unpalatable moral with greater bite and vividness.

The background and imagery of the parables have changed. The original figure of the sower is here replaced by that of a king — who, moreover, in the course of the story becomes a banker or some other kind of wealthy citizen. The style displays a change, too: it is fuller, more colorful. Jesus' original simple parables have given way to dramatic, picturesque stories, in which every character is a sharply drawn and original creation. Yet when we turn to the parable of the importunate friend, we find the old simplicity once more: "And he said unto them, 'Which of you shall have a friend, and shall go unto him at midnight, and say unto him, Friend, lend me three loaves; for a friend of mine in his journey is come to me, and I have nothing to set before him? And he from within shall answer and say, Trouble me not: the door is now shut, and my children are with me in bed; I cannot rise and give thee. I say unto you, Though he will not rise and give him, because he is his friend, yet because of his importunity he will rise and give him as many as he needeth.' "

The simple comparison of a man at his prayers with an importunate friend here germinates into a full-fledged story, and shows Jesus' fondness for making up such tales on the spur of the moment. He visualizes the friend knocking at the door, sketches in the small but telling details of his request for the loan of three loaves, the sudden arrival of an old friend on his travels. He lets us know that the victim is a family man, with children, but that his wife is away. In the East everyone shares the same bed, which explains why he has the children in with him. Given the slightest encouragement, Jesus would tell us how many children there were and what each of them was called, besides giving a full account of that nocturnal conversation through the barred front door. He knew how much the listening crowd — and his disciples — enjoyed such details; and he had a personal liking for the simple daily round of ordinary people's lives, which he portrayed with such taste, affection, and poetic insight.

On another occasion, when discussing the same topic, he once more indulged his love of picturesque detail, to a degree which suggests not only character portrayal for its own sake but also conscious social satire: "There was in a city a judge, which feared not God, neither regarded man: and there was a widow in that city; and she came unto him, saying, 'Avenge me of mine adversary.' And he would not for a while: but afterward he said within himself, 'Though I fear not God, nor regard man; yet because this widow troubleth me, I will avenge her, lest by her continual coming she weary me.'" If Jesus had told the people that God would see justice done to them, they would have nodded agreement; but in fact what he said, by implication, was: *At least God is no worse than a crooked judge.* Such an approach is typical of his manner; and it shows an apt sense of humor (especially in an Eastern country where justice tends to require *baksheesh*) to hold up a judge to ridicule by making him yield to a widow's importunate lamentations.

But this was a relatively simple lesson; and Jesus soon probed beyond it to reveal another, altogether more profound, aspect of the Kingdom — God's divine mercy. Perhaps because he foresaw his own future sufferings, he treated the subject with greater persuasiveness and power than he had ever before displayed.

7

THE GREAT PARABLES OF DIVINE MERCY

WE CANNOT BE CERTAIN at what precise point in Jesus' life the parables of divine mercy are to be located. They appear to predate the final visit to Jerusalem; and in their expression of the deepest truths concerning the Kingdom they mark so great an advance on the early Galilaean parables that it seems probable St. Luke was right, and that they were expounded during the journey to the Holy City.

The proposition that one element of the Kingdom of Heaven was God's infinite, all-powerful compassion for mankind had been expressed by Jesus previously, in Galilee. He had spoken of a God who "sendeth rain on the just and on the unjust." Sometimes, rather than speak in the synagogue, he had chosen to dine with some social outcast whom public opinion condemned. But now the light at the heart of the Kingdom was to spread its rays worldwide: the day of forgiveness was at hand, the great reconciliation of God and man.

Not that Jesus made any reference to the Biblical account of man's Creation and subsequent Fall. If he came to tell men their sins were forgiven them, his concern was always for the individual conscience separated from God: those who had turned their backs on their Maker and cut themselves off from the family of the faithful, the children of God. Jesus' listeners were for the most part either shepherds, or at least the owners of a few sheep. He began by appealing to their personal experience: "What man of you," he asked them, "having an hundred sheep, if he lose one of them, doth not leave the ninety and nine in the wilderness, and go after that which is lost, until he find it? And when he hath found it, he layeth it on his shoulders, rejoicing. And when he cometh home, he calleth together his friends and neighbours, saying unto them, Rejoice with me; for I have found my sheep which was lost. I say unto you, that likewise joy shall be in heaven over one sinner that repenteth, more than over ninety and nine just persons, which need no repentance."

The little anecdote embodies what is even today a daily occurrence throughout all the Mediterranean countries, especially in semi-barren regions, where there is much sheepherding. If a sheep goes astray, the shepherd corrals the rest of his flock or leaves a sheepdog in charge of them, and himself goes off, very often on a lengthy trek, to search for the absentee. The loss can be serious, and it is easy to understand the delight of the shepherd who has found his sheep and invites the neighbors in for a celebratory meal. This image of the shepherd was a traditional term in the Bible, applied equally to a king or to God; but Jesus was using it in a quite different sense from the prophet Ezekiel. The shepherd in the parable represents neither God nor Jesus, and the lost sheep is not to be equated with the sinner. The only analogy is between the delight of the shepherd and the joy in heaven over a sinner's conversion. There is no reason for respectable folk to be shocked — as they invariably are — at the thought of being abandoned in favor of the lost sheep; and Jesus' harsh reference to "just persons, which need no repentance" has in fact no direct link with the parable, which teaches a very simple lesson — that finding something you have lost gives you more pleasure than the mere enjoyment of what you have. God is very human in His understanding.

Jesus made a habit of doubling up his parables. To ensure that the point went home well and truly he would repeat the same theme with different characters. On this occasion his second example dropped the idea that in order to search for what you have lost you must abandon what remains to you: "Either what woman having ten pieces of silver, if she lose one piece, doth not light a candle, and sweep the house, and seek diligently till she find it? And when she hath found it, she calleth her friends and her neighbours together, saying, 'Rejoice with me; for I have found the piece which I had lost.' Likewise, I say unto you, there is joy in the presence of the angels of God over one sinner that repenteth."

A *drachma* was of the same value as a *denarius*; that is, in modern currency, rather less than a dollar. The woman would be a poor villager whose house consisted of a single room with a beaten earth floor. She lit her only lamp, swept the floor from corner to corner, and found the missing coin. Her joy stemmed not so much from its intrinsic value — though to her it represented a considerable sum — as from sheer relief: to have lost something was embarrassing enough, to have diminished her savings in so stupid a way was even worse.

Jesus made up another, longer parable in much the same vein: "A certain man had two sons: and the younger of them said to his father, 'Father, give me the portion of goods that falleth to me.' And he divided unto them his living. And not many days after the younger son gathered all together, and took his journey into a far country, and there wasted his substance with riotous living. And when he had spent all, there arose a mighty famine in that land; and he began to be in want. And he went and joined himself to a citizen of that country; and he sent him into his fields to feed swine. And he would fain have filled his belly with the husks that the swine did eat: and no man gave unto him. And when he came to himself, he said, 'How many hired servants of my father's have bread enough and to spare, and I perish with hunger! I will arise and go to my father, and will say unto him, Father, I have sinned against heaven, and before thee, and am no more worthy to be called thy son: make me as one of thy hired servants.' And he arose, and came to his father. But when he was yet a great way off, his father saw him, and had compassion, and ran, and fell on his neck, and kissed him. And the son said unto him, 'Father, I have sinned against heaven, and in thy sight, and am no more worthy to be called thy son.' But the father said to his servants, 'Bring forth the best robe, and put it on him; and put a ring on his hand, and shoes on his feet: and bring hither the fatted calf, and kill it; and let us eat, and be merry: for this my son was dead, and is alive again; he was lost, and is found.' And they began to be merry. Now his elder son was in the field: and as he came and drew nigh to the house, he heard musick and dancing. And he called one of the servants, and asked what these things meant. And he said unto him, 'Thy brother is come; and thy father hath killed the fatted calf, because he hath received him safe and sound.' And he was angry, and would not go in: therefore came his father out, and intreated him. And he answering said to his father, 'Lo, these many years do I serve thee, neither transgressed I at any time thy commandment: and yet thou never gavest me a kid, that I might make merry with my friends: but as soon as this thy son was come, which hath devoured thy living with harlots, thou hast killed for him the fatted calf.' And he said unto him, 'Son, thou art ever with me, and all that I have is thine. It was meet that we should make merry, and be glad: for this thy brother was dead, and is alive again; and was lost, and is found.' "

It has been suggested that this story represents "the gospel of the Gospel"; but to allegorize it in such a fashion is to misconstrue its purpose. None of the incidents of properties in the narrative have any symbolical value — the contrast between the children; the younger brother's journey and subsequent dissipated life; the crusts he craved, the swine he herded; the kiss of greeting that his father bestowed on him, together with a ring and clean raiment; the fatted calf, the elder brother's resentment and reference to a kid. There is no question here of equating the elder son with the Jews and the younger with the Gentiles. All such details are put in for their own sake — for the sheer pleasure of storytelling, and because of Jesus' liking for intrigue, adventure, poetry, and that clash of personalities essential to a good plot.

The father is a big landowner. What a striking contrast we find between the feast with which he celebrates his son's return and the poor wretch's way of life as a swineherd in a foreign land — like those pagan herdsmen Jesus had met one day on the coast near Gadara! Above all, what a difference there is between the father's welcome and that of the elder son, who stayed at home so loyally! Jesus' intention was, precisely, to point up this unpalatable home truth: that God's joy over the conversion of His errant children, the sinners and heathens alike, is seldom shared by the faithful, who feel they have a lien on His divine munificence.

The line of thought continues and develops Jesus' two previous parables. Lost sheep and lost drachmas were animals and inanimate objects; the parable of the prodigal son demonstrates the reactions of the "just men." From now on Jesus tends to base his stories on human lives and human relationships: his character drawing becomes progressively deeper. The protagonists in the parable of the prodigal son are etched in with great vividness; and the father who "had compassion, and ran, and fell on his neck, and kissed him" was to remain engraved forever in men's memories, perhaps as basic an image in the life of Jesus as the Cross itself.

Never had the Master's poetic genius manifested itself in quite so brilliant a manner; never before had he displayed so deep and poignant an understanding of the human heart. A new sort of urgency quivered in his words: never before had he attained such complete mastery over the scribes and the Pharisees. Though his own relentless destiny was already beckoning him, he could still be moved to pity by the moral plight of his unfortunate human brethren. The God he depicted for them was a being possessed by deep compassion and pity, a God who welcomed errant souls and held them clasped to his heart in a long, warm embrace. Even in the most heartrending passages of the Old Testament, mankind had never discovered anything quite like this before.

8

THE WEALTHY

IF ANYONE SUPPOSED that because Jesus was now teaching
the principle of divine mercy he had therefore surrendered
any of his more exacting requirements, they mistook their
man. He was to prove this during the course of his present
journey, in his dealings with the rich. Poor but not indigent
himself, he felt neither scorn nor hatred for those with great
possessions. There was no trace whatever in him of that
inverted cupidity which characterizes so many apologists of the
people — those who wish to see the proletariat overthrow the
bourgeoisie so that they can one day enjoy the same tinsel
luxury. Jesus' primary feeling towards the rich was one of pity.
He saw most of them as slaves to the cult of gold, what he
called *mammon*, or profit. He felt sorry for them in their
bondage.

During his progress to Jerusalem he was often asked questions about wealth, and those who possessed it. In Palestine,
as in the Middle East, India, and many other countries today,
one found vast and lavish riches cheek-by-jowl with the most
incredible poverty. This juxtaposition was something from
which Jesus privately revolted, since — like slavery, suffering
and death — it did not form part of God's plan. Jesus saw in
such a state of affairs a victory by Satan over mankind, the
establishment of the Devil's dominion on earth. Yet he did not
believe that revolution or mere brute force would ever bring
this dominion to an end: he knew that a slave dictatorship
would be as ruthless as an Emporer's autocracy. Nor would his
Kingdom depend on organizing the production and distribution
of wealth. How wealth was to be shared out must remain the
concern of politicians and legislators, whose duty embraced

such decisions. For Jesus, money was no more than a useful instrument of which he took advantage. He advised people to give it readily to those in need. Every individual should make it his aim to live soberly yet without undue restraint: never refusing or scorning a good meal or a good bottle of wine, but taking care to give away any surplus over and above his immediate needs.

One day a young man asked him: "Good Master, what shall I do that I may inherit eternal life?" Jesus' initial response was a snub. He had no great liking for the smooth good manners of the rich, the well-nourished charm which they exuded. He said: "Why callest thou me good? there is none good but one, that is, God. Thou knowest the commandments." And Jesus than ran rapidly through the Decalogue, as though impatient at the elementary nature of the question. This interview was beginning to bore him. The young man really ought to be more familiar with his catechism, or its Jewish equivalent.

But the young man replied: "Master, all these have I observed from my youth." His sincerity was now apparent. He had not asked Jesus this question to catch him out, or as a result of mere ignorant stupidity. He was one of those absolutely upright young men who belong to a very rare group — people with a spontaneous love of God. "Then," says Mark, "Jesus beholding him loved him, and said unto him, 'One thing thou lackest: go thy way, sell whatever thou hast, and give to the poor, and thou shalt have treasure in heaven: and come, take up the cross, and follow me.' And he was sad at that saying, and went away grieved: for he had great possessions."

Then Jesus, as was his wont, glanced round at his disciples, and they gathered closer, and he delivered himself of this crucial statement: "How hardly shall they that have riches enter into the Kingdom of God!" His disciples were astounded. Never before had Jesus been so explicit. Among the Jews the wealthy were regarded as God's favorites, and money itself as a blessing. The Patriarchs had been rich men. Wealth was good in itself. But Jesus took the argument one step further: "Children, how hard it is for them that trust in riches to enter into the Kingdom of God! It is easier for a camel to go through the eye of a needle, than for a rich man to enter into the kingdom of God." He enjoyed using such humorous and mildly shocking paradoxes. This time, however, his proposition had really taken the Twelve aback; they stood there dumbfounded.

"Who then can be saved?" they asked each other. Jesus' reassurance, when it came, had disturbing implications: "With men it is impossible," he said, "but not with God: for with God all things are possible." Not unnaturally, Peter was thinking of his own position: "Lo," he said, "we have left all, and have followed thee." To which Jesus replied: "Verily I say unto you, There is no man that hath left house, or brethren, or sisters, or father, or mother, or wife, or children, or lands, for my sake, and the gospel's, but he shall receive an hundredfold now in this time, houses, and brethren, and sisters, and mothers, and children, and lands, with persecutions; and in the world to come eternal life."

Such is the great law: by renouncing all we regain all, since the Kingdom is a reality already with us. We rediscover our families and our property, but transformed, increased — not into a hundred fields and a hundred wives and a hundred sons, as the millenarist heretics were to claim (the Kingdom they awaited bears a distinct resemblance to *Alice in Wonderland*), but according to the order of spiritual realities. The man who forswears mammon possesses the world and walks through it as a free man. He knows that for him every heart will open. Though he may have cast off the overrestrictive ties imposed by wife and children, he quickly discovers that this new fraternal spirit makes him part of a vaster and more truly human family.

On the subject of money Jesus produced endless aphorisms and parables. "And one of the company said unto him, 'Master, speak to my brother, that he divide the inheritance with me.' And he said unto him, 'Man, who made me a judge or a divider over you?' And he said unto them, 'Take heed, and beware of covetousness: for a man's life consisteth not in the abundance of the things which he possesseth.' And he spake a parable unto them, saying, 'The ground of a certain rich man brought forth plentifully: and he thought within himself, saying, What shall I do, because I have no room where to bestow my fruits? And he said, This will I do: I will pull down my barns, and build greater; and there will I bestow all my fruits and my goods. And I will say to my soul, Soul, thou hast much goods laid up for many years; take thine ease, eat, drink, and be merry. But God said unto him, Thou fool, this night thy soul shall be required of thee: then whose shall those things be, which thou hast provided? So is he that layeth up treasure for himself, and is not rich toward God.' "

Viewed in the context of the Kingdom's imminent coming, Jesus' reply to the man who asked him to arbitrate over the division of a legacy is readily understandable. What does a little cash or property matter compared with eternal life? And Jesus at once widened the field of discussion by repeating the exhortation to place one's trust in Providence that he had made during the Sermon on the Mount. Trust those whose trust is in God: beware of them who defy Him. Hence the parable. If a man relies upon earthly treasure, which is liable to be stolen or spoiled, then God may, without warning, reclaim the life He gave that man. On the "security" afforded by money Jesus echoes the disenchanted words of Ecclesiastes.

If some rich men are hoarders, others do not scruple to behave in a harsh and inhuman manner. Jesus made up a story to illustrate this: "There was a certain rich man, which was clothed in purple and fine linen, and fared sumptuously every day: and there was a certain beggar named Lazarus, which was laid at his gate, full of sores, and desiring to be fed with the crumbs which fell from the rich man's table: moreover the dogs came and licked his sores. And it came to pass, that the beggar died, and was carried by the angels into Abraham's bosom: the rich man also died, and was buried; and in hell he lift up his eyes, being in torments, and seeth Abraham afar off, and Lazarus in his bosom. And he cried and said, 'Father Abraham, have mercy on me, and send Lazarus, that he may dip the tip of his finger in water, and cool my tongue; for I am tormented in this flame.' But Abraham said, 'Son, remember that thou in thy lifetime receiveth thy good things, and likewise Lazarus evil things: but now he is comforted, and thou art tormented.'"

Jesus here borrowed the plot of an old folktale which turns up at an earlier date in ancient Egyptian literature: the deaths of a rich and a poor man, with their contrasting lot in the hereafter. The role allotted to Abraham shows that the theme had been taken up by the rabbis and loaded with various moral considerations on such topics as hell and resurrection. Jesus kept only the bare essentials.

The obvious, superficial moral of this story would seem to be that wealth always incurs penalties in a future life, while poverty is invariably rewarded. But this was not what Jesus had in mind. The name Lazarus, which he made up, signifies "God is our help," and puts a label of piety on its owner; the rich man, on the other hand, is presented as a debauchee. His worst offense is to have remained unmoved by a case of the most appalling misery when it was right under his nose. (The beggar's condition had reached a point where dogs came and licked his sores, thus adding impurity to disease: the Jews regarded these animals with repugnance and held them to be taboo.) What Jesus was saying was that hardness of heart brings inevitable retribution on itself. It is the most obvious symptom of the harm which riches can wreak upon our souls.

Nevertheless, Jesus did, from time to time, display admiration for the intelligence with which men went about their moneymaking affairs: if they would only apply such perseverance and ingenuity to the conquest of the Kingdom! To impress this point upon his followers, Jesus had no qualms about taking an example from the dishonest financial dealings of an unscrupulous overseer: "There was a certain rich man, which had a steward; and the same was accused unto him that he had wasted his goods. And he called him, and said unto him, 'How is it that I hear this of thee? give an account of thy stewardship; for thou mayest be no longer steward.' Then the steward said within himself, 'What shall I do? for my lord taketh away from me the stewardship: I cannot dig; to beg I am ashamed. I am resolved what to do, that, when I am put out of the stewardship, they may receive me into their houses.' So he called every one of his lord's debtors unto him, and said unto the first, 'How much owest thou unto my lord?' And he said, 'An hundred measures of oil.' And he said unto him, 'Take thy bill, and sit down quickly, and write fifty.' Then he said to another, 'And how much owest thou?' And he said, 'An hundred measures of wheat.' And he said unto him, 'Take thy bill, and write fourscore.'"

Jesus had finished his story. Now he — like the steward's employer — "commended the unjust steward, because he had done wisely: for the children of this world are in their genera-

tion wiser than the children of light." This parable has continued to embarrass all Pharisees throughout history. They
fail to perceive the ironic smile with which Jesus applauds
a man's ingenuity, not for robbing his employer twice over
but for displaying such diplomatic finesse. If only the affairs
of the Kingdom loomed as large in men's lives as their business deals! Why could they not develop the same skill and
adaptability in pursuing the way of truth as they brought to
their financial ambitions?

So Jesus pondered, as he expounded the principle of spiritual
freedom to a world over which slavery reigned supreme —
and not only in the mines and the prisons, where thousands
were starving to death, but also in palatial mansions, where the
rich led their luxurious lives as bond slaves of wealth.

9
JERICHO

ABOUT A MONTH BEFORE the Jewish Passover, Jesus reached
the outskirts of Jericho. Today it is a palm-studded oasis
between the Jordan and the first desert foothills; but at this
time it was a prosperous town, with many Biblical associations.
It lay only a few miles from the Essene monastery of Qumran,
above the ford where John had once baptized Jesus in Jordan
water — and where he was afterward to be arrested. Here, too,
there rose that rocky hill which had been the scene of Jesus'
visionary temptations by the Evil One. Standing on its summit
today, you see the whole Plain of Jericho unfolding before
your eyes in a splendid panorama, with the trees so many green
dabs against the white, dusty expanse of desert. In the south the
horizon is broken by the shimmering mirror of the Dead Sea.

Here Jesus had a fortunate encounter. He had entered
Jericho, and was on his way through the town, when he was

accosted by a man called Zacchaeus: the name signifies "pure" and was perhaps an abbreviated form of Zacharias. He was, we are told, "the chief among the publicans," or in other words an excise commissioner, what the Romans called a *magister*; his duties, we may surmise, included the supervision of both *portitores* and *publicani*. Jericho was a frontier town and a trading center for balsam.

Zacchaeus had heard of Jesus and was anxious to see him; but he was a very small man, and there was a big crowd pressing round the Master. Then he had the idea of clambering up a sycamore tree. (This detail is surely authentic: there would be no point to it otherwise, since it contains no symbolic significance.) People in the crowd looked up, and — to their surprise and amusement — spotted the well-known figure of the excise commissioner perched on a branch overhead. They drew Jesus' attention to this phenomenon, telling him the man's name and explaining what an important official he was. Jesus, susceptible as always to engaging humor of this sort, called out: "Zacchaeus, make haste, and come down; for today I must abide at thy house." This time Jesus was not merely having a meal with a *publicanus* but accepting the hospitality of his roof. He no longer bothered to placate the strict sectarians.

Zacchaeus came down with all speed, "and received him joyfully." Not surprisingly, the scandal rocked Jericho. But Zacchaeus stood his ground, and told Jesus: "Behold, Lord, the half of my goods I give to the poor; and if I have taken any thing from any man by false accusation, I restore him fourfold." To which Jesus replied: "This day is salvation come to this house, forsomuch as he also is a son of Abraham."

Jesus could not stay long in Jericho. Perhaps we should ascribe to this period a parable — that of the king spurned by his people — which we have only in fragmentary form. It certainly fits the occasion: "A certain nobleman went into a far country to receive for himself a kingdom, and to return. . . . But his citizens hated him, and sent a message after him, saying, 'We will not have this man to reign over us.'" This embassy failed of its purpose, and the claimant obtained his crown. When he returned, he gave audience to those who had remained loyal. To the first he said: "Well, thou good servant: because thou hast been faithful in a very little, have thou authority over ten cities." To another he said: "Be thou also over five cities . . . But those mine enemies, which would not that I should reign over them, bring hither, and slay them before me."

This parable is nothing more nor less than a faithful version of the career of Herod Antipas. In the year 4 B.C., on the death of his father, Herod the Great, he traveled to Rome to obtain from the Emperor and the Senate confirmation of his claim as *de jure* ruler over Judaea. An embassy consisting of fifty Jews at once followed him there, with the intention of thwarting his diplomatic intrigues. By alluding to this incident Jesus did not mean to draw an allegory from it. He himself is not to be identified with the nobleman who goes in search of a crown, nor are his apostles that nobleman's loyal supporters; the cities do not stand for any sort of paradisal government, and the slaughter of the king's enemies has no bearing on the Last Judgment.

Jesus would have found it profoundly distasteful to compare his role with that of the "old fox": what had he in common with a cruel Oriental tyrant such as Antipas, who slit his political opponents' throats? What Jesus wanted to emphasize was this. Not so long ago there had been a notorious political take-over bid, which ran into considerable trouble and suffered several delays — yet nevertheless succeeded, despite everything. His followers should not, therefore, let this long waiting period discourage them: matters would take their inevitable course. Had not this already been guaranteed in the parable of the sower? Though some grain might fall among stones, and some by the wayside, this could not hold up the harvest — any more than the embassy sent by his opponents could prevent Herod's ascending the throne.

Thus, the nearer he drew to Jerusalem, the more Jesus tended to take the subject matter of his parables from human situations and transform them into anecdotes of intrigue or psychological conflict. Furthermore, this change of tone fitted the social climate of Judaea very well. It was a more urbanized and politically conscious region: passions ran high there, and often had a bloody aftermath.

It is possible that Jesus' frequent allusions to kings — and this one in particular — may have provoked the request which the sons of Zebedee made: "And James and John, the sons of Zebedee, come unto him, saying, 'Master, we would that thou shouldest do for us whatsoever we shall desire.' And he said unto them, 'What would ye that I should do for you?' They said unto him, 'Grant unto us that we may sit, one on thy right hand, and the other on thy left hand, in thy glory.' But Jesus said unto them, 'Ye know not what ye ask: can ye drink of the cup that I drink of? and be baptized with the baptism that I am baptized with?' And they said unto him, 'We can.' And Jesus said unto them, 'Ye shall indeed drink of the cup that I drink of; and with the baptism that I am baptized withal shall ye be baptized: but to sit on my right hand and on my left hand is not mine to give; but it shall be given to them for whom it is prepared.' "

The baptism which Jesus speaks of here bears a remarkable resemblance to a *noyade*, or execution by drowning:* death

* As carried out by Carrier, at Nantes in 1793, during the French Revolution. [Tr.]

beneath a "deluge" of sufferings. The same applies to the cup. In the normal way drinking from a cup is, throughout the Old Testament, a metaphor used to express joy: but there are passages in the prophetic poems where we also read of the cup of folly and the cup of chastisement, much akin to that from which Socrates drank the hemlock. Jeremiah and Ezekiel depicted a personified Jerusalem as drinking deep from it, till she became intoxicated, and slashed herself with the splinters of the broken vessel.

Jesus used the request made by James and John as an excuse to reconsider his views on authority. "And when the ten heard it, they began to be much displeased with James and John. But Jesus called them to him, and saith unto them, 'Ye know that they which are accounted to rule over the Gentiles exercise lordship over them; and their great ones exercise authority upon them. But so shall it not be among you: but whosoever will be great among you, shall be your minister: and whosoever of you will be the chiefest, shall be servant of all. For even the Son of man came not to be ministered unto, but to minister, and to give his life a ransom for many.' "

Jesus regarded this question of authority as so important that he came back to it again and again. Can an authority exist which inspires those set under it to such blind devotion that it virtually enslaves them? Jesus had few illusions about this; but he still expressed his hope and desire for such an ideal, in words which now were tinged with melancholy.

On his way out of Jericho towards Jerusalem, Jesus had one of those encounters which are all too frequent in the East: "Blind Bartimaeus, the son of Timaeus, sat by the highway side begging. And when he heard that it was Jesus of Nazareth, he began to cry out, and say, 'Jesus, thou Son of David, have mercy on me.' And many charged him that he should hold his peace: but he cried the more a great deal, 'Thou Son of David, have mercy on me.' And Jesus stood still, and commanded him to be called. And they call the blind man, saying unto him, 'Be of good comfort, rise; he calleth thee.' And he, casting away his garment, rose, and came to Jesus. And Jesus answered and said unto him, 'What wilt thou that I should do unto thee?' The blind man said unto him, 'Lord, that I might receive my sight.' And Jesus said unto him, 'Go thy way; thy faith hath made thee whole.' And immediately he received his sight, and followed Jesus in the way."

The oddest detail in this vivid episode is the way the blind man cried out, "Thou Son of David." This is the only occasion in the whole of St. Mark's Gospel — based on Simon Peter's personal recollections — when Jesus is given this title, with its political and Messianic associations. It looks very much as though the subject of the Messiah, the "son of David," had been brought up during Jesus' stay in Jericho. The folk accompanying Jesus were expecting a Messianic demonstration in Jerusalem. The healing of Bartimaeus — who, contrary to Jesus' normal practice, was allowed to follow him thereafter — might even have been taken as a prelude to the Messiah's entering upon his kingdom. Jesus would, at long last, accept those political and kingly prerogatives which hitherto he had steadfastly refused. His entourage foresaw that this journey to Jerusalem would result in decisive — and, as they thought, glorious — action.

four

The
Tragedy
of
Jerusalem

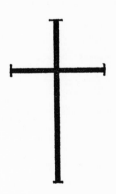

1

A TRIUMPHAL ENTRY

AT THE BEGINNING of the Christian era, Jerusalem was not only the undisputed capital of Judaea but the center and fountainhead of international Judaism. As such it was one of the most important cities in the Empire, though it could scarcely be compared, for size and beauty, with Antioch, Ephesus, Alexandria, Corinth, or Rome. Its buildings did not extend as far as the present-day site of the old Arab town, still encircled by the ramparts and crenelations which Suleiman constructed: ancient Jerusalem covered the southern hill, Ophel, and the juncture, beneath it, of three valleys — Cedron, Tyropaeon, and Ben-Hinnom, which we know better as Gehenna. It was protected by imposing fortifications and huge city gates set in the ramparts. The Temple towered over it, dominating the scene more effectively than its modern successor, the Dome of the Rock, or Q'ubbet-es-Sakhra, an elegant sky-blue cupola set over the old sacrificial rock altar.

Ever since Pompey's conquest of Jerusalem, the city had been under Roman occupation, and a military garrison was quartered just north of the Temple, in the stoutly built Antonia fortress. Their presence was, however, rendered as unobtrusive as possible. The legions left their eagles and other such pagan idols behind. The Procurator had his residence in Caesarea, and only came to Jerusalem for great feast days. The Roman administration was well aware of the sullen resentment which Rome's authority engendered among the nationalists, and took care not to provoke trouble. Jewish fanati-

cism was always on the brink of an explosion: best to leave
it alone. The Romans knew that if they took one false step
they might well have a Holy War on their hands — a situation
similar to that which later prevailed when Christians came to
occupy Arab countries. As a result they left the religious affairs
of Jerusalem entirely in the hands of the Sanhedrin Council;
and since more pilgrimages were made to Jerusalem than to
anywhere else, this implied a considerable degree of autonomy.

It is hard to visualize the swarming, motley crowds that
must have filled the Temple's great forecourts and thronged
the streets around it. This was the site of what we might
describe, in modern parlance, as the biggest Jewish university
in the world. The lofty colonnades of the forecourts were
used for lectures and discussions; besides which a brisk trade
in various commodities went on there. There were bankers
and money changers who handled religious taxes; there were
butchers to supply the material for sacrificial offerings; there
were guides for the pilgrims, merchants of every sort, inter-
preters — not to mention soapbox casuists, lawyers, rabbis,
and priests. Between them they transformed this "cathedral
of Judaism" into something midway between an exchange mart
and a commercial bank.

The Jews have always enjoyed a good argument, and the
traffic in ideas that went on beneath the shadow of the Temple
was at least as great as that in hard cash. The people one
met there, busily refuting each other's propositions with
characteristically subtle Eastern arguments, were the future
begetters of the Talmud: a far cry from the peasants and
fisherfolk of Galilee. Many of them were students, from every
part of the known world. They much resembled the crowds
who throng the streets of Tel Aviv today — polyglot, sophisti-
cated, well-traveled men who had read all the books and knew
all the answers. This was a complex, intelligent society, rich

in contrasting elements, where Jews of every description — Roman, Egyptian, Cappadocian, Greek, even travelers from Mesopotamia and the Arab countries — jostled one another in the street.

Though there were some aspects of Jerusalem that Jesus detested, on the whole he loved the place. He was passionately attached to the Sanctuary, the relics of the Holy City, the cult of the Divine Presence, the abiding truth of the Old Testament, of which Jerusalem was the emblem and spiritual center. He almost certainly was attracted by the city's cosmopolitanism; what he found repellent was the overweening pride that marked out its inhabitants, their fantastic hairsplitting subtleties and endless disputes, their scorn for the rest of mankind, their avarice, and the unscrupulous manner in which the priestly caste of the Sadducees exercised their great authority.

He entered the city by the old road which runs south from Jericho, through Bethphage and Bethany to the east of the Mount of Olives. He spent some time in these villages: he had friends there. One morning he sent two of his disciples on ahead with the following instructions: "Go your way into the village over against you," he told them: "and as soon as ye be entered into it, ye shall find a colt tied, whereon never man sat; loose him, and bring him. And if any man say unto you, 'Why do ye this?' say ye that the Lord hath need of him; and straightway he will send him hither." Such borrowings are common in the East. The disciples found the ass's colt and brought it back to Jesus. He mounted, and then, surrounded by his followers, he rode the short distance — just over a mile — to Jerusalem. The crowd of Galilaeans accompanying him were highly elated. People threw their garments or palm branches in his path as they would for a royal procession; and those who were most carried away sang psalms which, with their allusions to David, clearly had Jesus' own Messianic claims in mind.

This procession of chanting pilgrims bore no resemblance whatsoever to a mass demonstration. The delight which his arrival evinced must have given Jesus much pleasure, but it was no more than a bit of exuberance on the part of this handful of Galilaeans who loved him. Such processions were a frequent sight in the vicinity of the Temple and the various shrines. The Romans paid no heed to them; nor did the Jewish priests or the Temple authorities. When Jesus' supporters spread the word through the crowd that this was Jesus of Nazareth, the prophet from Galilee, perhaps a few guards grumbled at the noise and confusion, but nothing more.

The little procession must have made its way, still singing, down the Cedron Valley, by the track which hugs the western flank of the Mount of Olives. Then the low-walled orchards were left behind, and they began the steep ascent of the Temple bastion, up to the Golden Gate. At this point Jesus' followers dispersed. The ass's colt which had served as a mount for the Master was sent back home, and Jesus himself went into the Temple. From Peter's testimony one gets the feeling that Jesus suddenly looked round the inner courts of the Temple as though he had never seen them before. But the hour was late, and he returned to Bethany with the Twelve.

2

UPROAR IN THE TEMPLE

IT IS A HARD TASK for us today to visualize how the great temples of antiquity looked in their heyday. Not one of them has survived except as an imposing ruin. Greek and Roman sanctuaries — not to mention those of Egypt or Babylon — were so different from our churches, from our mosques even,

that to picture them defies the imagination: their magnificent
ruins are dead forever. The nearest modern equivalent is,
perhaps, a crowded Hindu temple on the banks of the Ganges:
here one can find some approximation to the atmosphere of
an ancient shrine, with its gilded pillars, sacrificial fires, thick
curling incense and prostrate worshippers — not to mention
the slaughterhouse stench of blood and raw meat which such
places always gave off, or the prostitutes who haunted them, or
the shouting of touts and hucksters, or the barbarous processions with their huge painted idols.

It is true that Jehovah's temple in Jerusalem was innocent of
any grossly repulsive effigy such as these; but strangers visiting
it for the first time were astonished by its colossal dimensions
and its positively overweening wealth. Temples on an equally
gigantic scale survive, though in ruins, at Pergamon and
Baalbek. The one in Jerusalem was enormous. By comparison
with the relatively cramped sanctuaries of Delphi, Eleusis,
Athens and Olympia, its site covered a very considerable area.
Its forecourts were just as extensive as those vast deserted
courts amid which today the Q'ubbet-es-Sakhra stands in
splendid isolation.

At this period, with Herod the Great not more than thirty
years dead, the walls and foundations of the Temple edifice
remained dazzlingly new. Great dressed blocks of stone, still
white from the chisel, glinted with golden bucklers. This
sumptuous work of restoration gave the Jews some cause for
pride. The over-all magnificence was enhanced by lofty colonnades in the forecourts, broad flights of steps, and richly
wrought doors.

This temple housed one of the richest treasuries in the
whole of the Roman Empire: every Jew throughout the
known world paid tribute to it. This annual levy, it has been
estimated, produced in the equivalent of modern currency

about a million dollars — a very substantial sum, especially when we set it against the monetary circulation of the period as a whole. Visiting pilgrims were not permitted to make their offerings or pay their tribute in foreign coin, since these were stamped with the images of the Emperor and various pagan gods and could not, therefore, be brought into the sanctuary. Hence the importance of the money changers, with their tables and scales, who were as prominent in Eastern countries then as they are today.

In addition, there was the cattle market. Because of its sacrifices, the Temple also constituted the most important abattoir in Palestine, and a flourishing trade in meat on the hoof had its center there. The beasts were sold under a priestly monopoly, and would-be sacrificers had to pay top prices for them. Some while before, Baba ben Buta had brought three thousand sheep there in an effort to bring down these prices and give ordinary poor people a chance to make sacrifice.

In the Court of the Priests was also located the market proper, sometimes known as the "bazaar of the sons of Ananias," which was later to be shifted from the Temple into the city. Naturally the priests, who held the monopoly and controlled this whole commercial venture, became fabulously rich. As the Talmud puts it, "the son of the High Priest acted as treasurer, and his sons-in-law as deputy treasurers."

Jesus decided the time had come for him to intervene. Minor scuffles and brawls were common enough here: we need only remember what effect the slightest political incident is liable to have in the North African *medinas* or the *suqs* of Damascus and Aleppo. (Apparently quarrels over the purchase of sheep in the precinct of the mosque at Mecca are still frequent and violent.) By overthrowing the tables of the money changers, Jesus intended to make them give up the places in the forecourt which they were occupying without any proper authorization, and to close certain unofficial rights of way through the Court of the Priests. The Temple police could hardly object to his action, since they should have stamped on these abuses themselves. Jesus (backed up by a few of his Galilaean followers) was in effect criticizing their inertia — or their complicity. He expressed his indignation in no uncertain terms. Who, he cried, could pray here nowadays? The place was nothing but a noisy commercial bazaar. "Is it not written, 'My house shall be called of all nations the house of prayer'?" Jesus asked, quoting Isaiah; and then added: "But ye have made it a den of thieves!"

Now this second comment was from Jeremiah, and those who knew their Bible well must have recalled the prophet's weighty discourse on the first Temple — that rabid and notorious attack which had led to Jeremiah's arrest and came within an ace of securing the death penalty for him. The brawl now quieted down into a verbal argument: this was exactly what Jesus wanted. Even the most hostile witnesses of his gesture would not dare to put themselves in the wrong by questioning the famous Biblical text he had invoked. Some of those present, indeed, must have had a very shrewd idea of what he was after. Herod's magnificent Temple was not fulfilling its proper role as a universal "cathedral," a house of prayer addressed to the one true God, the Father of mankind. Therefore it must be reformed, or even — who knew? — actually suppressed. Did not the Essenes already regard it as superfluous? "Destroy this temple," Jesus asserted in the course of the argument, "and in three days I will raise it up." So he wanted the Temple to survive — but in a radically different form.

His followers recalled the occasion when he had been accosted, at Jacob's well in Sychar, by a woman of Samaria, who said to him: "Our fathers worshipped in this mountain

[Gerizim]; and ye say, that in Jerusalem is the place where men ought to worship." Which were right, Jews or Samaritans? Jesus answered her: "Woman, believe me, the hour cometh, when ye shall neither in this mountain, nor yet at Jerusalem, worship the Father. Ye worship ye know not what: we know what we worship: for salvation is of the Jews. But the hour cometh, and now is, when the true worshippers shall worship the Father in spirit and in truth."

Through his quotation from Isaiah, Jesus seemed to be offering Judaism the chance to become, at last, a truly universal creed, a faith for the whole world.

But this incident in the Temple had (as it was bound to have) certain repercussions. The day after the brawl Jesus was approached in the forecourt by a group of what, today, we would call university professors. Politely but firmly they stopped him and asked the pertinent question: "By what authority doest thou these things? and who gave thee this authority to do these things?" They were not so naïve as to question the justice of Jesus' intervention: in such a case Jesus could have counted upon considerable public support. Instead they asked him in whose name he had intervened.

The reply Jesus made was a masterpiece of diplomacy. He said: "I will also ask of you one question, and answer me, and I will tell you by what authority I do these things. The baptism of John, was it from heaven, or of men? answer me." This question caused his interrogators considerable embarrassment. None of them had been baptized by John: their abstention demonstrated their lack of faith in the Kingdom's imminent reality. But how could they make a public avowal of such an attitude? And how could they admit even indirect responsibility for the prophet-martyr's bloody death — especially before a crowd of bystanders who believed both in John's mission and in his personal sanctity? Their answer, therefore,

was evasive: "We cannot tell," they said. To which Jesus, sensing he had the crowd on his side, made the prompt and triumphant retort: "Neither do I tell you by what authority I do
these things." The implication was plain. If these priests and
scribes and elders could not solve a question so vitally important for Jewry as the nature of John the Baptist's mission,
what right had they to call Jesus to account? Their incapability
robbed them of all credit and authority. Yet this polemical
victory on Jesus' part was far from solving the problem. His
questioners were powerful men, who were beginning to detest
this nobody of a Galilaean rabbi and had made up their minds
to find out without delay just what Jesus was up to.

3

THE SANHEDRIN

THE ONLY AUTHORITY that Jesus at present had to deal with was
a religious one: the Sanhedrin, or supreme tribunal, of Jerusalem. There were several lesser sanhedrins or local senates in
existence, but the Great Sanhedrin took precedence over them
all. The Romans, it was true, maintained absolute political
authority over the protectorate, but they left the Jews a free
hand in the running of the Temple and the enforcement of
religious laws.

The Grand Council of Jerusalem had seventy members,
drawn from widely divergent backgrounds, including aristocratic
laymen, Sadducee priests, and Pharisee jurists. The High Priest
acted as ex officio president of the council; other members were
co-opted. Those Jerusalem families which had built up fortunes
out of the priesthood had a sizable voting majority. One man in
particular dominated the Sanhedrin at this period: Ananias, or
Annas, the son of Sethi, who had been High Priest from A.D. 6
to 15. After him, five of his sons — Eleazar, Jonathan, Theo-

philus, Matthew, and Ananias the Younger — had also discharged this supreme office. When Jesus arrived in Jerusalem, the High Priest was Joseph, son of Caiaphas. He had been appointed by Valerius Gratus in A.D. 18; and it was not until the year 36, when Pontius Pilate, the Roman Procurator of Judaea, was recalled from his command, that Vitellius terminated Joseph's appointment. The fact that only he and Ananias contrived to remain High Priest for so long a period (their rivals held the position down for a few months, on the average, and never more than a year or two) indicates Joseph's extraordinary political flair and the diplomatic skill which he brought to his dealings with the Roman occupation authorities. Common report had it that he carried servility one degree too far, and acted as an informer.

Ananias and his whole family were detested by the people, and the Talmud was afterwards to describe them as infamous High Priests. On the slightest pretext they would turn their police loose on some hapless victim; and these policemen were not sparing with their clubs. An old Jewish lamentation used to run: "Woe is me because of the house of Ananias! Woe is me because of their bludgeons!"

The news of the arrival in Jerusalem of a Galilaean prophet named Jesus — who had presumed not only to lay hands on the Temple money changers but also to snub those persons indiscreet enough to query his conduct — had been reported back to Joseph and Ananias without delay. They most likely had already heard about Jesus, from the reports submitted by agents of Herod Antipas at least: they watched Galilee with a very wary eye, since though they considered all Galilaeans to be simpleminded clods, they were nevertheless rather frightened of them. Galilee was the place where revolutions were liable to begin, and Jesus' followers were not exactly calculated to assuage official fears. Had not Simon, James, John, and several others been disciples of John the Baptist and sympathetic to the nationalist resistance movement? Nor did Jesus' dynamic energy bode well for the future; but at present there was no adequate pretext on which he could be arrested and expelled from the Holy City. Besides, Jesus could count on solid support in certain aristocratic circles. Several influential persons were either among his followers or giving him active backing and protection. Finally, it looked as though Jesus had received some warning of official intentions, since he was now behaving in the most circumspect manner imaginable. But once let this provincial rabbi step out of line, even in the slightest degree, and Joseph would not hesitate to act.

Did Joseph and Ananias make up their minds to put an end to Jesus' activities at this early stage, only a few days after his arrival in Jerusalem? It is more than likely, though as yet the decision may have been restricted to a few influential people behind the scenes. Joseph was a corrupt and unscrupulous skeptic: he sent his secret agents into action. There must be a criminal dossier opened on the fellow. The police would frame him. No trouble about finding suitable charges: ask this Galilaean bumpkin a few really subtle questions, and it would be surprising indeed if he failed to swallow the bait. This sort of devious hairsplitting was something all Jerusalem rabbis had brought to a fine art. As for the police frame-up, Joseph was quite wealthy enough to buy a perjurer or two.

At this point a curious and hitherto self-effacing character comes into the limelight. Against all the odds, one of the Twelve offered his services to the police. The strangest aspect of this affair is that Jesus' other disciples never afterward discovered a thing about it. They knew the traitor's identity: it was Judas the *sicarius*. But that was all. Why had he decided to make contact with the High Priest's secret agents? Was there some crime in his record for which he was promised a pardon?

Had his affection towards Jesus changed into hatred? Or was it that he wanted to force his Master's hand by cornering him, to *make* Jesus display his true and manifest powers? No one has ever known. The theory that he was bribed is generally rejected, and there is nothing in St. Mark's Gospel to support it. There are two different versions of his subsequent death. But the very necessity of his intervention proves just how cautious Jesus was and how closely his followers protected him. Every night he left Jerusalem and slept at a safe distance from the city. Everyone could sense a trial of strength in the air.

Jesus had no intention of stirring up the people to revolt; he did not propose to attack the Romans or destroy the High Priest's authority by violent means. But he did make speeches, and huge crowds listened to him. His prestige in Jerusalem was growing daily. The brush fire kindled in Galilee could well set the entire Holy City ablaze. A revolution was afoot indeed, no less dangerous than violent sedition for all its pacific nature; a mass movement very similar to those afterward led by St. Francis of Assisi and by Gandhi. If Jesus had his way, the Jewish populace would welcome heathens into the Temple. They would even become reconciled with those hated and despised enemies of theirs the Samaritans, and hold feasts in their honor. Blood sacrifice would in all probability be abolished, and the rich would become responsible for maintaining orphans and poor persons generally. The Kingdom of God would be established not only in Judaea but throughout the Empire and the whole world: a Kingdom of gentleness, peace, and goodwill towards men. The leaders of Judaism saw all this with quite terrifying clarity: and it was something which they were determined to avoid at all costs.

So the decision to conduct a life-and-death campaign against Jesus was taken by a small group of extremely unpopular priests in Jerusalem, and by them alone. It was a terrible misfortune for Israel — the worst, perhaps, in her whole history — that at this particular juncture she had two such men as Joseph Caiaphas and Ananias ruling over her. Yet the reasons put forward at the time for rejecting Jesus' doctrines still strike a modern Jew as perfectly cogent. He is impressed by the moral stature of the Gospels, but unwilling to accept their universal application. "Humanity was everything to Jesus," Klausner writes: "for his own people, for his national group, he cared nothing." Such is a contemporary Jewish historian's main objection to him; and in part, at least, this objection is surely erroneous. Jesus was Jewish to his fingertips, to the innermost fiber of his being. But he could not stand by while his people monopolized the God who belonged to all mankind, denied the great brotherhood of nations, and — this above all — rejected the Messiah sent from heaven on their behalf. Jesus would fight back with every ounce of strength he possessed.

4

SOME DEVIOUS QUESTIONING

THE EMISSARIES SENT by Joseph Caiaphas had a very simple plan: it consisted in getting other people to ask Jesus trick questions while they themselves kept quiet and prepared their official report. They began with a commonplace enough incident — the case of a woman caught committing adultery. How, it might be asked, could such a matter concern Jesus? For such a crime the Mosaic Law prescribed the death penalty: but it could not be enforced, because the Romans reserved for themselves the right to impose capital punishment. Jesus was a rabbi. Supposing he said: "You know the Mosaic Law: apply it. Kill her!" This would make a good excuse for a report to the Roman authorities, alleging that Jesus had preached disobedience to the laws of the Empire. If, on the other hand, he advised against executing the adulteress, this would constitute open defiance of the Torah.

A group of scribes and Pharisees brought the woman to where Jesus was sitting, engaged in discussion, and set her, as St. John tells us, "in the midst." Then they said: "Master, this woman was taken in adultery, in the very act. Now Moses in the law commanded us, that such should be stoned: but what sayest thou?" Jesus' only response was to stoop down, without saying a word, and write — the usual practice among judges recording a sentence. But Jesus, unlike them, wrote with his finger in the dust. His questioners pressed their point. Then Jesus straightened up and said, with some irony: "He that is without sin among you, let him first cast a stone at her." Such was his "written judgment."

The first stone was the heavy block that felled the condemned person, and had to be cast by his accuser. Jesus' stinging retort sums up all he had ever taught concerning the nature of sin and forgiveness, and God's role as the merciful Father of mankind. After this one remark Jesus stooped down again and resumed his writing in the dust, as though preoccupied by other, more important matters. "And they which heard it, being convicted by their own conscience, went out one by one, beginning at the eldest, even unto the last: and Jesus was left alone, and the woman standing in the midst. When Jesus had lifted himself up, and saw none but the woman, he said unto her, 'Woman, where are those thine accusers? hath no man condemned thee?' She said, 'No man, Lord.' And Jesus said unto her, 'Neither do I condemn thee: go, and sin no more.' " The police spies and the old men must have slipped out together.

But they soon made another attempt, and this time they laid a more cunning trap, connected with the vexed matter of taxation. The Jews were extremely money-conscious; moreover,

to pay Roman taxes was by implication to recognize the legiti-
macy of a hated foreign occupation. But to refuse payment was
tantamount to preaching a holy war of independence. What
reply would Jesus make? "And when they were come, they say
unto him, 'Master, we know that thou art true, and carest
for no man: for thou regardest not the person of men, but
teachest the way of God in truth: Is it lawful to give tribute to
Caesar, or not? Shall we give, or shall we not give?' But he,
knowing their hypocrisy, said unto them, 'Why tempt ye me?
bring me a penny, that I may see it.' And they brought it. And
he saith unto them, 'Whose is this image and superscription?'
And they said unto him, 'Caesar's.' And Jesus answering said
unto them, 'Render to Caesar the things that are Caesar's, and
to God the things that are God's.' "

Jesus' followers observed the discomfiture of the sly rogues
who had asked this question. What reply could they possibly
make to Jesus? He had revealed the essential hypocrisy of his
interrogators. They themselves, by pocketing money from the
Romans, implicitly condoned a Roman occupation; and the
coins they accepted bore the inscribed titles of the Emperor
whose emissaries they now were. Let them then give Tiberius
his due share, but also render to God all that appertained to
Him — in other words, the entire world, Caesar included.

Jesus was proving himself a very difficult man to confound
in argument. Some Sadducees accordingly came to him with a
real moral teaser, the sort of grotesque problem of conscience
which these academic theorists found irresistible. A woman
married seven husbands in succession: whose wife would she
be at the Resurrection? "When they shall rise from the dead,"
Jesus replied, "they neither marry, nor are given in marriage;
but are as the angels which are in heaven." Then, moving over
to the offensive, he went on: "And as touching the dead, that
they rise: have ye not read in the book of Moses, how in the

bush God spake unto him, saying, 'I am the God of Abraham, and the God of Isaac, and the God of Jacob'? He is not the God of the dead, but the God of the living: ye therefore do greatly err."

Jesus' argument proved that Abraham, Isaac and Jacob were living and, indeed, already risen, since the Jews had no conception of the soul's immortality apart from the body. Here again, what could Jesus' questioners say in reply? For a Jew, his argument was unanswerable. As for belief in the Resurrection, here Jesus ranged himself on the side of the Pharisees. He did the same in regard to the Messiah, whose absolute superiority he emphasized by a reference to the royal line of David: "Jesus asked them, saying, 'What think ye of Christ? whose son is he?' They say unto him, 'The Son of David.' He saith unto them, 'How then doth David in spirit call him Lord, saying, The Lord said unto my Lord, Sit thou on my right hand, Till I make thine enemies thy footstool? If David then call him Lord, how is he his son?' "

Each of these lucid retorts served to improve Jesus' standing among the rabbis of Jerusalem: he excelled them all. Some of them, it is true, hated him even more as a result, but others conceived a deep admiration for him.

Jesus took great care to avoid identifying himself with the Messiah in public. On the contrary, he had spoken of the Messiah in a detached way, rather as though discussing some mere academic point. He never applied the prophecies to his own case, but left this task to be carried out, at a later date, by his disciples. Much time would need to elapse before men understood the Old Testament in its full historical sense and perceived his presence shining through almost every page of it. He knew himself to be king, priest, prophet, judge and sage; soon he would add to these the role of victim and hostage. But for the present he had to engage in the most fearful struggle: to fight back, even to counterattack.

5
JESUS DEFENDS THE SAMARITANS

THERE WERE CERTAIN topics on which Jesus knew he could safely express himself without any risk of provoking a Messianic insurrection. He even, at times, made statements which ran flatly counter to popular nationalist prejudices. One such opportunity was given him by a certain scribe. According to Simon Peter's testimony, this learned person had heard Jesus discussing the Resurrection; and after observing the admirable way in which he dealt with the Sadducees, asked him: "Which is the first commandment of all?" Jesus answered: "What is written in the law? how readest thou?" The scribe answered with the Jewish profession of faith, still known today by its opening Hebrew words *Shema Israel* — "Hear, O Israel: The Lord our God is one Lord: and thou shalt love the Lord thy God with all thy heart, and with all thy soul, and with all thy strength, and with all thy mind; this is the first and great commandment. And the second is like, namely this: Thou shalt love thy neighbour as thyself." And Jesus said: "Thou hast answered right: this do, and thou shalt live."

But the scribe was not willing to let the matter drop there. He asked Jesus: "And who is my neighbour?" The Aramaic word he used carried the connotation of comrade, friend, companion: so did its Hebrew equivalent. Instead of answering him directly, however, Jesus launched into a story: "A certain man went down from Jerusalem to Jericho, and fell among thieves, which stripped him of his raiment, and wounded him, and departed, leaving him half dead. And by chance there came down a certain priest that way: and when he saw him, he passed by on the other side. And likewise a Levite, when he was at the place, came and looked on him, and passed by on the other side. But a certain Samaritan, as he journeyed, came where he was: and when he saw him, he had compassion on him, and went to him, and bound up his wounds, pouring in oil and wine, and set him on his own beast, and brought him to an inn, and took care of him. And on the morrow when he departed, he took out two pence, and gave them to the host, and said unto him, 'Take care of him; and whatsoever thou spendest more, when I come again, I will repay thee.' "

In order to get the extremely apposite point of Jesus' story, those who heard it would have to have noticed one detail which, we may be sure, did not escape the scribe. Jesus had said that the victim was left "half dead." Now the Law forbade a priest to defile himself by contact with a corpse, "even by the way-side." Both the priest and the Levite had assumed that the man *was* dead. After they had gone their way, the audience probably expected Jesus to bring on some broadminded member of the Jewish laity and give his parable an anticlerical punchline. In the event Jesus went further than this. The man who showed compassion was a Samaritan — a person whom all Jews would execrate as an enemy. This Samaritan outcast was to become an exemplar for the application of the Law's greatest single commandment — while in order to avoid ritual defilement a priest and a Levite, pious folk *par excellence*, disregarded the fundamental precept of the *Shema Israel*. The lesson this parable taught was a hard one — so hard, indeed, that to Jesus' question: "Which now of these three, thinkest thou, was neighbour unto him that fell among the thieves?" the scribe could not bring himself to reply: "The Samaritan"; the word would have burned his lips. Instead he said: "He that shewed mercy on him." Whereupon Jesus retorted: "Go, and do thou likewise."

The Samaritan becomes an embodiment of charity at its very highest: the outcast proves himself more loving than any of God's chosen faithful. Never before had Jesus dared to launch so open an attack upon Jewish fanaticism, the Jew's hatred for the Samaritan and the goy. Such a parable must have infuriated some who heard it; they probably regarded it as a calculated act of defiance.

Jesus seemed to take every available opportunity now of hammering home a series of truths and paradoxes that were bound to cause offense. For instance, he "sat over against the treasury, and beheld how the people cast money into the treasury: and many that were rich cast in much. And there came a certain poor widow, and she threw in two mites, which make a farthing. And he called unto him his disciples, and saith unto them, 'Verily I say unto you, That this poor widow hath cast more in, than all they which have cast into the treasury: for all they did cast in of their abundance; but she of her want did cast in all that she had, even all her living.'" Jesus was touched by this incident, for he loved the poor, the humble, the ignorant: once again he had, by way of a parable, expressed his preference for those whom most would regard as failures or outcasts.

"For the kingdom of heaven," he said, "is like unto a man that is an householder, which went out early in the morning to hire labourers into his vineyard. And when he had agreed with the labourers for a penny a day, he sent them into his vineyard. And he went out about the third hour [between 8 and 9 A.M.], and saw others standing idle in the marketplace, and said unto them; 'Go ye also into the vineyard, and whatsoever is right I will give you.' And they went their way. Again he went out about the sixth and ninth hour [midday and 3 P.M.], and did likewise. And about the eleventh hour [between 5 and 6 P.M.] he went out, and found others standing idle, and saith unto them, 'Why stand ye here all the day idle?' They say unto him, 'Because no man hath hired us.' He saith unto them, 'Go ye also into the vineyard; and whatsoever is right, that shall ye receive.' So when even was come, the lord of the vineyard saith unto his steward, 'Call the labourers, and give them their hire, beginning from the last unto the first.' And when they came that were hired about the eleventh hour, they received every man a penny. But when the first came, they supposed that they should have received more; and they likewise received every man a penny. And when they had received it, they murmured against the goodman of the house, saying, 'These last have wrought but one hour, and thou hast made them equal unto us, which have borne the burden and heat of the day.' But he answered one of them, and said, 'Friend, I do thee no wrong: didst not thou agree with me for a penny? Take that thine is, and go thy way: I will give unto this last, even as unto thee. Is it not lawful for me to do what I will with mine own? Is thine eye evil, because I am good?' "

This parable gives a very clear picture of the Eastern agricultural labor market — the out-of-work peasants waiting around the village square all day long in the hope that someone will hire them. (The spectacle is a familiar one to this day throughout Sicily and southern Italy, where thousands of workers have to face an identical problem.) The employer is a big landowner: his vineyards are extensive and the work urgent. The rate he is offering, a *denarius* for a day's work, is high by contemporary standards. Besides, he is a just employer, a "good man." His sharp retort to those who grumble at his generosity with late-comers springs from his distaste for envy and jealousy. He offers us an excellent image of one aspect of God — the God who, as Jesus proclaimed, shows tolerance for the tardy, just as (in another guise) he welcomed home the prodigal son. Repentance, and toil for the Kingdom's sake — these things are within everyone's reach. The only thing that incurs God's wrath is the jealousy of those who regard themselves as having a special claim on Him, and presume to restrict his benefits to sinners, loafers, the unemployed — all those poor folk whom the world despises and rejects.

6

FURTHER PARABLES

WE SEE, THEN, that Jesus was still producing new parables during his stay in Jerusalem. They were as memorable as ever, though harsher in their implications. Their constant theme was the rejection of the Kingdom by those who were its rightful and natural inheritors: a good example is the parable of the unwilling guests: "A certain man made a great supper, and bade many: and sent his servant at supper time to say to them that were bidden, 'Come; for all things are now ready.' And they all with one consent began to make excuse. The first said unto him, 'I have bought a piece of ground, and I must needs go and see it: I pray thee have me excused.' And another said, 'I have bought five yoke of oxen, and I go to prove them: I pray thee have me excused.' And another said, 'I have married a wife, and therefore I cannot come.' So that servant came, and shewed his lord these things. Then the master of the house being angry said to his servant, 'Go out quickly into the streets and lanes of the city, and bring in hither the poor, and the maimed, and the halt, and the blind.' And the servant said, 'Lord, it is done as thou hast commanded, and yet there is room.' And the lord said unto the servant, 'Go out into the highways and hedges, and compel them to come in, that my house may be filled. For I say unto you, That none of those men which were bidden shall taste of my supper.' "

It has been assumed, on good evidence, that when Jesus

portrayed this would-be host, with his grandiose ideas, he had in mind some parvenu millionaire such as Zacchaeus: if the man's wealth had been dubiously acquired, it would explain why his guests — who themselves were men of substance — made excuses for turning down a dinner invitation from him. Palestine farmers were not in the habit of buying five yoke of oxen every day of the week.

It is also clear that the invitations had been issued at the shortest possible notice: the master of the house was trying to force his guests to accept. The excuses they proffered were transparently feeble: they had no desire to come. The rich man thereupon recruited his guests from "the poor, and the maimed," who would be hanging about the highways and village squares, either as beggars or in search of work. The guest list was finally made up by including some tramps, who had to be brought in by force. This presented no difficulties: the master was a power-ful man.

Jesus' listeners could hardly have helped laughing at the story of a rich man whose guests had the temerity to turn down his invitation. But for Jesus himself this parvenu host, who only turned to beggars and cripples after his gesture of friendship had been snubbed by his well-to-do neighbors, was exactly in the same position as God. And yet, Jesus knew, God was not merciless or unfeeling: he even forgave those who failed to per-form what he expected from them. "A certain man," he said, "had a fig tree planted in his vineyard; and he came and sought fruit thereon, and found none. Then said he unto the dresser of his vineyard, 'Behold, these three years I come seeking fruit on this fig tree, and find none: cut it down; why cumbereth it the ground?' And he answering said unto him, 'Lord, let it alone this year also, till I shall dig about it, and dung it: and if it bear fruit, well: and if not, then after that thou shalt cut it down.' "

God grants a respite before condemning the barren tree; and some very surprising changes of heart are possible, as the parable of the two sons makes clear. Once again Jesus left his hearers to work out the moral for themselves. "But what think ye?" he asked them. "A certain man had two sons; and he came to the first, and said: 'Son, go work to day in my vineyard.' He answered and said, 'I will not'; but afterwards he repented, and went. And he came to the second, and said likewise. And he answered and said, 'I go, sir'; and went not. Whether of them twain did the will of his father?" "The first," they answered.

This parable was not an allegorical account of the Jews' refusal of Christ's teaching and its subsequent acceptance by the pagans, since the Jews would have been represented as the *elder* son. It was far simpler than that: a reminder, merely, of the great truth that human nature is liable to change, uttered at a time when resistance to Jesus was daily becoming more vigorous. A willful or disobedient soul may turn back to the truth, while a just man may, equally, go astray.

But the richest and most circumstantial parable which Jesus expounded during this period was the one concerning the murderous vine dressers: "A certain man planted a vineyard, and set an hedge about it, and digged a place for the winefat, and built a tower, and let it out to husbandmen, and went into a far country. And at the season he sent to the husbandmen a servant, that he might receive from the husbandmen of the fruit of the vineyard. And they caught him, and beat him, and sent him away empty. And again he sent unto them another servant; and at him they cast stones, and wounded him in the head, and sent him away shamefully handled. And again he sent another; and him they killed, and many others; beating some, and killing some. Having yet therefore one son, his wellbeloved, he sent him also last unto them, saying, 'They will reverence my son.' But those husbandmen said among themselves, 'This is the heir; come, let us kill him, and the inheritance shall be our's.' And they took him, and killed him, and cast him out of the vineyard. What shall therefore the lord of the vineyard do? he will come and destroy the husbandmen, and will give the vineyard unto others."

The parable began with a phrase which everyone would remember and place: the words were borrowed from Isaiah's poem about the vineyard of Jehovah.* But very quickly Jesus changed his essential theme. Where Isaiah was concerned with the retribution which befell the vine, Jesus had something quite different in mind — a dramatic story of personal relationships, between a landowner and his husbandmen. The landowner must have been living abroad, and his vineyard was obviously in some brigand-haunted area of Palestine, such as Trachonitis. This background to Jesus' stark tale would make its twists of plot more than credible.

The first servant sent to collect the farm profits was given a good working over; the second was severely wounded; and the third killed. Finally, the landowner sent his own son. But such a state of anarchy prevailed in the region that the vine dressers murdered the boy without a moment's hesitation — rather like nationalist guerrillas revenging themselves on a *colon* — and, having done so, lugged his body off the estate and left it lying there without burial. They argued that no further emissaries would come to bother them, and the estate would be theirs by default. Such peasant risings were not unknown in countries which the Romans had colonized, but the central authorities put them down ruthlessly. The lord of the vineyard called in military assistance: he recovered his property, had the murderers executed, and took fresh husbandmen onto his payroll. It would not have occurred to the bulk of those who heard this story that Jesus had portrayed himself in it, as the landowner's son;

* Chapter 5, especially verses 1-7.

or even, indeed, that he was making any allusion to the Messiah.
The point of the parable was that God's servants were prepared to commit murder rather than have to obey Him; and the
members of the Sanhedrin, when this story was reported back to
them by their agents, could hardly fail to take the point. They
recognized the murderous vine dressers as a representation of
themselves, and resented the charge. But soon enough they were
to hear a good many more home truths about themselves.

7
JESUS ATTACKS THE SCRIBES AGAIN

JESUS NOW BEGAN to attack openly: the next parable he made
up was the harshest he had ever uttered: "And he spake this
parable unto certain which trusted in themselves that they
were righteous, and despised others: 'Two men went up into
the temple to pray; the one a Pharisee, and the other a publican.
The Pharisee stood and prayed thus with himself, "God, I
thank thee, that I am not as other men are, extortioners, unjust, adulterers, or even as this publican. I fast twice in the
week, I give tithes of all that I possess." And the publican,
standing afar off, would not lift up so much as his eyes unto
heaven, but smote upon his breast, saying, "God be merciful to
me a sinner." I tell you, this man went down to his house
justified rather than the other: for every one that exalteth himself shall be abased; and he that humbleth himself shall be
exalted.' "

The Pharisee's prayer is an act of thanksgiving. This strict
sectarian is not, however, thanking God for helping him to carry
out the commandments of the Decalogue, but because he is
"not as other men." From the list of the commandments he
omits charity; indeed, he actively flouts it. He only retains two
of the Decalogue's prohibitions, those against theft and adul-

tery: the two sins — along with murder — which "respectable" people throughout the ages have always regarded as dishonorable. Above all, the Pharisee thanks God that he is what he is, a member of the sect. He observes fast days and pays special supplementary tithes; he concentrates on the least important and most debatable requirements of the Law. The *publicanus*, on the other hand, contents himself with begging for God's divine mercy, in words borrowed from the Fifty-first Psalm, known today as the *Miserere*.

In the Talmud (and indeed in certain other manuals of devotion) we find a prayer which much resembles that uttered by the Pharisee: "I thank Thee, O Lord my God," it runs, "for that Thou hast placed my lot amongst those who sit in the seat of learning, and not amongst those who sit at street-corners. From the dawn I am about my work, as are they; but what I labour at from daybreak is the matter of the Law; whereas the matter they labour at is nothingness, and its words are vain. Like them, I grow weary with toil; but to me good accrues therefrom, whereas they strive to no profit. They run, as do I; but I hasten towards the Life that is to come, while they plunge headlong in the well which drains the ditch."

Now, Jesus was here making a unique assertion, without precedent in his previous parables. He claimed — and in the name of God — that the Pharisee, whose prayer was not on the face of it at all objectionable, failed to achieve sanctity, whereas the *publicanus* "went down to his house justified." "To those who first heard it," a modern scholar writes, "the parable must have seemed inconceivably shocking," so frontal an assault did it make upon those who passed for the very embodiment of piety and religious zeal.

Some contemporary Jewish writers admit that Jesus' criticisms were justified. "The casuistical spirit," one of them observes, "together with a strict adherence to every least detail of reli-

gious ritual, led certain Pharisees into error, by making them
believe that such practical shibboleths were what really mattered, and that rules of moral conduct possessed only secondary
importance." Jesus went further still. He did not by any means
include *all* the Pharisees in his condemnation, for there were
some very sincere and honorable men among them, including a
number whom Jesus regarded as his friends; he did not criticize
them, either, over many of their articles of faith, since these he
himself subscribed to. What he objected to was the "Pharisaical
spirit," that is, the attitude maintained by a sect of self-styled
perfecti who looked down on their fellow-men and felt they
had an exclusive lien on the Almighty. This attitude Jesus regarded as being diametrically opposed to his own often reiterated
precept: faith in a kindly, compassionate God, who cared for
the humble and the contrite, and was determined to widen the
Law of the Torah until it embraced all mankind in brotherhood, as children of one Father.

This was why Jesus, in the course of a lengthy diatribe, did
not fear to attack the scribes and the Pharisees directly, or to
stiffen his criticism with sharp invective, even with formal
execration. "The scribes and the Pharisees," he declared, "sit in
Moses' seat: all therefore whatsoever they bid you observe, that
observe and do; but do not ye after their works: for they say,
and do not. For they bind heavy burdens and grievous to be
borne, and lay them on men's shoulders; but they themselves
will not move them with one of their fingers."

When Jesus advised his hearers to obey the learned elders
who taught the Mosaic Law, he had in mind the basic commandments of this Law, the Decalogue. His opposition to the
absurd manner in which they interpreted the laws relating to
the Sabbath remained constant and implacable. The Pharisees
multiplied a whole host of prohibitions, which were easy enough
for the wealthy to observe but inapplicable to ordinary poor

people. The image of porters or carriers is an excellent one with which to depict such wretches, crushed by countless rules and regulations. "But all their works they do for to be seen of men," Jesus went on; "they make broad their phylacteries, and enlarge the borders of their garments, and love the uppermost rooms at feasts, and the chief seats in the synagogues. And greetings in the markets, and to be called of men, Rabbi, Rabbi."

Jesus' main criticism here is leveled against their passion for ceremony and ritual. He hated the way they would scramble for the highest places; their love of honorifics; their habit of ostentatiously binding prayer-inscribed fillets around head and wrists when they prayed in public. He heaped insult upon insult: "But woe unto you, scribes and Pharisees, hypocrites! for ye shut up the kingdom of heaven against men: for ye neither go in yourselves, neither suffer ye them that are entering to go in.

"Woe unto you, scribes and Pharisees, hypocrites! for ye devour widows' houses, and for a pretence make long prayer: therefore ye shall receive the greater damnation.

"Woe unto you, scribes and Pharisees, hypocrites! for ye compass sea and land to make one proselyte, and when he is made, ye make him twofold more the child of hell than yourselves.

"Woe unto you, ye blind guides, which say, 'Whosoever shall swear by the temple, it is nothing; but whosoever shall swear by the gold of the temple, he is a debtor!' Ye fools and blind: for whether is greater, the gold, or the temple that sanctifieth the gold? And, Whosoever shall swear by the altar, it is nothing; but whosoever sweareth by the gift that is upon it, he is guilty. Ye fools and blind: for whether is greater, the gift, or the altar that sanctifieth the gift? Whoso therefore shall swear by the altar, sweareth by it, and by all things thereon and whoso shall swear by the temple, sweareth by it, and by him that dwelleth therein. And he that shall swear by heaven, sweareth by the throne of God, and by him that sitteth thereon.

"Woe unto you, scribes and Pharisees, hypocrites! for ye pay tithe of mint and anise and cummin, and have omitted the weightier matters of the law, judgment, mercy, and faith: these ought ye to have done, and not to leave the other undone. Ye blind guides, which strain at a gnat, and swallow a camel.

"Woe unto you, scribes and Pharisees, hypocrites! for ye make clean the outside of the cup and of the platter, but within they are full of extortion and excess. Thou blind Pharisee, cleanse first that which is within the cup and platter, that the outside of them may be clean also.

"Woe unto you, scribes and Pharisees, hypocrites! for ye are like unto whited sepulchres, which indeed appear beautiful outward, but are within full of dead men's bones, and of all uncleanness. Even so ye also outwardly appear righteous unto men, but within ye are full of hypocrisy and iniquity.

"Woe unto you, scribes and Pharisees, hypocrites! because ye build the tombs of the prophets, and garnish the sepulchres of the righteous, and say, If we had been in the days of our father, we would not have been partakers with them in the blood of the prophets. Wherefore ye be witnesses unto yourselves, that ye are the children of them which killed the prophets. Fill ye up then the measure of your fathers. Ye serpents, ye generation of vipers, how can ye escape the damnation of hell?"

By a strange anomaly, Jesus' invective, or some of it, finds echoes in the Jewish tradition. The Talmud criticizes the "seven sorts of Pharisees," and refers to "those pestilential Pharisees who counsel orphans to deprive the widow of her livelihood." But Jesus listed his complaints in some detail, objecting, for instance, to the casuistical arguments by which the relative value of various oaths was determined. He practically cited official

authority in places; there was a rabbinical dictum which declared that "to kill a flea on the Sabbath day was no less a sin
than to kill a camel." The violence of the charges which Jesus
brought against these Jewish savants (and the passionate language in which they were couched) destroyed any hope of
reconciliation. Either Jesus would spread Judaism to the farthest
corners of the globe, and thus triumph over the sectarians; or
else they would pull him down and destroy him.

8

THE TEMPLE AND THE COMING ORDEAL

ONE MORNING, on his way from Bethany to Jerusalem, Jesus
made a detour from the road that skirted the Mount of Olives
and climbed until the Temple and the whole of the city lay
before him in one magnificent panorama. Humanly speaking,
he had no hope left; and he began to lament over the Holy
City: " 'O Jerusalem, Jerusalem, thou that killest the prophets,
and stonest them which are sent unto thee, how often would I
have gathered thy children together, even as a hen gathereth
her chickens under her wings, and ye would not! . . . If thou
hadst known, even thou, at least in this thy day, the things
which belong unto thy peace! but now they are hid from thine
eyes. . . .' And as he went out of the temple, one of his
disciples saith unto him, 'Master, see what manner of stones
and what buildings are here!' And Jesus answering said unto
him, 'Seest thou these great buildings? there shall not be left
one stone upon another, that shall not be thrown down.' And
as he sat upon the mount of olives over against the temple, Peter
and James and John and Andrew asked him privately, 'Tell us,
when shall these things be? and what shall be the sign when all
these things shall be fulfilled?' And Jesus answering them began
to say . . . 'When ye shall see the abomination of desolation,

spoken of by Daniel the prophet, standing where it ought not, (let him that readeth understand,) then let them that be in Judaea flee to the mountains: and let him that is on the house top not go down into the house, neither enter therein, to take any thing out of his house: and let him that is in the field not turn back again for to take up his garment. But woe to them that are with child, and to them that give suck in those days! And pray ye that your flight be not in the winter.' "

Jesus envisaged a local and specific catastrophe, in which the world of Judaism and the Temple would perish forever. Though Jerusalem's capture by Nebuchadnezzar and the burning of the first Temple were events in the distant past, their terrible memory still lingered on. According to Jesus, Rome would now take the place of Babylon. God, using some foreign general as his instrument, would destroy the religious center he loved so dearly. For all his sober restraint over details, Jesus managed to evoke all the horrors of war. He carefully refrained from making any allusion to the apocalyptic writers' fantasies and visions, which frequently hovered on the verge of surrealism. But for all that, he was very much to the point.

His followers were overeager, anxious to equate the fall of Judaism with the end of the world. But Jesus did not share their preoccupations: he knew nothing of the end of the world, he told them bluntly, nor did it concern him: "But of that day and that hour knoweth no man, no, not the angels which are in heaven, neither the Son, but the Father." Some Christians have evinced embarrassment at this remark, though it cannot be taken as indicating anything other than Jesus' complete indifference towards a pointless question, which happened to excite avid speculation among his people. In any case he himself —Jesus the man, who knew he was the Son of God — had no intention of revealing the Creator's mysterious designs. His sole center of interest still remained the Kingdom. When we strip away these apocalyptic fantasies, he was saying in effect: We see that the Kingdom is near at hand, within our grasp; men can enter it whenever they so desire; it is a new way of life, here and now. Jesus produced an image to match the occasion: "Now learn a parable of the fig tree," he said. "When her branch is yet tender, and putteth forth leaves, ye know that summer is near." The fig, in point of fact, is Palestine's one deciduous tree, the only one that looks dead during the winter. Then suddenly, in late spring, it buds into fresh life — a symbol of the Kingdom, which is always present, and soon will become manifest. But this visible inauguration of an ever-present Kingdom required a terrible ordeal, and Jesus was anxious to prepare his followers for the tragic crisis which his clash with official Judaism would precipitate. He ceaselessly advised them to be vigilant, and not to let themselves be taken unawares by the dramatic events now impending. Every one of them risked being caught up in this desperate and agonized situation. "Take ye heed," he told them, "watch and pray: for ye know not when the time is. For the Son of man is as a man taking a far journey, who left his house, and gave authority to his servants, and to every man his work, and commanded the porter to watch. Watch ye therefore: for ye know not when the master of the house cometh, at even, or at midnight, or at the cockcrowing, or in the morning."

The parable alludes to the ordeal which Jesus' followers will shortly be called upon to endure, and which will descend on them like the unexpected return of the master to his house, setting the servants by the ears. Elsewhere Jesus gives the image a fresh twist: "But know this, that if the goodman of the house had known in what watch the thief would come, he would have watched, and would not have suffered his house to be broken up." This confrontation of Jesus and the leaders of Judaism was to be the crucial test, in which hearts and minds alike would be

judged; and Jesus therefore produced as many images as possible
that might alert his disciples to the seriousness of this test of
souls.

9

THE PARABLES OF THE ORDEAL

JESUS' FOLLOWERS were still expecting him to seize Messianic
power in Jerusalem. He would be a king, they thought. Jesus
knew he had not succeeded in ridding them of their illusions.
At Caesarea, Simon Peter had saluted him as a king; and when
Jesus had tried to show Peter that his royal function would be
that of Jehovah's suffering servant, he had run up against his
disciple's frank skepticism. Jesus knew that his sojourn in Jerusalem was to have a tragic end. The Son of Man's royal consecration would not involve that celestial, cloudborne epiphany
which Jesus had refused at the time of his temptation by the
Devil; nor would it take the form of a military or political victory, but of death. And as men bore themselves when faced with
this death, so could they be judged.

Jesus continued to predict this disaster by means of parables.
Once, for a change, he drew his metaphor from a country
wedding. In Palestine these often took place during the evening, by torchlight. "Then shall the kingdom of heaven be
likened unto ten virgins, which took their lamps, and went forth
to meet the bridegroom. And five of them were wise, and five
were foolish. They that were foolish took their lamps, and
took no oil with them: but the wise took oil in their vessels
with their lamps. While the bridegroom tarried, they all
slumbered and slept. And at midnight there was a cry made,
'Behold the bridegroom cometh; go ye out to meet him.' Then
all those virgins arose, and trimmed their lamps. And the foolish
said unto the wise, 'Give us of your oil; for our lamps are gone

out.' But the wise answered, saying, 'Not so; lest there be not enough for us and you: but go ye rather to them that sell, and buy for yourselves.' And while they went to buy, the bridegroom came; and they that were ready went in with him to the marriage: and the door was shut. Afterward came also the other virgins, saying, 'Lord, Lord, open to us.' But he answered and said, 'Verily I say unto you, I know you not.'"

What an expert storyteller Jesus was! Here were ten bridesmaids, waiting for the arrival of the wedding procession, which had gone to fetch the bridegroom from the bride's house. All of them had dozed off in the mild, subtropical night air. At midnight the improvident ones were still clutching their little clay lamps, but they had run out of oil. While they were away getting more, the wedding procession arrived. The bridegroom dealt with these latecomers much as a master in the rabbinical school was wont to treat pupils who arrived late or were sent out: "I know you not," he told them.

No one listening would have for one moment supposed that Jesus intended them to regard the bridegroom as a self-portrait. The point of this little tale was to show how disconcerting the bridegroom's arrival could be for those who were still unprepared — just like the master's nocturnal return in the parable of the vigilant servant, or that of the thief in the hole-in-the-wall story.

On another occasion Jesus used the image of hard cash to make his point. No possible question here that Jesus was referring to his own glorious coming as the Messiah, attended by his followers; the test was that of fidelity, of looking after one's employer's capital to best advantage in a difficult situation. The story concerned a man who was going abroad, and who entrusted his five servants with all his financial reserves. To one he gave five talents (almost six thousand dollars in modern currency). To another he gave two talents, and to the last one talent only. When the man returned home he asked his servants to account for these sums. The first had doubled what was given him, and the second likewise. Their master invited them to his table, saying to each: "Enter thou into the joy of thy lord." But the last one had buried the money left with him, and simply returned it as it was. He was promptly shown the door. In other words, Jesus was telling his disciples that when the time of trial came, their real capabilities would become apparent.

Jesus did not speak openly of the Son of Man's glorious advent as predicted in the prophetic Book of Enoch; but he did once allude to the subject in a parable, and no doubt surprised everyone a great deal by doing so. He made no reference to heavenly signs or a victory over Satan: he was discussing a king who had spent some time away from his country. The parables of this last period in Jerusalem are full of absentee masters.

On his return the king in question gathered his subjects before him and divided them into two groups, whom he set one on his right hand, the other on his left. To those on the right he said: "Come, ye blessed [of my Father*], inherit the kingdom prepared for you from the foundation of the world: for I was an hungred, and ye gave me meat: I was thirsty, and ye gave me drink: I was a stranger, and ye took me in: naked, and ye clothed me: I was sick, and ye visited me: I was in prison, and ye came unto me. Then shall the righteous answer him, saying, 'Lord, when saw we thee an hungred, and fed thee? or thirsty, and gave thee drink? When saw we thee a stranger, and took thee in? or naked, and clothed thee? Or when saw we thee sick, or in prison, and came unto thee?' And the King shall answer and say unto them, 'Verily I say unto you, Inasmuch as ye have done it unto one of the least of these my brethren, ye have

* The French text omits these crucial words, which firmly attach the passage (Matthew 25, 34 ff.) to a Messianic context: the king is identified with the Son of Man in his glory. [Tr.]

done it unto me.' " Those on his left hand, however, the king upbraided bitterly for failing to take him in and succor him.

Jesus was moving back to the central theme of his teaching in Galilee. What mattered above all was charity, love for all humble and suffering people. Was he alluding to himself in the person of the king? Not directly. He was telling the story of a king who loved poor people and regarded everything that was done for their sakes as being done for him. In Jesus' view this king's action provided a useful image of the Messiah's role: he was conceived as an absent overlord, and the degree of closeness to the Kingdom which each individual attained was directly proportionate to his qualities as a Good Samaritan.

Spring, and the Passover, drew daily nearer. Jesus knew that his decisive test, foretold so insistently in the last parables, would take place during that great feast for which pilgrims flocked to Jerusalem from the four corners of the world.

10

PREPARATION FOR THE PASSOVER

FOR WEEKS NOW Jesus had regularly left the city at nightfall and slept in the village of Bethany. According to St. Mark, he stayed with a man known as Simon the Leper, and it was in this man's house that the most extraordinary incident took place. While they were at supper, a woman came in with an alabaster flask containing pure spikenard, a most expensive oil perfume. Breaking the neck of the flask, she poured the perfume over Jesus' head. Some of those present were angry at her gesture. "Why was this waste of the ointment made?" they asked. "For it might have been sold for more than three hundred pence, and have been given to the poor." And, says St. Mark, they "murmured against her."

But Jesus said: "Let her alone; why trouble ye her? she hath wrought a good work on me. For ye have the poor with you always, and whensoever ye will ye may do them good: but me ye have not always. She hath done what she could: she is come aforehand to anoint my body to the burying." Long before, in Galilee, another woman had anointed Jesus' feet. Now this woman of Bethany — as anonymous as her predecessor — had come and poured spikenard on his head. Perhaps her intention was to show recognition of Jesus' royal dignity, and to make a gesture that symbolized the anointing at his Messianic consecration. In her own fashion she was saluting him whom she acknowledged King of the Jews.

Some guests — it is not on record whether or not they were the Twelve — protested at her action, and Jesus answered their complaints. Far from emphasizing the Messianic significance of what she had done, he treated it simply as a gesture of affection towards one whom they would not always have with them. A certain deep melancholy pervades his remarks. He went so far as to say that the woman had foreseen his death, and was dealing with him as though he were a corpse ready for the embalmer. Was there a touch of irony about this suggestion? Did his hearers still labor under so many illusions where he was concerned? Could he talk of his death, yet have them all convinced that the remark was a pleasantry merely? Given half a chance, Simon Peter would once more charge Jesus with succumbing to his pet obsession.

The date of the Passover Feast was determined by the first new moon in the spring solstice. In ancient Israel this had marked the beginning of the year; but in Jesus' day the Palestinian Jews had adopted the "Greek reckoning," and with it the habit of pushing the New Year back to the beginning of October. Nevertheless, as happened later with the Russian *raskolniki*, the old sacerdotal calendar retained certain firm adherents, in particular the monastic communities of the Essenes. These archaizing splinter groups celebrated the Passover on the Tuesday evening prior to the official Paschal Sabbath. Jesus himself observed the older custom.

His enemies had only a week in which to act. They were now determined to arrest him. Did they genuinely fear a popular uprising at the time of the Passover, when thousands of Jews from abroad would be coming up to Jerusalem? Perhaps their main concern was lest Jesus find a ready audience in these visitors. It was true that afterward the nuclei of the first Christian communities were established by proselytes and the Jews of the Diaspora.

Since Jesus' enemies had decided to strike quickly, they took advantage of the offer made them by Judas. It was essential that the arrest should be made with a minimum of fuss. Jesus knew quite well that Judas had betrayed him; he could easily have eluded capture. All he needed to do was to leave Jerusalem. But in fact he did nothing of the sort: he made up his mind to stay in Jerusalem for the Passover, and to walk into his betrayer's trap of his own free will.

When his disciples asked him where they would eat the Paschal Supper together, Jesus, as was his wont, sent two of them on ahead, with these instructions: "Go ye into the city, and there shall meet you a man bearing a pitcher of water: follow him. And wheresoever he shall go in, say ye to the goodman of the house, 'The Master saith, Where is the guestchamber, where I shall eat the passover with my disciples?' And he will shew you a large upper room furnished and prepared: there make ready for us." Jesus had already warned the owner of the house, who was one of his friends — clearly, since Jesus was familiar with the guest chamber. He knew that his disciples would meet the water carrier near the spring known as Gihon, or the Virgin's Well, down the Cedron Valley towards the Tower of Siloam.

Apart from this mission, the two disciples, Peter and John, had also to buy unleavened bread, salad vegetables, fruit (such as grapes and figs) for dessert, and wine. They would fill up the water jars and lay out cushions for the supper guests.

11

THE LAST SUPPER

THE PASCHAL SUPPER should be a joyful festival, a celebration of freedom. But that night, when the guests climbed up to the chamber on the second floor and settled themselves on their couches, there was an atmosphere of tragedy in the air. Scarcely had supper begun before Jesus uttered the melancholy words: "Verily I say unto you, One of you which eateth with me shall betray me." The Twelve were thunderstruck by this. One after another, they uneasily asked Jesus: "Is it I?" But Jesus did not reply. He was eating the *charoset*, a dish of stewed fruit in which pieces of bread were dipped. At last he said: "It is one of the twelve, that dippeth with me in the dish. The Son of man indeed goeth, as it is written of him: but woe to that man by whom the Son of man is betrayed! good were it for that man if he had never been born."

Judas was there, eating with the other disciples, talking to Jesus. It was to him that the words of the Master were addressed. Was their purpose to arouse remorse in him at the eleventh hour? Had they done so, the whole course of history would have been altered. But Judas had taken an irrevocable decision. He felt nothing for the Galilaean rabbi now except sardonic contempt. What harm was there, he asked himself, in turning the fellow over to the official authorities or their representatives?

Faced with Judas' stubborn silence, Jesus realized the die was cast. At that point, seeing what the future held for him, he "took bread": one of those round, soft, flat loaves known in Jerusalem nowadays as Arab bread, which can be torn to pieces as easily as a pancake and is used to pick up mouthfuls of food from the dish with one's fingers.

Jesus pronounced the blessing: "I thank Thee, O heavenly Father, for giving us this day our daily bread." Then he broke the loaf into pieces, saying: "Take, eat: this is my body." Afterward he took the cup, probably wrought of bronze and filled with coarse red wine. Rabbinical law, and indeed general custom throughout the ancient world, would require this wine to be diluted. Again he pronounced the benediction: "Blessed be thou, O Lord God, who hast created the fruit of the vine." Then he passed the cup around, and each of them drank in turn. "This," he said, "is my blood of the new testament, which is shed for many." And he added: "Verily I say unto you, I will drink no more of the fruit of the vine, until that day that I drink it new in the Kingdom of God."

These final words — like all that had gone before — expressed not only his absolute certainty of dying but also the equal certainty that this death would open the gates of the Kingdom to him. Jesus, declaring that his blood was that of the "new testament," said: "This do in remembrance of me."

What in fact had he done? Anticipated his death by a few days. But this was no ordinary death; it was a genuine human sacrifice, which for all its cruelty nevertheless remained the supreme sacramental act performed by primitive man. There are numerous traces of human sacrifice in the Bible; it was still practiced here and there during Jesus' lifetime. What else, when one comes to think of it, were the gladiatorial combats in Rome? The Mosaic Law had substituted animal sacrifices for the human rite — in particular the sacrifice of the Paschal Lamb. The shedding of blood had sealed God's pact with His chosen people on Mount Sinai. Jesus knew himself to be the suffering and martyred Servant of God, the innocent hostage slain for the sake of mankind. That night, in all probability, the flesh of the Paschal Lamb was missing from his table, since the priests had not yet slaughtered their multitudinous victims in the Temple. He, Jesus, was himself the Lamb of the New Testament between God and man; and this covenant too would be sealed with blood. The Twelve were made one with him by the act of Communion in "flesh and blood." This Semitic phrase meant "the whole man," since the flesh was equated with the body, and the blood contained the soul.

Jesus therefore regarded himself as already dead to the world of men; his sacrificial death opened up for these men the Kingdom of God which they had not sought or desired. Jesus' martyrdom, moreover, was to be provoked by just this same prophecy of his concerning the Kingdom that stood for tolerance and forgiveness. It was for this that the leaders of Judaism were to strike him down. His disciples were to survive him — and to repeat the gesture he made. Thus they established on earth that heavenly Kingdom which was now to become incarnate among men of "flesh and blood."

As the night progressed, Jesus still talked with his disciples. He was in a melancholy mood. He must have alluded in some way to the coming persecutions and the fellowship of the Kingdom. Then they all rose and the lights were put out. Judas slipped away; the others accompanied Jesus across the Cedron Valley.

12

GETHSEMANE

A FULL MOON SHONE down coldly on the olive trees in the gardens. The Orthodox Passover was not due to begin for another three days, so all was still quiet in Jerusalem. They walked through the Ophel quarter, down narrow, twisting alleyways, till they reached the Cedron Valley. Then they turned north and began the ascent towards the Mount of Olives. As they went Jesus said: "All ye shall be offended because of me this night." Unusually for him, he capped this remark with a phrase from the prophet Zechariah, which came into his mind just then: "I will smite the shepherd, and the sheep shall be scattered."

Simon Peter, true to form, saw this as just another of his Master's temporary fits of depression. "Although all shall be offended," he declared firmly, "yet will not I." But Jesus replied: "Verily I say unto thee, that this day, even in this night, before the cock crow twice, thou shalt deny me thrice." Peter would have none of this: "If I should die with thee," he exclaimed, "I will not deny thee in any wise." In any case (Peter must have told himself), the whole idea is ridiculous. He is on the eve of his triumph, and he talks of *dying!* Granted that he does have one or two enemies: he is well guarded.

Instead of going back to Bethany, Jesus decided to spend this particular night out of doors, on the property of a friend of his: an olive grove which lay along the lower flank of the mountain, just beside the road to the village. Its name was Gethsemane, which means oil press. As one scholar puts it, "it was a typical country estate, such as could — and still can — be found in large numbers throughout Palestine." The grove was surrounded by a wall; it was also guarded, for it lay so close to Jerusalem that without adequate protection it ran a grave risk of being plundered. Jesus knew the watchman. Followed by his disciples, he entered the garden. Beneath the trees, among the gray calcareous stones, on a springtime carpet of the flowers — red spearwort, white behen — which grew so thickly in that rich soil, Jesus showed them a spot where they could roll up in their coverings for the night. "Sit ye here," he said, "while I shall pray."

They were still under the impression that he intended to recite the Psalms celebrating the joyful accomplishment of the Passover, the liberation of the people thanks to the blood of the immolated Paschal Lamb. But he took Peter, James, and John aside; and when they were out of earshot of the rest, he was, visibly, seized by some appalling nameless fear. He appeared physically prostrated, in agony. All he could find the strength to tell his three dearest friends was: "My soul is exceeding sorrowful unto death: tarry ye here, and watch."

Then he went on a little farther, alone, and collapsed. He gave in to his weakness, and knelt as a suppliant before his invisible God. Groaning, he begged to be released from his personal ordeal. All human will and strength had ebbed from him. He saw a night of horror looming ahead, a ghastliness that brought tears to his eyes. His crouching body trembled, and sweat streamed down it. Half asleep, Peter heard him whisper: "Abba, Father, all things are possible unto thee; take away this cup from me: nevertheless not what I will, but what thou wilt." Later Peter was awakened by Jesus: "Simon, sleepest thou? couldest not thou watch one hour? Watch ye and pray, lest ye enter into temptation." But then, with a glance at their sleeping figures, he added: "The spirit truly is ready, but the flesh is weak."

He went back to his solitary prayer. He felt, as never before in his life, that he was engaged in a struggle with the Evil One. The temptation in the wilderness was far behind him; it had been easy enough to refuse a triumph over men. But this night was different.

Twice more he approached his sleeping followers. But what was the point of rousing them? They would wake soon enough. And at that moment there came a confused shouting, the tramp of feet in the darkness. It all happened very quickly. The men who had burst into the garden were all talking in loud voices. Jesus and his three companions were surrounded. Their assailants carried weapons. Suddenly Judas advanced on Jesus and — like any pious disciple greeting his master — said, "Rabbi!" and kissed him.

At once the soldiers of Ananias who accompanied Judas laid their heavy hands on Jesus. He was under arrest, they said, and must come with them. An abortive scuffle now took place. Someone drew his sword and struck out. A guard received a minor injury. But with one word Jesus put an end to this resistance. He had recovered his self-control. In contemptuous tones he addressed the soldiers who formed his escort: "Are ye come out, as against a thief, with swords and with staves to take me? I was daily with you in the Temple teaching, and ye took me not."

He still possessed all his old authority: the police detachment eyed him with uneasy respect. For some reason unknown to them, he alone was to be arrested. Judas by now must have taken himself off. The eleven other disciples, seeing Jesus talking to the soldiers, slunk nervously away into the shadow of the trees and debated what all this could mean. Some of them decided to follow the group at a distance in order to find out what was happening.

At this point a ridiculous incident took place. As the escort emerged from the olive grove a young man tagged on behind them, wearing nothing but a sheet which he had wrapped round himself. The police decided to arrest him too, but he left the sheet in their hands and ran off stark-naked. Was this boy John Mark, son of the man who owned Gethsemane, or one of his friends, who told him the story afterward? We do not know.

Ananias' men took Jesus straight to the house of the former High Priest.

13
BEFORE THE SANHEDRIN

ANANIAS HAD SUMMONED only a small group of people on this fatal night, all of them Jesus' sworn enemies. He was an extremely powerful old rogue, whose authority matched the degree of his corruption: he wanted to tie up every detail of the trial himself, in advance. We have, naturally, no evidence as to the relentless interrogation which Jesus must have undergone during the course of that night. There were few witnesses, and none of them talked. There is only one thing we can be sure of. Faced with the silence of the accused, and the impossibility of extracting any incriminating statement from him, Ananias and his accomplices doubtless resorted to the time-honored device of torture, which has been practiced ever since the idea of a police force first began. However, Ananias could not afford to be too violent; he certainly could not risk leaving the accused covered with open wounds, since the hearing was next morning, and the members of the tribunal would be bound to ask for an explanation, even though Jesus was the person they had assembled to try. The former High Priest was extremely unpopular and did not intend to provide any excuse whatsoever for an inquiry.

Accordingly, he turned Jesus over to his men for a little roughing-up: what the French nowadays call *un passage à tabac*. Ananias' police were notorious for their skill with a truncheon. In some back alley or guardroom Jesus was gone over thoroughly. Truncheons and fists both played their part. Someone spat in his face.

Late that night — in fact, in the early hours of the morning

— two of Jesus' followers, Simon Peter and John, tried to find out what was going on. They slipped into the courtyard of Ananias' house — John may have had friends among the servants — where they found a fire blazing away: spring nights in Jerusalem can turn very chilly. Those of the staff who had stayed up were, naturally, discussing the previous evening's arrest; perhaps they were guffawing over the rough treatment being handed out to this so-called prophet from Galilee. Bandits and cutthroats, Galilee was full of them: this was the way to deal with such riffraff. Then, suddenly, a woman caught sight of Peter's face in the firelight, and felt sure she had seen him before, in Jesus' company.

She said: "And thou also wast with Jesus of Nazareth."

Caught off his guard, Peter replied, "I know not, neither understand I what thou sayest," and backed away into the shadows. But the woman's curiosity was now thoroughly aroused. She was on to something and refused to drop it. She pointed Peter out, saying: "This is one of them." This time Peter flatly denied it. But others gathered around, from the guardroom perhaps, and said: "Surely thou art one of them: for thou art a Galilaean, and thy speech agreeth thereto." Then Peter, terrified by the prospect of the torture chamber, had recourse to a desperate resort, and swore by Almighty God: "I know not this man of whom ye speak." At once people left off questioning him, and he went out. Dawn was breaking: a cock crowed. There in the narrow street, as the pale half-light quickened, Peter stood, and wept bitterly.

That supreme religious tribunal, the Jerusalem Sanhedrin, had been convened to meet the following forenoon. We have no precise evidence as to where the meetings were held at this period. One detail the Talmud tells us is that forty years before the destruction of the Temple, the place of assembly was shifted from the "Chamber of the Cloven Rock" to another hall situated "by the market of the sons of Ananias." Of the seventy members, twenty-three formed a quorum: below that number no finding or sentence was valid. Naturally, Ananias had arranged matters so that those members of the High Court who were sympathetic towards Jesus — and we know that several such existed — were not called upon to attend.

Furthermore, the Sanhedrin was not empowered to pronounce sentence of death. On capital charges its sole function was to conduct the preliminary examination, after which the dossier on the case, together with the court's findings, was sent up to the Roman Procurator.

Two clerks of the court sat facing the judges. The High Priest — by title if not by right — presided. On this occasion it was Joseph Caiaphas. Jesus was brought in, and the hearing began. The main difficulty was in finding any really crushing testimony against him. Any isolated remark could be dragged in as evidence. Witnesses declared that they had heard him say: "Destroy this temple, and in three days I will raise it up." This was a genuine saying of Jesus', but quoted out of context. He had prophesied the destruction of the Temple, but only to his followers. He could hardly be brought to trial on the strength of one ill-argued accusation over which the witnesses themselves were not in complete agreement.

Now came the question of his Messianism. Here too Jesus had skillfully and ironically sidestepped all the trick questions put to him by informers before the time of his arrest. There was nothing on this score in his dossier; and Jesus himself refused to say anything, preferring to let these pettifogging jurists thrash around helplessly on their own. But Joseph, the High Priest, decided to ask Jesus one direct and crucial question: "Art thou the Christ, the Son of the Blessed?"

Not all the Jews by any means thought that the Messiah

was the Son of God. They did not even believe in the Son of God's existence, except in the general sense that all men are adopted sons of their Father in heaven. But Joseph was well informed about Jesus' teaching, and knew that he sometimes referred to his Father. Could this Galilaean nobody have been toying with the outrageous notion that he had special affiliations with Almighty God? That he was, in fact, the Messiah?

This time Jesus broke silence. "Thou sayest it," he told Joseph. And he added a quotation from the Book of Daniel: "Ye shall see the Son of man sitting on the right hand of power, and coming in the clouds of heaven." Once more, as he had done at Caesarea, Jesus countered the labels of "Messiah" and "Son of God" by representing himself as the "Son of Man"; and to foretell his triumph he had recourse to a favorite prophecy, that which predicted his reign here on earth. But at this Joseph burst out before the whole assembly: "He hath spoken blasphemy; what further need have we of witnesses? behold, now ye have heard his blasphemy." And in a theatrical, characteristically Jewish gesture, he tore the border of his robe. He took Jesus' reply to be a "profanation of the Holy Name," or *Hillel hasshem*, as it was then termed.

The accused was taken out and the Sanhedrin proceeded to deliberate the matter. Judgment could not be given that same day; they had to wait another twenty-four hours and then present the complete dossier to the Roman authorities for action. Their best line, Joseph and Ananias considered, was to stick to the charge of Messianism. To the Romans this meant participation in a revolutionary plot, an appeal to a Holy War. It should not prove too difficult to secure a death sentence on this count.

We do not know whether Joseph met any opposition from those members of the Sanhedrin who gathered on Wednesday morning. If opposition there was, it had probably already been stifled by Ananias, with a discreet mixture of pressurizing and intrigue: the old man was not exactly a beginner in these matters. "From start to finish," writes one shrewd modern scholar, "the trial of Jesus is stamped with the mark of Sadducee rather than Pharisee influence."

14
Pontius Pilate

JESUS PROBABLY SPENT a day and a night in prison. Next morning — that is, on Thursday — he was once more summoned before the Sanhedrin, where he was informed that the charge against him was one of Messianism. Since this offense carried the death sentence, the case was to be referred to the Roman Procurator. If the Jews had been at liberty in the matter, they would have condemned Jesus, stoned him to death, and hung his corpse from a gibbet. But they no longer had executive authority in matters of life and death, and were forced to leave the sentence to Pilate.

The closeness of the Passover made this step somewhat easier than usual. Normally the accused person, together with his accusers, had to be sent to Caesarea, the Procurator's permanent residence. But Pilate had come up to Jerusalem for the Passover Feast and was lodged in Herod's palace, at the northwest corner of the city. The reason for his presence was simple: the capital was dangerously overcrowded at this time, and if an uprising did take place, he could deal with it in person, on the spot. Therefore, to accuse Jesus of revolutionary activities was only too likely to procure results — always providing the Roman governor could be persuaded to swallow so grossly palpable a falsehood.

Pontius Pilate is a character about whom history has a fair

amount to tell us. He had been Governor of Judaea since A.D. 25, and was immediately responsible to the Imperial Legate (*legatus pro praetore*) of Syria. In a letter to Caligula, Herod Agrippa I attributes every sort of vice to him. He was, we gather, cruel, corrupt, arrogant, of ungovernable temper and slanderous tongue, a man who pronounced sentence first and heard the case (if he heard it at all) afterward. In fact, Pilate was, first and foremost, a senior administrator on the make: opportunistic, and afraid of the Jews, whom he thought ripe for revolt. He therefore took a deliberately tough line, though at the same time he was suspicious of the influence which some of his more powerful subjects had at the Imperial court in Rome.

Jesus and his accusers from the Sanhedrin were taken to the *praetorium*, the paved forecourt of the palace fortress where the Procurator was residing. The Sanhedrin's formal charge was then read out before him. At the conclusion of this preamble Pilate interrogated Jesus himself.

"Art thou the King of the Jews?" he asked him.

As he had done to Joseph, Jesus replied: "Thou sayest it."

The accusers pressed their charges. As Jesus made no reply to the accusations brought against him, Pilate questioned him once more: "Answerest thou nothing? behold how many things they witness against thee." These "many things" no doubt included Messianism, revolutionary activities, and conspiring with the *sicarii* of the resistance. But Jesus still said nothing. Pilate was surprised. The Easterners normally were all too loquacious. Those who were in danger of crucifixion were wont to defend their lives with desperate energy. They would deploy every possible argument, true or false, and swear black was white in their efforts to convince the Procurator of their innocence or, failing that, to melt his heart with compassion. Why was *this* defendant remaining so obstinately mute?

Pilate was by no means a fool, and he must very soon have come to the conclusion that Jesus, far from being politically dangerous, was — as he saw it — a harmless mystic. He sent him back to prison and reserved his judgment till the following day. It looks as though in the intervening period he was approached by various influential people, all pressing him to show Jesus clemency. There is even a tradition that his wife was among them.

Next morning, Friday, the verdict in the case had to be given. Jesus was once more brought before the Procurator. Pilate began by upholding the Sanhedrin's recommendations: he sentenced Jesus to death for subversive political activities, attempted rebellion, and usurping the title King of the Jews in defiance of the Emperor's authority. Having thus covered himself against the possible eventuality of someone's denouncing him to Tiberius, he then attempted to foil the Sanhedrin by exercising his prerogative of pardon. He went out and addressed the crowd, which had gathered on the eve of the Paschal Feast to pay him their respects and to demand the release of one prisoner. Now, a certain *sicarius* named Jesus Barabbas had been condemned to death for taking part in a nationalist uprising and committing murder during it. The Zealots were eager to get Barabbas freed, and started manipulating the crowd for their own purposes. This hardly helped Jesus. When Pilate proposed to release him, the crowd yelled for the other Jesus — Barabbas. "What will ye then," asked Pilate, "that I shall do unto him whom ye call the King of the Jews?"

The crowd, sensing the Procurator's contempt and indifference, screamed: "Crucify him!" So Pilate, in his anxiety to avoid trouble, gave the order to release Barabbas and crucify Jesus. To Romans, crucifixion was a commonplace. Besides, Pilate probably thought, what does one Jew more or less matter?

How strange life is: all Pilate felt he had done was to settle the fate of some wretched Jew whose survival was a matter of almost complete indifference to him. Yet, without knowing it, he had come face to face with his destiny, and pronounced sentence in the most momentous trial of all human history. He was to become more famous than Tiberius, more famous even than Julius Caesar, enshrined in men's memory forever as the symbol of craven cowardice: the man who washed his hands.

Beyond all question, it is this Imperial Roman administrator who must bear the entire responsibility, legally speaking, for Jesus' death. Yet he was not the truly guilty one; nor were the Jewish people, who knew nothing of the matter and whose opinion was not solicited, collectively responsible; not even the Sanhedrin as a whole can be blamed. No, the guilt rests entirely upon Ananias, together with his family and accomplices, who detested the people of Jerusalem. Though the Jewish people as such were innocent of Jesus' death, it was beyond a doubt their unworthy leaders who knowingly, and by a combination of stupidity, cowardice, fanaticism and ruthlessness, accomplished the greatest crime in history.

15

THE CROSS

CRUCIFIXION, we are told, originated as a form of punishment in Persia, and was adopted by the Roman army as a method of torturing slaves, deserters, and brigands to death. It was not a punishment that could be inflicted upon Roman citizens: they had the right to be beheaded. The word *crux*, or cross, simply means one of those wooden posts, about six feet in length, which were used by the legionaries to build a palisade when they pitched camp. The condemned man was simply nailed to this post; when it proved too small, a crosspiece was fitted to one end and the victim's arms nailed out along it, horizontally. Sometimes, to prevent the weight of his body tearing his nailed hands free, the crucified man had a projecting wooden "saddle" fixed between his thighs as an additional support.

The execution squad was made up of Roman troops; appropriately, since Jesus was a political prisoner, sentenced for supposed crimes of rebellion and terrorism which came under the aegis of what we would nowadays term military justice. So Pilate detailed a detachment from one cohort and issued orders that the execution was to be carried out without delay.

While these preparations were going forward, Jesus was left under military guard. In accordance with a barbarous Roman custom, the condemned man was tortured and scourged with lictors' rods before his execution took place. Jesus was beaten till the blood flowed. Then the soldiers engaged in a curious sport, part ritual, part mockery. These "Romans" who garrisoned Jerusalem were themselves of Eastern origin, and hated the Jews. Their contempt and fear were largely conditioned by their knowledge that the Jews hated *them*. Jesus had been sentenced as a Jewish royal pretender; they were eager to scoff at him for having had the mad temerity to defy a Roman army and the Roman Empire. They were also taking a leaf from the Saturnalia, a feast to which the ancients generally, and soldiers in particular, were well used. During this period of carnival a condemned man became — for one day only — a sort of Lord of Misrule, who received every public honor and was subsequently executed.

Before they dressed Jesus' bruised and naked body, the soldiers made a crown from the thorns kept as fuel out by the fire in the *praetorium*, and put it on his head. Round his body they wrapped a scarlet military cloak, and then they proceeded to punch him and spit in his face by way of homage. If Jesus was not by now completely unconscious, he may have glimpsed that high cliff in the wilderness where he had heard the voice of Satan offering him all the kingdoms of the world; and perhaps he remembered how he had refused them. Now he was undergoing a savage and ironic humiliation: these brutes were the first to bend the knee before Him whom, for centuries to come, millions of men of all races would adore as King of the World.

Early that Friday morning a small procession emerged from the fortress and set off on the few hundred yards' journey to the city walls. Three condemned men were being taken for execution. From the start it was clear that Jesus would not be strong enough to carry the T-piece of his cross. The centurion in charge whistled up a passer-by, Simon of Cyrene, a non-Palestinian Jew coming in from the fields, and gave him the job of carrying the heavy wooden beam instead.

Outside the northwest side of the city there stood a hill, close beside the road, called Golgotha, or the Place of Skulls. Several crosses already planted there, just outside a cemetery, denoted an execution site, rather in the manner of a gibbet.

A crucifixion was a disgusting spectacle which attracted every sort of idler. The three condemned men were stripped of their clothes and, about nine in the morning, nailed alive to the crosses. Above Jesus' head was fixed a notice giving the reason for his execution: it read, *The King of the Jews.* His two fellow-victims were thieves. A detachment of soldiers was posted to keep watch over this tortured trio. There was nothing to prevent passers-by stopping and staring, or even addressing remarks to the crucified men.

Some such hapless creatures made their ghastly situation an excuse for screaming insults and blasphemies at the crowd.

They often went into fits of raving madness; these were sometimes provoked by the onset of tetanus, which finished them
off. Others were limp and exhausted. Normally the guard
remained with them until death ensued; but some victims
of crucifixion survived for several long days afterwards, in agonies
of thirst, tortured by both racking cramps, which made them
scream aloud, and the flies that swarmed on their still bleeding
wounds. They were only too happy when a sudden hemorrhage
freed them from the awful pain, the sadistic pleasure of the
bystanders, the cruel folly of men who proved themselves
less civilized than so many mad dogs.

Jesus was exhausted, finished. He had refused the soporific
wine that they gave condemned men to drink as a crude
anesthetic when they were actually driving the nails through
their limbs. It was all he could do to murmur a few broken
words from time to time. Not far from the foot of the cross
there stood a group of women who had followed him ever
since the early days in Galilee; a different tradition from that
which ultimately goes back to Peter includes among them
his mother Mary, and places John, one of the Twelve, with the
group. Both Mary and John had relatives among the Temple
priests and were therefore safe from arrest.

Some of Jesus' enemies had worked up such a keen edge of
hatred against him that they came and shouted jeering insults before this torn and bleeding rag of human flesh: " 'Ah,' "
they cried, "wagging their heads . . . 'thou that destroyest
the temple, and buildest it in three days, save thyself, and come
down from the cross . . . that we may see and believe.' "

After six hours of this torture, Jesus began to recite a psalm
in Aramaic — *Eloi, Eloi, lama sabachthani?* it begins: "My
God, my God, why has thou forsaken me? why art thou so
far from helping me, and from the words of my roaring? O
my God, I cry in the daytime, but thou hearest not; and in

the night season, and am not silent. But thou art holy, O thou that inhabitest the praises of Israel. Our fathers trusted in thee: they trusted, and thou didst deliver them. They cried unto thee, and were delivered: they trusted in thee, and were not confounded. But I am a worm, and no man; a reproach of men, and despised of the people. All they that see me laugh me to scorn: they shoot out the lip, they shake the head, saying, 'He trusted on the Lord that he would deliver him: let him deliver him, seeing he delighted in him.' But thou are he that took me out of the womb: thou didst make me hope when I was upon my mother's breasts. I was cast upon thee from the womb: thou art my God from my mother's belly. Be not far from me; for trouble is near; for there is none to help. Many bulls have compassed me: strong bulls of Bashan have beset me round. They gaped upon me with their mouths, as a ravening and a roaring lion. I am poured out like water, and all my bones are out of joint: my heart is like wax; it is melted in the midst of my bowels. My strength is dried up like a potsherd; and my tongue cleaveth to my jaws; and thou hast brought me into the dust of death. For dogs have compassed me: the assembly of the wicked have inclosed me: they pierced my hands and my feet. I may tell all my bones: they look and stare upon me. They part my garments among them, and cast lots upon my vesture." Had Jesus time to complete this terrible prayer, with its joyous conclusion? About three in the afternoon he gave a cry, and died.

This sudden death spared him the *coup de grâce* which the soldiers would have inflicted on him before nightfall, because of the feast that was about to begin. Furthermore, the centurion in charge of the Roman execution party had felt a growing respect during these past few hours for so long-suffering a victim; he guessed that Jesus had been wrongly condemned, by some error of judgment. "Truly," he said, "this man was the Son of God."

Jesus' friends did not remain inactive. The body of a crucified criminal was normally cast into a common grave, but they were powerful enough to avert this final insult. Joseph of Arimathaea, an influential member of the Sanhedrin, went at once to see Pilate, and got his permission to take Jesus' body. Then Jesus was removed from the cross, quickly washed and anointed, and placed in a nearby rock tomb.

As night fell, and the lights began to twinkle all over Jerusalem, the noisy nocturnal celebrations of the Passover Sabbath began. The priests sat down to their cheerful banquet, symbolically free once more; as far as they were concerned, the little matter of Jesus of Nazareth was over and done with. The saddest reflection is that the Eleven, and all Jesus' many other friends and followers, those who had loved him and stood by him, shared this view. They were all convinced that the glorious adventure had finished forever.

16

The Resurrection

The Passover, as celebrated by Orthodox Jews, ended at nightfall on Saturday. At dawn the following day, the women who had witnessed Jesus' death decided to visit the tomb where his body had been so hastily interred. They came to the conclusion that no great risk was involved. The disciples had gone into retreat, prostrate with grief after the tragic events of the past few days, and scarcely capable of measuring the depth of their despair. Some of Jesus' friends had hastily fled the city before the Passover, convinced that they too were liable to be arrested. Nobody could be quite sure where Ananias' desire for vengeance would stop. But the old priest had no reason to hunt down Jesus' supporters. Jesus himself had died on the cross, and the whole of Jerusalem knew it. The idea of his being the Messiah could no longer be entertained even by his most fanatical adherent. It had become so absurd that the mere mention of it brought tears to his friends' eyes — tears of pain and regret for what was lost.

When the women came back and sought out the disciples, with a wild story of having found Jesus' tomb empty, the Eleven thought they had gone out of their minds. An angel had appeared to them, they said, and told them that Jesus was risen again, that he would meet the Eleven in Galilee. Then Mary of Magdala arrived, ready to swear she had seen Jesus himself, alive. Peter went along to the tomb, found it empty, and also met Jesus, though in what circumstances we do not know. Other disciples met him on the road. James saw him, and all the Eleven did so later in Jerusalem. There were further manifestations in Galilee, on an unnamed mountain, and others again by the lakeside.

The first of these incidents had been the women's discovery of the empty tomb. One Jewish historian writes:

Some Christian scholars have conjectured that the Jews removed Jesus' body by night, and buried it in some unknown grave, to prevent the rock-tomb becoming a shrine. But at this stage they could have had no such fears. The very idea of a "crucified Messiah," someone "accursed of God and hanged," was so monstrous to the Jews' way of thinking that it would never have occurred to them that anyone might be impelled to come and worship at his tomb. It is equally hard to believe that the disciples themselves hid the body; during those early days they were far too terrified by the frightful death of their Messiah. If they *had* gone about such a task that night, with the object of proclaiming next day that Jesus was risen again, we should be forced to admit that the faith they displayed in the period which followed was nothing but falsehood and hypocrisy. Now this is quite out of the question. You cannot found a religion that commands the belief of countless millions on an imposture.

According to the same author, a similar verdict must be given on the appearances of Jesus after his resurrection. Indeed, no historian well acquainted with early Christian literature denies the actuality of these manifestations. Mary of Magdala, Peter, James, the Eleven and "above five hundred brethren at once" (as St. Paul tells us in his first Epistle to the Corinthians) all truly saw the risen, living Christ. These visions are the one thing that made Christianity possible. No Jew, however passionately devoted to Jesus he might have been, would have dared to identify the Messiah with a crucified man — unless this Messiah had given conclusive proof of his victory over death. A yawning gulf lies between the corpse of Christ crucified and what has been termed the "Easter faith."

What was the *reality* behind the manifestations of the risen Jesus? Collective hallucinations, or something equally insubstantial? An ineffable proof of the validity of mysticism? Physical reanimation of a sort that defies all known scientific laws? When we begin to ask such questions the historian finds himself without an answer. As a Christian philosopher has lately reminded us:

If we define the historical by saying that only what is *universally* verifiable can be admitted as a historical phenomenon, then these manifestations do not belong to history. For although their subject was a man known, before his death, to large numbers of people, nevertheless in his risen state he no longer appeared to everyone without distinction, as he had done prior to his trial. History in the strict sense can only admit events capable of verification by a normal person. A conversation between Napoleon and General Bertrand on St. Helena, even though the sole witness to it was Las Cases, is a historical datum, since any other witness, had he been present, would have heard what Las Cases heard. In this sense the most private history becomes, to all intents and purposes, public. But if Tiberius, Tacitus, Philo, Pilate, or Josephus had been present in the room when Jesus "appeared," it seems very probable that they would have seen nothing.

The life of a man beyond the grave penetrates that realm of mystery where God Himself dwells. Faith alone can perceive its light. Confronted with the risen Jesus, each man must make his own decision. Millions upon millions of men throughout the ages have believed the testimony of those witnesses who themselves saw Christ after his resurrection. They have "verified" their faith in terms of the meaning it gives their own lives, and man's destiny as a whole. Countless others, not only in our own times but from antiquity onward, have taken the opposite view. No, they say, they would rather see life as Macbeth saw it:

> . . . a walking shadow, a poor player,
> That struts and frets his hour upon the stage,
> And then is heard no more; it is a tale
> Told by an idiot, full of sound and fury,
> Signifying nothing.

By exalting Jesus' works at the expense of his crucified body, Renan failed to perceive that this death was a sign, a portent. Jesus has the unique privilege of forcing every man who reaches a verdict upon him to do likewise upon his own life and death. Is this existence of ours a mystery, or an absurdity? What is the meaning of death? Where does man's ultimate destiny lie — with God, or the void? According to how they answer these questions, men on earth will be forever divided beneath the sign of the Cross.

An Afterword

To SET ABOUT WRITING a life of Jesus in 1959 seems a task as paradoxical as it is presumptuous. One great, indeed insurmountable obstacle, we are told, is the "literary" character of the Gospels. It is generally agreed that they are not, in the modern sense at least, biographies of Christ. Rudolf Bultmann's work *Die Geschichte der Synoptischen Tradition* offers a balanced summing-up of the extreme critical position, which rejects the whole traditional mass of evidence concerning Jesus as a historical character. Albert Schweitzer had previously conducted a very similar inquiry, which he published under the title *Geschichte der Leben-Jesu Forschung*.

But Bultmann's approach (like that of Dibelius and, at an earlier date, Alfred Loisy) suffers from two most disadvantageous assumptions. It deals with texts as though they were wholly divorced from real life; and it embodies a number of *a priori* notions concerning the development of the primitive Christian community. Such a radical revaluation does, indeed, pose various necessary critical problems — problems which can no longer be ignored. But a truly exhaustive study of the sources must collate the Gospels with other evidence — written testimony concerning the Jews in Palestine; recent archaeological discoveries, with particular reference to the Dead Sea Scrolls; and daily life in the Near East.

The best answer to this radical spirit, represented in France by Guignebert's big, recently published book on Jesus, is Joseph Klausner's *Jésus de Nazareth*, the work of a Jewish scholar who can hardly be accused of natural bias in favor of Jesus and Christianity. Klausner is Professor of Jewish Literature in the University of Jerusalem, and writes in modern Hebrew. He concludes his analysis of the sources with the following remarks (page 184):

The further we enlarge our detailed knowledge of Judaism during the period of the second Temple, the more impossible it becomes to challenge the value of the Synoptic Gospels as historical evidence. Despite very considerable effort, on the part of those who wrote the Gospels, to accentuate the opposition between Jesus and Pharisaical Jewry, nevertheless every move Jesus makes, every word he utters, everything he does reminds us (by contrast on occasion, though most often directly) of the Palestine he knew during the period of the second Temple, the Jewish way of life, the teaching of the Pharisees.

Whether his acts and words and arguments support or contradict some *halaka* or *haggada* or *midrash* is, surely, quite unimportant. The fact remains that we cannot understand them without knowing the oral tradition of the Law way back to Hillel or Shammai; and that is the best proof that Jesus was an actual historical figure, that the Synoptic Gospels are authentic.

There are in existence today various excellent and up-to-date critical studies of Jesus' life — works which are solidly rooted in the texts and can be used as the foundation of any serious study. The Gospel commentaries by Lagrange, Strack and Billerbeck are somewhat out of date. Goguel has written a book on Jesus, and also played a leading part as co-translator of the *Nouveau Testament de la Bible du Centenaire*. Taylor's outstanding *The Gospel According to St. Mark* (London 1953) is the best available commentary on the most valuable source for Jesus' life. A recent survey of Catholic scholarship entitled *La Bible de Jérusalem* has appeared from the authoritative pen of Father Benoit. An old but still useful study is Alfred Edersheim's *The Life and Times of Jesus, the Messiah*. There is much to appreciate, also, in Joseph Klausner's *Jésus de Nazareth*. But the list could go on indefinitely: the bibliography of this subject knows no bounds.

Perhaps I should make some reference at this point to the extreme thesis advanced by certain amateur critics, according to whom Jesus never really existed. About twenty years ago P.-L. Couchoud tried, without much success, to argue this case before the French public, first in a short and entertaining little monograph called *Le Mystère de Jésus*, and latterly in a vast (and vastly boring) tome with the title *Jésus le Dieu fait Homme*, which was unanimously rejected by all critics and historians, whether they professed Christianity or not. But it should not be dismissed out of hand: it provides some trenchant criticism of critical excesses. If one is to believe Guignebert, Jesus was "the man who either could not, or would not, speak effectively to the people; a prophet who had done no more than arouse some sympathetic curiosity, and perhaps an occasional glimmer of hope, among the jobbing workmen of Galilee." In short, Jesus was a failure. Yet Christianity itself still exists today: no one could deny that, and its survival is a central premise in Couchoud's counterargument:

If we turn back now to the peasant of Galilee, or the Jerusalem rabble-rouser, we cannot but feel daunted by the huge gulf he would have to leap — before the appearance of St. Paul's letters — in order to breach and raid the Divine Citadel. Impossibilities abound on all sides . . . The first Christian whose voice we hear, Paul, was a Hebrew and the son of a Hebrew; yet he could, in the most casual manner, associate a man's name with that of Jahweh! *That* is the miracle I jib at; those in the Gospels could be explained without much difficulty. Even if they were multiplied a hundredfold, I still would not regard so small a matter as adequate grounds for challenging the historical reality of Christ. The invincible obstacle is the *cult* of Christ — that is, the Christian faith . . . How can anyone seriously maintain that a Cilician Jew — educated moreover as a Pharisee — could have mentioned another Jew, a contemporary of his from Galilee, in the same breath as the sacred texts referring to Jahweh, and without any apparent perturbation? To make such an assumption implies either total ignorance or total disregard of Jewish customs.

Couchoud's weighty reasoning argues directly against the portrait — or rather caricature — of Jesus drawn for us by the late M. Guignebert, whose near-offensive apologia on behalf of petty-mindedness cannot, surely, be treated with any serious respect. The demands of Christian faith on the one hand and rigorous criticism on the other are not beyond reconciliation — always provided that a fair balance is struck between them.

I have attempted, therefore, to write a life of Christ based on the generally accepted findings of critical scholarship. His historical existence is beyond dispute. No historian, be he Christian or nonbeliever, will challenge the proposition that most of the statements attributed to Jesus in the synoptic Gospels are authentic, though they may at times have been deliberately rearranged and completed. But when the historian begins to weigh up his evidence, must he make no distinction between the Sermon on the Mount and the discourses in the Fourth Gospel — or, indeed, the anecdotes concerning Jesus' childhood? No one today would dream of maintaining such an indiscriminate thesis. Two traditions can derive from wholly different sources, and yet be of equal significance and value. The discourses in the Fourth Gospel stand, from a literary viewpoint, far closer to St. Paul's Epistles than to the sayings of Jesus as reported by the synoptic tradition. Despite the apparent genuineness of the sayings collected in these Gospels, they are grouped in a manner which displays the hand of the

Evangelist at work. The same applies to the interpretation of
the parables. I owe a considerable debt in this field to Dodd
and Jeremias, each of whom has made the parables the subject
of a special treatise; and my chronology of Our Lord's Passion follows the illuminating hypotheses advanced by Mlle.
Jaubert in her excellent book on the date of the Last Supper.

In order to write a life of Jesus, then, it seems best to base
oneself on the synoptic Gospels, following St. Mark wherever
possible, filling out his account with trustworthy material
stemming from the common source on which both St. Matthew
and St. Luke drew, and including one or two reliable passages
which we find in St. Luke and nowhere else. I have taken St.
Mark as my main guide, but have not restricted myself to him
entirely.

A biographer has to marshal the facts he relates into some sort
of chronological order, and cannot be perpetually justifying his
chosen sequence. Did the summoning of the apostles take
place before or after the Sermon on the Mount? Can the
parables be disentangled from the Evangelists' commentary
on them? Did Jesus make one visit to Nazareth, or several?
Was it on a Wednesday or a Thursday that he appeared before
the High Priest? Did Pontius Pilate sit in judgment upon him
once or twice? I have digested the views expressed by scholars
in each instance, and then made up my mind. When the
answer seems cut and dried, I say so. If there is a reasonable
doubt, I leave the question open. But to the best of my knowledge I nowhere advance an opinion which lacks the support
of some recognized authority.

I have tried to stick to the historical facts at all times. I
do not consider it honest to use faith as the solution to historical
uncertainty. I have done my best to produce an objective,
well-documented life of Christ: one that aims at clarity and
readability, and avoids burdening the reader with pointless

displays of erudition. My aim has been to achieve a Gospel-like simplicity, but at the same time to dispense with those technical Jewish terms which sometimes make the Gospels themselves unintelligible. The Messiah was a King, but something more than a King besides. The Pharisees regarded themselves as religious purists. The scribes were learned scholars, while the Sanhedrin acted as both High Court and Council of State. The Sadducees were priests, the Zealots terrorists. I have not, therefore, hesitated to employ such modern terminology, though I am aware that at times it has an anachronistic ring about it. But nevertheless, it remains true to say that the essential details of Jesus' life could be related as though they had taken place during our own lifetime, in some Israeli or Jordanian village — or even, perhaps, in its French equivalent: Aubervilliers, say, or Romorantin. Every masterpiece contains an element of the timeless and eternal qualities which historical scholarship, valuable though it may be in itself, cannot ignore without falsifying some essential part of the truth.

JEAN STEINMANN

Notes

5 "The Jews . . . went to make up the Empire." See J. Juster, *Les Juifs dans l'empire romain: Leur condition juridique, économique et sociale.* 2 vols. Paris: 1914. See also, especially, E. Schürer, *Geschichte des jüdischen Volkes im Zeitalter Jesu Christi.* 3 vols. Leipzig: 1901-1908 (fourth edition).

10 "Then . . . incarnate in a Man." On the "Son of Man," see S. Mowinckel's study *He That Cometh.* Oxford: 1956.

11 " 'He seized . . . a dog's death.' " Quoted by J. Klausner, *Jésus de Nazareth*, p. 211. Paris: Payot, 1933 (Coll. Historique).

21 ". . . the old traditional calendar . . ." See Mlle. Jaubert's *La Date de la Cène.* Paris: 1957.

27 "The Temple of Jerusalem . . ." English-speaking readers will find an excellent account of the history, topography, and Herodian transformation of the Temple in *The Life and Times of Herod the Great*, by Stewart Perowne, pp. 129-142. London: 1956. [Tr.]

27-28 " 'When the Messianic King . . . as it is written.' " Quoted by Alfred Edersheim, *The Life and Times of Jesus the Messiah*, vol. I, p. 293. 2 vols. Grand Rapids, Michigan: 1953.

28-29 " 'All the requirements . . . in abeyance.' " *Ibid.*, p. 296.

30 " 'In a similar fashion . . . its moral point.' " M. J. Lagrange, *L'Evangile de Jésus-Christ*, p. 74. Paris: 1930.

35 " 'Crowds had gathered . . . Machaerus.' " *Antiq. Jud.* XVIII, 118-119.

36 " 'The northern flank . . . Josephus.' " F. M. Abel, *Une Croisière autour de la Mer Morte*, pp. 37-38. Paris: 1911.

39 " 'On the Sabbath day . . . length.' " Edersheim, *op. cit.*, vol. I, p. 443.

50 " 'The Pharisees . . . based on them.' " Klausner, *op. cit.*, p. 588.

54 " 'Jesus obviously . . . spiritual powers.' " *Ibid.*, p. 395.

56-57 " 'It was noised . . .' " For the following narrative, see, in addition to Mark 2, 1-12, V. Taylor, *The Gospel According to St. Mark*, pp. 191ff. London: 1953.

58 "He was a *publicanus* . . ." On the various *publicani*, see Edersheim, *op. cit.*, vol. I, p. 515.

68 " 'We may well . . . quite possible.' " O. Cullmann, *Dieu et César*, p. 18. Neuchâtel: 1956.

70 "The Hebrew name for them was *sheluhim* . . ." See V. Taylor, *op. cit.*, p. 621.

82 " 'The sabbath . . . the sabbath.' " See *ibid.*, p. 219.

82-83 " 'The Talmud . . . the Sabbath.' " See Edersheim, *op. cit.*, vol. I, p. 778.

83 " 'For the Pharisees . . . the greater offense.' " Klausner, *op. cit.*, p. 318.

103 "Not only is Jesus . . . the parable." See Edersheim, *op. cit.*, vol. I, p. 589.

109 "He began . . . ocular disorders." See *ibid.*, vol. II, p. 48; and M. J. Lagrange, *Evangile selon saint Marc*, p. 212. Paris: 1929.

125 "He is the Chosen One of God . . ." See S. Mowinckel, *op. cit.*, p. 378.

127 " 'There can be . . . divinity.' " *Ibid.*, p. 426.

172 "As the Talmud . . . treasurers." Edersheim, *op. cit.*, vol. I, p. 372.

175 "The only authority . . . Jerusalem." See Schürer, *op. cit.*, vol. II, p. 218.

176 "An old Jewish lamentation . . . bludgeons." See Klausner, *op. cit.*, p. 489.

179 " 'Humanity . . . nothing.' " *Ibid.*, p. 331.

185-186 " 'For the kingdom of heaven . . . I am good.' " There is a lengthy analysis of this passage in J. Jeremias, *The Parables of Jesus*, pp. 23-25 and especially p. 108. London: 1954.

189 "But the richest . . . the murderous vine dressers . . ." For further discussion of this parable see G. H. Dodd, *The Parables of the Kingdom*, p. 125. London: 1953.

192 "In the Talmud . . . uttered by the Pharisee . . ." Quoted by Jeremias, *op. cit.*, p. 113.

192 " 'To those who first heard it . . . shocking . . .' " *Idem.*

192-193 " 'The casuistical spirit . . . importance.' " Klausner, *op. cit.*, p. 318.

195 "The Talmud . . . livelihood." *Ibid.*, p. 467.

208 "As one scholar . . . Palestine." Lagrange, *Evangile selon saint Marc*, p. 386.

213 "One detail . . . Ananias." See Klausner, *op. cit.*, p. 491.

213 "Of the seventy . . . valid." See Edersheim, *op. cit.*, vol. II, p. 554.

214 "He took Jesus' reply . . . then termed." See *ibid.*, p. 555.

215 " 'From start to finish . . . influence.' " See Klausner, *op. cit.*, p. 487.

224-225 " 'Some Christian scholars . . . imposture.' " *Ibid.*, p. 517.

225-226 " 'If we define . . . seen nothing.' " Jean Guitton, *Jésus*, p. 306. Paris: Bernard Grasset Editeur, 1956.

Biblical References in the Text

(Citations are to the King James Version)

PAGE

10	"as the stars"	Genesis 22, 17
15	"The Kingdom"	Matthew 3, 2
16	"I say unto you"	Luke 3, 8
17-18	"There cometh one mightier"	Mark 1, 7
18	"I am not" and following lines	John 1, 19-22
18-19	"I am the voice"	Matthew 3, 3 (see also Isaiah 40, 3)
21-22	"the Lamb of God"	John 1, 29
22	"Thou art my beloved Son"	Mark 1, 11
26	"If thou be"	Matthew 4, 3-11
26	"Give us this day"	Matthew 6, 11
27	"It is written"	Matthew 4, 4 (see also Deuteronomy 8, 3)
27	"If thou be"	Matthew 4, 6 (see also Psalm 91, 11-12)
28	"It is written again"	Matthew 4, 7 (see also Deuteronomy 6, 16)
28	"all the kingdoms"	Matthew 4, 8
30	"Get thee hence"	Matthew 4, 10 (see also Deuteronomy 6, 13; 10, 20)
43-44	"sons of thunder"	Mark 3, 17
44	"Come ye after me"	Mark 1, 17
45	"The time is fulfilled"	Mark 1, 15
45	"And he came to Nazareth"	Luke 4, 16-22
47	"Lay not up for yourselves"	Matthew 6, 19-21
47	"No man can serve"	Matthew 6, 24
47-48	"I say unto you"	Matthew 6, 25
48	"Behold the fowls"	Matthew 6, 26
48	"Which of you"	Matthew 6, 27
48-49	"Consider the lilies"	Matthew 6, 28-29
49	"Seek ye first the kingdom"	Matthew 6, 33
49	"Take therefore no thought"	Matthew 6, 34
49	"Ask, and it shall be given"	Matthew 7, 7-8
49	"What man is there of you"	Matthew 7, 9-10
49-50	"Therefore all things whatsoever"	Matthew 7, 12

PAGE

52	"Let us alone"	Mark 1, 24
52	"Hold thy peace"	Mark 1, 25
55-56	"If thou wilt"	Mark 1, 40-44
56-57	"It was noised"	Mark 2, 1-12
58	"Follow me"	Matthew 9, 9
59	"They that are whole"	Mark 2, 17
60	"No man putteth new wine"	Mark 2, 22
61	"Art thou he that should come"	Luke 7, 19
61	"Go your way"	Luke 7, 22 (see also Luke 4, 18; Isaiah 35, 3-6; and Isaiah 61, 1)
64	"Hearken; behold, there went out a sower"	Mark 4, 3-9
65	"So is the Kingdom of God"	Mark 4, 26-29
65	"Whereunto shall we liken"	Mark 4, 30-32
66	"Whereunto shall I liken"	Luke 13, 20-21
66-67	"Is a candle brought"	Mark 4, 21
67	"The kingdom of heaven is"	Matthew 13, 44-46
71-72	"Blessed are the poor"	Matthew 5, 3-12 (corrected in part on the basis of Luke 6, 20-23)
74-75	"Think not that I am come"	Matthew 5, 17-18
75-76	"For I say unto you"	Matthew 5, 20-48
78-79	"Take heed"	Matthew 6, 1-4
79	"And when thou prayest"	Matthew 6, 5-6
79	"Moreover when ye fast"	Matthew 6, 16-18
80	"Judge not"	Matthew 7, 1-5
80	"Beware of false prophets"	Matthew 7, 15-20
81	"And it came to pass"	Mark 2, 23
81	"Behold, why"	Mark 2, 24
82	"Have ye never"	Mark 2, 25-26
82	"The sabbath was made for man"	Mark 2, 27
83	"And he entered again into the synagogue"	Mark 3, 1-4
84	"And when he had looked"	Mark 3, 5-6
84	"Why walk not thy disciples"	Mark 7, 5
84	"Well hath Esaias"	Mark 7, 6-8 (see also Isaiah 29, 13)
85	"Blind guides, which strain at a gnat"	Matthew 23, 24
85	"There is nothing from without a man"	Mark 7, 15
85	"Is it lawful to heal on the sabbath day"	Luke 14, 3

PAGE

85	"Which of you"	Luke 14, 5
86	"Go not into the way of the Gentiles"	Matthew 10, 5-7
87	"Provide neither gold, nor silver"	Matthew 10, 9-10
87	"shod with sandals"	Mark 6, 9
87	"The labourer is worthy"	Luke 10, 7
87-88	"I thank thee, O Father"	Matthew 11, 25
88	"Come unto me"	Matthew 11, 28-30
89	"Come ye yourselves apart"	Mark 6, 31-32
89	"This is a desert"	Mark 6, 35-38
90	"give us this day"	Matthew 6, 11
90	"What was it that ye disputed"	Mark 9, 33-37
91	"And when he was come out of the ship" and following quotations	Mark 5, 2-12
93-94	"And behold, there cometh"	Mark 5, 22-34
94-95	"While he yet spake"	Mark 5, 35-43
96	"By the prince of the devils"	Mark 3, 22
96	"If a kingdom"	Mark 3, 24-26
96-97	"No man can enter"	Mark 3, 27
97	"Behold, thy mother"	Mark 3, 32-35
98	"He that loveth father"	Matthew 10, 37
98	"Whence hath this man this wisdom"	Matthew 13, 54-56
98	"A prophet is not without honour"	Matthew 13, 57-58
99-100	"And one of the Pharisees desired"	Luke 7, 36-50
101	"The publicans and the harlots"	Matthew 21, 31
101	"Mary called Magdalene"	Luke 8, 2-3
101	"deeply in his spirit"	Mark 8, 12
101-102	"When it is evening"	Matthew 16, 2-4
102	"Verily I say unto you"	Mark 8, 12
102	"The men of Nineveh"	Matthew 12, 41
102-103	"The kingdom of heaven"	Matthew 13, 24-30
104	"I will make you"	Matthew 4, 19
104	"The kingdom of heaven"	Matthew 13, 47-48
105	"And when a convenient day was come"	Mark, 6, 21-29
106	"What went ye out into the wilderness"	Luke 7, 24-26 (see also Malachi 3, 1)
106	"Among those that are born"	Luke 7, 28
107	"And from the days of John the Baptist"	Matthew 11, 12
107	"But whereunto shall I liken"	Matthew 11, 16-19
108	"Get thee out"	Luke 13, 31-33
108	"Take heed"	Mark 8, 15-16
108-109	"And he cometh to Bethsaida"	Mark 8, 22-26

PAGE

109-110	"The harvest truly is great"	Luke 10, 2-3
110	"Be ye therefore wise as serpents"	Matthew 10, 16
110	"The disciple is not above his master"	Matthew 10, 24-27
110	"And fear not them"	Matthew 10, 28-31
110	"Think not"	Matthew 10, 34-36 (see also Micah 7, 6)
111	"But I tell you of a truth"	Luke 4, 25-30
111-112	"Woe unto thee, Chorazin!"	Matthew 11, 21-24
118	"entered into an house"	Mark 7, 24-30
119	"Ephphatha"	Mark 7, 34
120-121	"I saw in the night visions"	Daniel 7, 13-14
121	"I will declare the decree"	Psalm 2, 7
121	"The Lord hath sworn"	Psalm 110, 4
122	"Whom do men say"	Mark 8, 27-28
123	"And he saith unto them"	Mark 8, 29
123	"Blessed art thou"	Matthew 16, 17-18
125	"one like the Son of man"	Daniel 7, 13
127	"Thou sealest up the sum"	Ezekiel 28, 12-15
128	"And he began to teach them"	Mark 8, 31
129	"I was not rebellious"	Isaiah 50, 5-6
129	"Surely he hath borne"	Isaiah 53, 4-8
130	"took him, and began"	Mark 8, 32-33 and Matthew 16, 23
131	"And when he had called"	Mark 8, 34
132	"Whosoever will save his life"	Mark 8, 35
132	"Whosoever hath"	Matthew 13, 12
132	"For what shall it profit a man"	Mark 8, 36-37
132	"Thou art an offence"	Matthew 16, 23
132-133	"If thy hand offend thee"	Mark 9, 43-47
134	"Up into an high mountain"	Mark 9, 2
134-135	"And after six days"	Mark 9, 2-8
136	"Thou art the Christ"	Matthew 16, 16
137	"Flesh and blood"	Matthew 16, 17
138	"And as they came down from the mountain"	Mark 9, 9-13
139-140	"And when he came to his disciples"	Mark 9, 14-29
140-141	"He stedfastly set his face"	Luke 9, 51-56
141	"Boanerges"	Mark 3, 17
141	"And it came to pass"	Luke 9, 57-62
141-142	"Lord, teach us"	Luke 11, 1-4
143-144	"Then came Peter to him"	Matthew 18, 21-35
145	"And he said unto them"	Luke 11, 5-8
146	"There was in a city"	Luke 18, 2-5
147	"sendeth rain"	Matthew 5, 45

PAGE

147	"What man of you"	Luke 15, 4-7
148	"Either what woman"	Luke 15, 8-10
149	"A certain man had two sons"	Luke 15, 11-32
153	"Good Master"	Mark 10, 17-30
155	"And one of the company"	Luke 12, 13-21
156	"There was a certain rich man"	Luke 16, 19-25
157-158	"There was a certain rich man"	Luke 16, 1-8
159	"the chief among the publicans"	Luke 19, 2
159	"Zacchaeus, make haste"	Luke 19, 5-9
160	"A certain nobleman"	Luke 19, 12-19, 27
161	"And James and John"	Mark 10, 35-40
162	"And when the ten heard it,"	Mark 10, 41-45
162-163	"Blind Bartimaeus"	Mark 10, 46-52
169	"Go your way"	Mark 11, 2-3
173	"Is it not written"	Mark 11, 17 (see also Isaiah 56, 7; Jeremiah 7, 11)
173	"Destroy this temple"	John 2, 19
173-174	"Our fathers worshipped"	John 4, 20-23 (see also Isaiah 2, 3)
174	"By what authority"	Mark 11, 28-33
180	"Master, this woman"	John 8, 3-11
181	"And when they were come"	Mark 12, 14-17
181-182	"When they shall rise"	Mark 12, 25-27
182	"Jesus asked them"	Matthew 22, 41-45
183	"Which is the first commandment"	Mark 12, 28
183	"What is written"	Luke 10, 26
183	"Hear, O Israel"	This passage is conflated from Matthew 22, 37-39; Mark 12, 29-31; and Luke 10, 27. In the accounts of Matthew and Mark, the text is attributed to Jesus rather than to his questioner. See also Deuteronomy 6, 4-5.
183	"Thou hast answered"	Luke 10, 28
183	"And who is my neighbor?"	Luke 10, 29
183-184	"A certain man went down"	Luke 10, 30-35
184	"Which now of these three"	Luke 10, 36-37
185	"sat over against the treasury"	Mark 12, 41-44
185-186	"For the kingdom of heaven"	Matthew 20, 1-15
187	"A certain man made a great supper"	Luke 14, 16-24

188 "A certain man had a fig tree"   Luke 13, 6-9
189 "But what think ye?"   Matthew 21, 28-31
189-190 "A certain man planted a vineyard"   Mark 12, 1-9
191 "And he spake this parable"   Luke 18, 9-14
193 "The scribes and the Pharisees"   Matthew 23, 2-5
194 "But all their works they do"   Matthew 23, 5-7
194-195 "But woe unto you, scribes"   Matthew 23, 13-33
196 "O Jerusalem"   Matthew 23, 37
196 "If thou hadst known"   Luke 19, 42
196 "And as he went out of the temple"   Mark 13, 1-5
196-197 "When you shall see the abomination"   Mark 13, 14-18
197 "But of that day"   Mark 13, 32
198 "Now learn a parable"   Mark 13, 28
198 "Take ye heed"   Mark 13, 33-35
198 "But know this"   Matthew 24, 43
199-200 "Then shall the kingdom of heaven"   Matthew 25, 1-12
201 "Enter thou into the joy"   Matthew 25, 23
201-202 "Come, ye blessed"   Matthew 25, 34-40
202-203 "Why was this waste"   Mark 14, 4-8
204 "Go ye into the city"   Mark 14, 13-15
205 "Verily I say unto you"   Mark 14, 18-21
206 "took bread"   Mark 14, 22
206 "Take, eat"   Mark 14, 22
206 "This is my blood"   Mark 14, 24
206 "This do in remembrance of me"   Luke 22, 19
208 "All ye shall be offended"   Mark 14, 27-31 (see also Zecheriah 13, 7)

209-210 "Sit ye here"   Mark 14, 32-38
210 "Are ye come out"   Mark 14, 48-49
212 "And thou also wast"   Mark 14, 67-72
213 "Destroy this temple"   Mark 14, 57-58 (see also John 2, 19)

213-214 "Art thou the Christ"   Mark 14, 61-62 (see also Daniel 7, 13)

214 "He hath spoken blasphemy"   Matthew 26, 65
216 "Art thou the King of Jews?"   Mark 15, 2-5
217 "What will ye then"   Mark 15, 12
217 "Crucify him"   Mark 15, 13
221 "Ah, thou that destroyest the temple"   Mark 15, 29-32
221-222 "My God, my God"   Psalm 22, 1-18
223 "Truly this man"   Mark 15, 39
225 "above five hundred"   I Corinthians 15, 6